INTIMATE RELATIONSHIPS ACROSS CULTURES

Intimate relationships exist in social domains, in which there are cultural rules regarding appropriate behaviors. But they also inhabit psychological domains of thoughts, feelings, and desires. How are intimate relationships experienced by people living in various types of romantic or sexual relationships and in various cultural regions around the world? In what ways are they similar, and in what ways are they different? This book presents a cross-cultural extension of the findings originating from the classic Boston Couples Study. Amassing a wealth of new data from almost 9,000 participants worldwide, Hill explores the factors that predict having a current partner, relationship satisfaction, and relationship commitment. These predictions are compared across eight relationship types and nine cultural regions, then uniquely combined in a *Comprehensive Partner Model* and a *Comprehensive Commitment Model*. The findings test the generalizability of previous theories about intimate relationships, with implications for self-reflection, couples counseling, and well-being.

Charles T. Hill is Professor of Psychology at Whittier College, California, where he won the Nerhood Teaching Excellence Award. He has a PhD in Social Psychology from Harvard University and is a member of Phi Beta Kappa, the American Psychological Association, and the American Sociological Association.

Advances in Personal Relationships

Christopher R. Agnew
Purdue University

John P. Caughlin
University of Illinois at Urbana-Champaign

C. Raymond Knee
University of Houston

Terri L. Orbuch
Oakland University

Although scholars from a variety of disciplines have written and conversed about the importance of personal relationships for decades, the emergence of personal relationships as a field of study is relatively recent. *Advances in Personal Relationships* represents the culmination of years of multidisciplinary and interdisciplinary work on personal relationships. Sponsored by the International Association for Relationship Research, the series offers readers cutting-edge research and theory in the field. Contributing authors are internationally known scholars from a variety of disciplines, including social psychology, clinical psychology, communication, history, sociology, gerontology, and family studies. Volumes include integrative reviews, conceptual pieces, summaries of research programs, and major theoretical works. *Advances in Personal Relationships* presents first-rate scholarship that is both provocative and theoretically grounded. The theoretical and empirical work described by authors will stimulate readers and advance the field by offering new ideas and retooling old ones. The series will be of interest to upper-division undergraduate students, graduate students, researchers, and practitioners.

Other Books in the Series

Attribution, Communication Behavior, and Close Relationships
Valerie Manusov and John H. Harvey, editors

Stability and Change in Relationships
Anita L. Vangelisti, Harry T. Reis, and Mary Anne Fitzpatrick, editors

Understanding Marriage: Developments in the Study of Couple Interaction
Patricia Noller and Judith A. Feeney, editors

Growing Together: Personal Relationships Across the Lifespan
Frieder R. Lang and Karen L. Fingerman, editors

Communicating Social Support
Daena J. Goldsmith

Communicating Affection: Interpersonal Behavior and Social Context
Kory Floyd

Changing Relations: Achieving Intimacy in a Time of Social Transition
Robin Goodwin

Feeling Hurt in Close Relationships
Anita L. Vangelisti, editor

Romantic Relationships in Emerging Adulthood
Frank D. Fincham and Ming Cui, editors

Responding to Intimate Violence Against Women: The Role of Informal Networks
Renate Klein

Social Influences on Romantic Relationships: Beyond the Dyad
Christopher R. Agnew, editor

Positive Approaches to Optimal Relationship Development
C. Raymond Knee and Harry T. Reis, editors

Personality and Close Relationship Processes
Stanley O. Gaines, Jr.

The Experience and Expression of Uncertainty in Close Relationships
Jennifer A. Theiss

Contemporary Studies on Relationships, Health, and Wellness
Jennifer A. Theiss and Kathryn Greene, editors

Power in Close Relationships
Christopher R. Agnew and Jennifer J. Harman, editors

Health and Illness in Close Relationships
Ashley P. Duggan

Intimate Relationships Across Cultures

A Comparative Study

Charles T. Hill

Whittier College, California

CAMBRIDGE
UNIVERSITY PRESS

University Printing House, Cambridge CB2 8BS, United Kingdom

One Liberty Plaza, 20th Floor, New York, NY 10006, USA

477 Williamstown Road, Port Melbourne, VIC 3207, Australia

314–321, 3rd Floor, Plot 3, Splendor Forum, Jasola District Centre, New Delhi – 110025, India

79 Anson Road, #06–04/06, Singapore 079906

Cambridge University Press is part of the University of Cambridge.

It furthers the University's mission by disseminating knowledge in the pursuit of education, learning, and research at the highest international levels of excellence.

www.cambridge.org
Information on this title: www.cambridge.org/9781107196629
DOI: 10.1017/9781108164832

© Charles T. Hill 2019

First published 2019

Printed and bound in Great Britain by Clays Ltd, Elcograf S.p.A.

A catalogue record for this publication is available from the British Library.

Library of Congress Cataloging-in-Publication Data
NAMES: Hill, Charles T., 1943– author.
TITLE: Intimate relationships across cultures : a comparative study / Charles T. Hill, Whittier College, California.
DESCRIPTION: New York : Cambridge University Press, [2019] | Series: Advances in personal relationships | Includes bibliographical references and index.
IDENTIFIERS: LCCN 2019002565 | ISBN 9781107196629 (alk. paper)
SUBJECTS: LCSH: Intimacy (Psychology) | Interpersonal relations. | Communication in marriage.
CLASSIFICATION: LCC BF575.I5 H55 2019 | DDC 306.7–dc23
LC record available at https://lccn.loc.gov/2019002565

ISBN 978-1-107-19662-9 Hardback
ISBN 978-1-316-64740-0 Paperback

"How do I love thee?
Let me count the ways."
–Elizabeth Browning (1850)

CONTENTS

List of Figures   *page* xi
List of Tables   xii
List of Spotlights   xiv
List of Collaborators   xvi
Foreword by Daniel Perlman   xix
Acknowledgments   xxvi

Introduction: Why Was This Book Written?   1

1 How Do We Know What Matters in Intimate Relationships?   4

2 Why Do People Seek Intimate Relationships?   36

3 How Are Intimate Partners Selected?   52

4 What Is Love and How Is Intimacy Expressed?   73

5 How Do Sexual Attitudes and Behaviors Matter?   84

6 What Are the Dynamics of Exchange and Power?   101

7 How Do Couples Cope with Conflict?   112

8 How Do External Factors Matter in Intimate Relationships?   131

9 How Do Intimate Relationships Relate to Well-Being?   155

10 How Do the Predictions Combine in Comprehensive Models?   173

11 How Much Do the Levels of Factors Vary?   183

12 What Are the Implications of the Study?   193

13 How Might the Findings Apply to Other Social Relationships?   198

    Epilogue: What Future Research Is Needed?   217

Glossary of Statistical Terms   219
Boston Couples Study Publications   221
References   223
Index   254

FIGURES

1.1. *Comprehensive Partner Model* being developed   *page* 6
1.2 *Comprehensive Commitment Model* being developed   6
1.3 Overlap of group distributions   14
1.4 Probability distribution of difference between two groups   16
1.5 Illustration of SEM Measurement Models   18
1.6 Illustration of SEM Structural Models   19
1.7 Illustration of correlations   34
10.1 *Comprehensive Partner Model*   175
10.2 *Comprehensive Commitment Model*   179
13.1 *Comprehensive Relationship Model*   204
13.2 Inner circle of support   205
13.3 Circles of support in decreasing intimacy   205

TABLES

1.1	Current partner groups	*page* 11
1.2	Relationship types	11
2.1	Reasons for being in a committed relationship	38
2.2	Importance of life goals	40
3.1	Mate selection factors	54
3.2	Mate selection SEM measures	54
3.3	Mate selection scale means	54
3.4	Partner similarity SEM measures	55
3.5	Partner similarity Scale means	55
3.6	Self and partner mean ratings	57
3.7	How partners meet	62
4.1	Four components of Love Scale items	75
4.2	Measures of Lee's Love Styles	75
4.3	Correlates of Lee's Love Styles	77
4.4	Correlates of knowing the partner	81
5.1	Approval of sex for unmarried partners	85
5.2	Physical activities with CP	86
5.3	Frequency of sexual activities with CP	87
5.4	Frequency of desired sex with CP	88
5.5	Who is more interested in sexual activities	88

5.6   Sex with others before relationship with CP   90

5.7   Sex with others during relationship with CP   91

5.8   Approval of outside sex   92

7.1   Mean sources of conflict   113

7.2   SEM measures for conflict factors   114

7.3   Mean violence behaviors   118

7.4   How often expressed jealousy   119

7.5   Times broken up and come back   119

8.1   Impacts of life domains   134

8.2   Racial-ethnic identities of participants   136

8.3   Religious identities of participants   137

9.1   Correlations between age 20 and age 58   162

10.1 Central Factors predicting Having a Current Partner   174

10.2 Comprehensive Factors predicting Having a Current Partner   175

10.3 Central Factors predicting satisfaction or commitment   176

10.4 SEM indexes for predicting satisfaction and commitment   177

10.5 Comprehensive Factors predicting satisfaction or commitment   179

11.1 Means for Having a Current Partner   184

11.2 Percentage variation in means for Having a Current Partner   184

11.3 Means for satisfaction and commitment   186

11.4 Percentage variation in means for satisfaction and commitment   187

13.1 Relevance of *Comprehensive Partner Model* for other relationships   201

13.2 Relevance of *Comprehensive Commitment Model* for
      other relationships   202

SPOTLIGHTS

Chapter 1
Filial Piety and Intimate Relationships in East Asia   *page* 25
  by Algae K. Y. Au and Sylvia Xiaohua Chen
Conflicting Views of Dating in Indonesia   30
  by Jenny Lukito Setiawan
Correlations Are Independent of Group Averages   34
  by Charles T. Hill

Chapter 2
Intimate Relationships of Youth in Russia   47
  by Victoria V. Ilchenko, Valery L. Sitnikov, Natalia V. Parnyuk, and
  Fatima G. Sanakoeva
Self-Transcendence Values   50
  by Cláudio V. Torres

Chapter 3
Partner Similarities in Romania   65
  by Loredana Ivan
Cross-Cultural Marriages in India   68
  by Suhas Shetgovekar

Chapter 4
Intimacy and Relational Mobility   82
  by Mie Kito

Chapter 5
Sexual Behaviors in Hungary   95
  by Zsuzsa F. Lassú

Chapter 6
Couple Power Dynamics in Mexico   109
by José Enrique Canto y Rodriguez

Chapter 7
Conflict Resolution in Spain and Colombia   121
by Andrés A. Fernández-Fuertes, Noelia Fernández-Rouco,
Anni M. Garzón, Rodrigo J. Carcedo, and José L. Martínez
Intimate Partner Violence   127
by Silvia Mari

Chapter 8
Parent-Choice vs. Own-Choice Marriages in Pakistan   141
by Charles T. Hill, Rukhsana Kausar, and Shehnaz Bano
Traditional Norms and Social Changes in China   143
by Xiaomin Li
Changes in Family Life in Greece   145
by Artemis Z. Giotsa
Family Tradition and Catholic Religion in Poland   149
by Karolina Kuryś-Szyncel and Barbara Jankowiak

Chapter 9
Well-Being of Partnered vs. Single People   164
by Claudia C. Brumbaugh
Spouses with a Special Needs Child   167
by Vered Shenaar-Golan and Ofra Walter
Implicit and Explicit Self-Esteem   170
by Takafumi Sawaumi and Tsutomu Inagaki (Fujii)

Chapter 13
Workplace Relationships in Africa and Elsewhere   207
by Olufemi A. Lawal

COLLABORATORS

The following collaborators made major contributions to the project in one or more of the following ways: by translating the questionnaire, by recruiting participants, by authoring Spotlights.

- Kâmile Bahar Aydın, Ankara Yıldırım Beyazıt University, Turkey
- Maria Rivas Barros, Universidad del Magdalena, Colombia
- Diana Boer, University of Koblenz-Landau, Germany
- Claudia C. Brumbaugh, Queens College, City University of New York, United States
- José Enrique Canto y Rodriguez, Universidad Autónoma de Yucatán, Mexico
- Rodrigo J. Carcedo and José L. Martínez, Universidad de Salamanca, Spain; Andrés A. Fernández-Fuertes and Noelia Fernández-Rouco, University of Cantabria, Spain; and Anni M. Garzón, University Foundation of the Andean Area, Colombia
- Elena Chebotareva, Moscow State University of Psychology and Education, National Research University Higher School of Economics, Russia
- Sylvia Xiaohua Chen, and Algae K. Y. Au, The Hong Kong Polytechnic University, Hong Kong SAR, China
- Artemis Z. Giotsa, University of Ioannina, Greece
- Victoria V. Ilchenko and Fatima G. Sanakoeva, North Ossetian State University, Vladikavkaz, Russia; Valery L. Sitnikov, Herzen State Pedagogical University, St. Petersburg, Russia; Natalia V. Parnyuk, University of the Ministry of the Interior, St. Petersburg, Russia; and Elena Sinelnikova, Emperor Alexander I St. Petersburg State Transport University
- Loredana Ivan, National University of Political Studies and Public Administration (SNSPA), Bucharest, Romania
- Ilona Kajokiene, Mykolas Romeris University, Vilnius, Lithuania
- Rukhsana Kausar, University of Management and Technology; and Shehnaz Bano, University of the Punjab, Pakistan

- Mie Kito, Meiji Gakuin University, Japan
- Karolina Kuryś-Szyncel and Barbara Jankowiak, Adam Mickiewicz University, Poznań, Poland
- Zsuzsa F. Lassú, Eötvös Loránd University, Hungary
- Olufemi A. Lawal, Lagos State University, Nigeria
- Xiaomin Li, University of Arizona, United States
- Guillermo Macbeth and Eugenia Razumiejczyk, Universidad de Salvador and Argentinian Council of Science and Technology, Argentina
- Silvia Mari, Università di Milano-Bicocca, Italy
- Takafumi Sawaumi, Ryutsu Keizai University, Japan; and Tsutomu Inagaki (Fujii), Kagoshima University, Japan
- Jenny Lukito Setiawan, Universitas Ciputra Surabaya, Indonesia; and Immanuel Yosua, Atma Jaya Catholic University of Indonesia
- Vered Shenaar-Golan and Ofra Walter, Tel Hai Academic College, Israel
- Suhas Shetgovekar, Indira Gandhi National Open University, India
- Mein-Woei Suen, Asia University/Chung Shan Medical University, Taiwan
- Cláudio V. Torres, University of Brasília, Brazil

FOREWORD

Leo Tolstoy wrote "Happy families are all alike; every unhappy family is unhappy in its own way." It is the first line of his novel *Anna Karenina*. Such openings in books and movies are often crafted to set the tone and signal what is ahead. In Chapter 1 of this book, *Intimate Relationships Across Cultures: A Comparative Study*, Charles T. (Chuck) Hill has an opening, elegant in its simplicity, that tells where his volume is headed:

This book reports the results of a comprehensive cross-cultural study of intimate relationships. The study was designed to do the following:
- Update the findings of the Boston Couples Study and other research
- Develop comprehensive models that combine the findings
- Compare the models across relationship types and cultures.

In broad strokes, the book accomplishes three things: (a) it builds on the foundation of a longitudinal study begun in the 1970s, (b) it provides a comprehensive model for predicting relationship commitment, and (c) it examines the extent to which predictors of commitment are similar or different in various types of relations and different world regions. Each of these goals merits comment.

THREE OBJECTIVES OF THE BOOK

Led by Zick Rubin along with Chuck Hill and Anne Peplau, the Boston Couples Study originally followed 231 dating couples for 25 years, which is extended to 38 years as part of the diverse sample in this book. In his 1969 doctoral dissertation, Rubin (1970) developed what became a groundbreaking social psychological measure of romantic love. In the Boston Couples Study, he and his coauthors set out to determine which couples stayed together and which terminated their relationships. Along the way, Rubin, Peplau, and Hill examined numerous aspects of the couples' relationships bearing on Rubin's central question. These included topics such as the couple factors in who volunteered to be research participants, how relationships developed, self-disclosure, partners' gender roles, sex differences, sex and contraceptive use, commitment, various factors predicting whether or not couples stayed together (e.g., premarital factors including cohabitation, romantic beliefs), and the associations of relationships with other variables (e.g., life satisfaction). In all, the Boston Couples Study Publications, listed in this volume, include twenty-five items. The study became one of the preeminent, most-cited social psychological studies of relationships done in the 1970s.

Apropos of Chuck Hill's first goal, replications of previous studies have clear advantages such as allowing examination of historical change. They can also have drawbacks such as when questionnaire items have dated referents. In being a partial replication with new elements, in this work Chuck Hill capitalized on the best of both worlds. He was able to have baseline historical results but also new measures and the ability to study a much larger, more diverse sample of participants.

A second of Hill's key goals for the book was to develop two overarching predictive models: one of being (vs. not being) in a relationship, the other of partners' commitment to the relationship. Regarding commitment, Hill looked for what predicts commitment directly as well as what predicts relationship satisfaction, which in turn predicts commitment. In focusing on commitment, Hill is aligning himself with an interdependence theory (IT) position as articulated by VanderDrift and Agnew (in press): "From an IT perspective, ... commitment, conceptualized as consisting of a long-term orientation, a motivation to persist, and an affective connection to a partner (Arriaga & Agnew, 2001) fuels an individual's expectation that they will persist 'through thick and thin.'"

An exciting feature of Hill's study, reported in the present book, is how well he was able to predict commitment. The late Caryl Rusbult's Investment Model is widely recognized as the leading theoretical perspective on commitment (Rusbult, Olsen, Davis, & Hannon, 2001). Rusbult believed that the amount partners invest in a relationship and how satisfied they are with it foster commitment, while the quality of the alternatives (e.g., other possible relationships) undermines commitment. Rusbult's model has enjoyed considerable predictive success, predicting nearly two-thirds of the variance in commitment (Le & Agnew, 2003). As readers will learn, Hill's empirically grounded, comprehensive model can do even better. Although advancing a theoretical model is different from advancing an empirical approach, Hill's unusually high level of predictive accuracy is certainly a kudo for his project.

Hill's third objective in doing the book was to test his model for predicting commitment in different types of relationships as well as different world regions. With male and female participants in heterosexual and same-sex relations as well as in married and non-married relationships, Hill had eight types of relationships. He also had participants from nine cultural regions across the globe.

The variability captured in Hill's global effort is relevant to two thrusts in contemporary social science research: using diverse samples and exploring core principles. In 2010, Henrich, Heine, and Norenzayan published their "weirdest people in the world" article. Henrich et al. noted that behavioral scientists routinely conduct their studies using participants from "Western, Educated, Industrialized, Rich, and Democratic (WEIRD) societies." They argued that these scientists then make broad claims about human behavior, but these claims are based on only a small, "unusual" proportion of the human species. Henrich et al. concluded, "WEIRD subjects may often be the worst population from which to make generalizations" (p. 79). They recommend, as Hill admirably does geographically, forging links to diverse samples.

A second thrust, this time in the relationship literature per se, is toward extracting a set of core principles from extant theories (Finkel, Simpson, & Eastwick, 2017). Finkel et al. do recognize the importance of cultural variation. Similar to Finkel et al. looking across theoretical perspectives, Hill's testing of findings across eight relational types and nine regional groups can help identify empirical regularities that might warrant being in the core set of phenomena that theorists should address.

When examining cultural variation, Hill primarily attends to how the association between variables is the same or different in various cultures. That is an important and frequently neglected part of how culture influences relationships. Other studies examining culture's impact on relationships often compare how cultures differ in average levels of key variables. In line with this more common approach, Hill also has a chapter on gender and cultural differences in the average levels of key variables. What do you think: are couple satisfaction and commitment pretty much the same across cultures, or do you think they vary between cultures? An intriguing part of Hill's analysis is this: do the two ways of comparing cultures produce similar conclusions, and what are the similarities and differences Hill finds?

STRENGTHS OF THE VOLUME

In an enlightening manner, the book provides a portrait of the universality and cultural specificity of personal relationships. For me, Hill's project and his report of it have two clusters of strength: (a) those of the study and (b) those of the book and its author. The laudable qualities of the study include the following:

- The study focuses on two of the most central aspects of close relationships: commitment and satisfaction.

- Whereas journal articles typically examine just a few factors, this project is comprehensive in exploring many factors related to its key outcome measures.
- It makes explicit comparisons across cultures instead of discussing each culture separately.
- It compares predictions across cultures instead of just average levels.
- It explores similarities as well as differences across cultures and relationship types.
- It considers effect sizes – the strength of predications, not just statistical significance.

Strengths of the author and the book include the following:

- Chuck Hill is an award-winning teacher who writes in a clear, direct style, which is apparent throughout and especially in his easily understood description of statistical and methodological issues.
- The book has a straightforward structure that builds across the chapters to an overall conclusion, the predictive model of commitment.
- The book balances a more Spartan statistical approach to reporting the study itself with a more detailed, more culturally sensitive set of SPOTLIGHTS.
- With its roots in the 1970s Boston Couples Study, for readers keeping track, the book uniquely illuminates a question that students, researchers, and members of the general public repeatedly ask: are our relationships changing?
- A short glossary of statistical terms assists readers who might want it.

THE BONUS FACTOR

Beyond Hill's investigation, the book features twenty SPOTLIGHTS as a bonus. These get into specific aspects of relationships in specific cultures. Various SPOTLIGHTS provide additional, country-specific data (e.g., Sexual Behaviors in Hungry), engage in theoretical analysis (e.g., Intimacy and Relational Mobility), summarize research conducted in specific cultural regions (Conflict Resolution in Spain and Colombia), depict historical change within a culture (Changes in Family Life in Greece; Traditional Norms and Social Changes in China), discuss atypical circumstances (e.g., Spouses with a Special Needs Child), and the like. Thus the SPOTLIGHTS expand the book's coverage, adding nuance and texture to the volume.

It is also interesting to consider these contributions from the perspective of the state of relationship science internationally. The number of international contributors testifies that relationship science is an area of research in many parts of the world. Personality and social psychology, a dominant contributing discipline in the personal relationships area (Perlman, Duck, & Hengstebeck, 2018), has been and continues to be dominated by American scholars, but that domination appears to be lessening throughout the world. Adair and Huynh (2012) reported that in leading personality and social psychology journals the percentage of US first authors dropped from 82 percent in the early 1980s to 58 percent by 2008. The proportion of US authors was lower in psychology journals with lower citation impact scores, dropping from 76 percent to 41 percent over time. The proportion of US first authors was considerably less and dropped less in international psychology journals, going from 41 percent to a percentage in the low 30s.

Independent of judgments about the merits of different styles of research, Adair, Puhan, and Vohra (1993) have differentiated between indigenous and endogenous research, a distinction somewhat akin to emic (from the perspective of those within the culture) vs. etic (from the perspective of an observer outside the culture). Indigenous research emanates from within the culture where it is conducted, frequently dealing with applied questions of local significance rather than more universal, scientifically driven inquiries. References to the culture are common and citation of international scientific literature is less prominent. The worldview and the methodology on which research is based may also vary across countries and world regions.

In the SPOTLIGHTS, I detect some signs of an indigenous view. For example, Setiawan's discussion of dating in Indonesia rests heavily on Muslim views. Some of the SPOTLIGHTS are largely region-specific, primarily descriptive reports (e.g., Hill, Kausar, and Bano's analysis of parent vs. own-choice marriages in Pakistan). An indicator of a highly developed level of indigenous research is a high ratio of references to publications by local researchers relative to psychologists from highly developed countries (Adair et al., 1993). The discussion of power dynamics in Mexican couples does this, especially referencing Rivera Aragon and Diaz-Loving's formulations.

Yet many of the authors of SPOTLIGHTS drew on concepts and use methods (e.g., questionnaires, basic statistics such as correlations) similar to those used in North American–led research. A further indication of the more universal, endogenous trend is evidence that previously in Latin American countries where a psychoanalytic perspective was ubiquitous (Benito, 2012), this influence has been replaced more recently by neuroscience research and cognitive and behavioral theories. The SPOTLIGHT on conflict in Colombia (and Spain) shows no discernible influence of psychoanalytic thinking.

In sum, the distinction between indigenous and endogenous research has fuzzy edges. Nonetheless, characteristics of an endogenous approach are frequent in the SPOTLIGHTS, even ones that help explain cultural differences (e.g., Intimacy and Relational Mobility).

INTERNATIONAL ASSOCIATION FOR RELATIONSHIP
RESEARCH SPONSORSHIP

This volume is sponsored by the International Association for Relationship Research (IARR), the leading international scientific society for the study of personal relationships. It is an exemplary addition to its *Advances in Personal Relationship Series*, joining some sixteen other published or soon-to-be-published books. The volumes in this series represent the culmination of years of scholarship on personal relationships. Contributing authors are internationally known scholars from a variety of disciplines, including social psychology, communication, family studies, human development, and sociology. Illustrating the ever-evolving yet cumulative nature of relationship science, this volume builds on the past from a fresh vantage point. It admirably achieves the standards and orientation of the series in presenting

first-rate scholarship that is both provocative and theoretically grounded. The theoretical and empirical work described by authors will stimulate readers and advance the field by offering up new ideas and retooling old ones. The series will be of interest to upper-division undergraduate students, graduate students, researchers, and practitioners. (IARR sponsorship page, this volume)

Other volumes in the series have addressed various aspects of personal relationships: their development, maintenance, and decline; specific types of relationships (e.g., romantic relations in emerging adulthood, marriage); external influences on relationships, including social networks; support; their role in health; abuse and other negative aspects of relationships; and ways of optimizing positive relationships. The book by Robin Goodwin (2008) entitled *Changing Relations: Achieving Intimacy in a Time of Social Transition* is an especially noteworthy complement to the current volume. Goodwin primarily focuses on historical change. He does this, however, by reviewing research from across the globe. In doing so, he examines the impact of macro-level variables such as social class and especially cultural variations on dyadic partners' everyday relationships. His book, like the present volume, reminds us that cultural milieus in which relationships function are not fixed but rather fluctuate over time. The take-home message is that scholars should attend to the way both time and culture, as macro-level factors, impact relationships.

CONCLUSIONS

Tolstoy's opening sentence warrants a refrain: "Happy families are all alike; every unhappy family is unhappy in its own way." Notarius and Markman (1993) have challenged the second part of the statement that every unhappy family is unhappy in its own way. From an overall vantage point, Hill's study seems to me to support Tolstoy's first assertion: satisfied and committed couples all share many attributes in common. Foster those conditions and qualities in your own life; you will have rewarding primary bonds.

I have studied relationships throughout my fifty-plus year professional career. Chuck Hill's book has given me a world tour that has taught me new information and focused my thinking on what most importantly predicts key elements of relationship success. The book provides clear answers to crucial questions that diverse audiences want addressed. I am grateful. It is my privilege to extend to you an invitation to dig into what the book offers.

Daniel Perlman, Former President (2012–2014)

International Association for Relationship Research

ACKNOWLEDGMENTS

Zick Rubin created the first love scale and initiated the Boston Couples Study in collaboration with his graduate students Anne Peplau and myself. It was enjoyable to work together with such great colleagues.

The original two-year data collection of the Boston Couples Study (1972–74) was supported by National Science Foundation grant GS27422 to Zick Rubin. Collection of the fifteen-year follow-up data was supported by grants to Charles T. Hill from the Haynes Foundation and from Whittier College, and by a University Research Grant from UCLA to Anne Peplau. The twenty-five-year and thirty-eight-year follow-ups were supported by faculty research grants to Charles T. Hill from Whittier College.

The present online cross-cultural study was supported by faculty research grants to Charles T. Hill from Whittier College. In addition to those listed as collaborators, the following have also translated the questionnaire or recruited participants: Klaus Boehnke, Giovanni Sadewo, and Donald Stull. The online database for storing participants' responses was created by Jeffrey Feng, Information Technology Services, Whittier College.

The following made helpful comments on drafts of book chapters: my students Tyrus Trevino and Richard Manjarres, my colleague Sean Morris, my wife Pam Hill who has been supportive throughout this project, and Dan Perlman who provided insightful comments in framing the book and provided additional references for each of the chapters.

I'd also like to thank Janka Romero of Cambridge University Press for inviting me to submit a book proposal, and Christopher R. Agnew, John P. Caughlin, C. Raymond Knee, and Terri Orbuch, editors of the *Advances in Personal Relationships* series, for advice on writing the book.

Introduction: Why Was This Book Written?

This book reports the findings of a cross-cultural study to update and extend the groundbreaking Boston Couples Study and other research on intimate relationships. It develops comprehensive models of relationship dynamics and makes explicit comparisons across relationship types and cultural regions, which are missing in the research literature. It is written in a style appropriate for college students, researchers, therapists, and others.

WHY WAS THIS STUDY CONDUCTED?

In 1972, Zick Rubin, Anne Peplau, and I began a pioneering longitudinal study of college-age dating couples, known as the Boston Couples Study. This research has been cited in numerous textbooks and journal articles. Our first of many articles (Hill, Rubin, & Peplau, 1976) has been cited more 750 times (Google Scholar, 2018).

In the four decades that I have been lecturing about the Boston Couples Study, my students have wondered: What about our generation? Do the findings apply to us? So I decided to update and extend the Boston Couples Study by conducting in collaboration with colleagues around the world an online study of intimate relationships that is cross-cultural and includes adults of all ages, with either opposite-sex or same-sex partners who are either unmarried or married.

This book presents the first published findings from this large and inclusive new study. In updating the Boston Couples Study, the book cites key findings of that pioneering study that have previously been scattered across many journal articles, book chapters, and conference presentations (see Boston Couples Study Publications). It also reports the results of a thirty-eight-year follow-up of some participants in the Boston Couples Study who participated in the new online study of intimate relationships, as well as unpublished results from the Boston Couples Study. In addition, the book reports unique findings about gay marriages, and additional findings about parent-choice versus own-choice marriages.

HOW DOES THE BOOK EXTEND THE RESEARCH LITERATURE?

Although there has been a great deal of research on close relationships, less is known about cross-cultural similarities or differences in romantic or sexual relationships. Recent books have reviewed intimate relationships (e.g., Bradbury & Karney, 2013; Fletcher, Simpson, Campbell, & Overall, 2013; Miller, 2017; Vangelisti & Perlman, 2018). One book focuses on stages of the life cycle (Khaleque, 2018) and cites some cross-cultural research. But none makes comprehensive comparisons across cultures.

Other textbooks have examined ethnic families in the United States (e.g., Coltrane & Adams, 2013; Knox & Schacht, 2015; Lamanna, Riedmann, & Stewart, 2014) and around the world (Ingoldsby & Smith, 2006; Queen, Habenstein, & Adams, 1961). A recent journal issue has explored interethnic marriages in the United States (Gaines, Clark, & Affful, 2015), and two online articles have discussed family variations and changes across cultures (Georgas, 2003; Kagitchibasi, 2002). Two edited volumes have discussed mate selection in various cultures, but neither makes explicit cross-cultural comparisons (Hamon & Ingoldsby, 2003; Scott & Blair, 2017). And an edited volume reviews research on marriage in selected cultures from an evolutionary psychology perspective (Weisfeld, Weisfeld, & Dillon, 2018).

There are a few older books and book chapters on relationships and culture (Dion & Dion, 1997; Gaines, 1997; Goodwin, 1999), as well as a few more recent book chapters (Gaines & Hardin, 2013; Gaines & Ketay, 2013; Heine, 2016). Also a few books deal with specific aspects of relationships and culture (Agnew, 2016; Goodwin, 2008; Hatfield & Rapson, 2005; Rosenblatt & Weiling, 2015); there are two books on relationships written in Mexico (Diaz-Loving & Sanchez Aragon, 2004, 2010), and a book on intermarriage (Singla, 2015).

In addition, a classic study compares same-sex and opposite-sex cohabiting couples in the United States (Blumstein & Schwartz, 1983), and there are two reviews of same-sex couples (Hunter, 2012; Diamond & Blair, 2018). Other books have explored the lives of persons who remain unmarried (DePaulo, 2006; Stein, 1981).

But currently, no other contemporary book exists that develops comprehensive models of relationship dynamics, with comparisons across cultures and across various types of romantic or sexual relationships.

FOR WHOM WAS THIS BOOK WRITTEN?

This book was written to be a supplemental textbook for undergraduate and graduate students studying social relationships, as well as for researchers and therapists. Hence it includes many references, measures, and statistical results. Key concepts are highlighted in bold when they are introduced, and measures have initial letters capitalized to distinguish them from concepts. For example, **relationship commitment** refers to the concept when it is introduced, while Relationship Commitment refers to the measure of it used throughout this book.

It is very important to study Chapter 1, to know the tools for thinking needed to understand the remainder of this book. These include conceptual tools for understanding the comparisons made, and statistical tools for understanding the results. But since the subject of the book is intrinsically interesting to almost anyone, the book attempts to explain these tools and the study in a way that will be understandable to other readers.

Readers are encouraged to think about each of the book's questions, and how they might apply to themselves. Participants in the Boston Couples Study reported thinking and talking about the questions in that study, which served as a form of couples counseling (Rubin & Mitchell, 1976). The first webpage (https://cf.whittier.edu/chill/ir) of this new online study described it as a way for participants to evaluate their intimate relationships and their well-being. I hope that reading this book, and thinking about its questions, will do the same. The overall goal of the study and the book is to provide insights that will help people have satisfying intimate relationships and meaningful lives.

How Do We Know What Matters in Intimate Relationships?

This book reports the results of a comprehensive cross-cultural study of intimate relationships. The study was designed to do the following:

- Update the findings of the Boston Couples Study and other research.
- Develop comprehensive models that combine the findings.
- Compare the models across relationship types and cultures.

Previous books have generally reported research conducted in one culture, or an anthology of separate studies in a few ethnicities or cultures without comprehensive comparisons among them.

To understand the present study, it is important to have certain tools for thinking. These include **conceptual tools**, which consist of the concepts used to categorize study participants for comparisons, as well as theoretical concepts for explaining which factors were measured and why they matter. They also include **statistical tools** for making comparisons and determining how much the factors matter. Statistical tools are used to reveal the results throughout this book. This chapter reviews these conceptual and statistical tools to facilitate the reader's understanding of this study, as well as other research on intimate relationships.

WHAT KINDS OF INTIMATE RELATIONSHIPS ARE FOCUSED ON IN THIS BOOK?

There are various ways of being intimate, including physical (touching, hugging, kissing, sexual), emotional (sharing feelings), cognitive (sharing thoughts), and experiential (sharing activities), as noted by Kakabadse and Kakabadse (2004). There are also many kinds of intimate relationships, including friendships, dating, marriage, and other relationships among family members or non-relatives. This book focuses primarily on dating, marriage, and other romantic or sexual relationships.

Sociologists have a long tradition of conducting research on marriage (e.g., Bossard, 1932; Burgess, Wallin, & Schultz, 1954; Winch & Goodman, 1968). Early research by psychologists examined interpersonal attraction (Berscheid & Walster, 1969; Rubin, 1973), and there was theorizing about what happens between initial attraction and marriage (Murstein, 1976).

The Boston Couples Study was one of the first to actually study dating relationships, following opposite-sex couples in college over time to see who stayed together or broke up (Hill, Rubin, & Peplau, 1976) and who eventually married (Hill & Peplau, 1998), as well as other aspects of their relationships (see Boston Couples Study Publications, p. 221 in this book). Many other studies of close relationships soon followed (Hendrick, 1989; Hendrick & Hendrick, 1983, 2000; Kelley et al., 1983; Perlman, Duck, & Hengstebeck, 2018).

HOW IS WHAT MATTERS DETERMINED IN THE PRESENT STUDY?

The present study investigates what matters using a questionnaire that has been online at https://cf.whittier.edu/chill/ir for participation in the study and is also available in pdf format at www.cambridge.org/0781107196629. The questions measure factors found to be important in the Boston Couples Study and other research. To determine whether these factors matter in this extended study, data analyses examine whether they predict **having a current partner**, and whether they predict **relationship satisfaction** and **relationship commitment**. Implications for well-being are also explored.

Previous research has studied people who are in an on-going intimate relationship, and people who are single, but little is known about comparisons between those who do or do not have a current partner. One goal of the present study is to develop a comprehensive model of factors that predict having a current partner, as indicated in Figure 1.1. For example, having a current partner might be predicted by one's desire to have a partner, one's confidence in approaching potential partners, one's readiness for a committed relationship, and one's opportunities to find a partner.

Prior research has examined factors that predict relationship satisfaction, which predicts relationship commitment (Rusbult, 1980; Rusbult, Agnew, & Arriaga, 2012). The present study expands this by exploring to what extent various factors predict relationship commitment indirectly through relationship satisfaction, and to what extent they predict relationship commitment directly, independent of relationship satisfaction. In other words, what factors predict commitment to a relationship whether relationship satisfaction is high or low? This is illustrated in Figure 1.2. For example, relationship satisfaction and relationship commitment might be predicted by characteristics of the

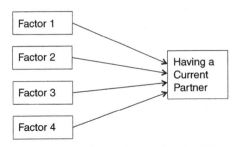

FIGURE 1.1   *Comprehensive Partner Model* being developed

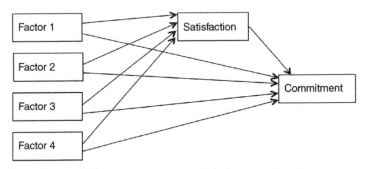

FIGURE 1.2   *Comprehensive Commitment Model* being developed

partner, feelings of love, equal involvement in the relationship, and positive ways of coping with conflict.

Studies comparing cultures, and studies comparing relationship types, have generally focused on differences in the **average levels** of various factors. For example, Sorokowski et al. (2017) focus on the average levels of marital satisfaction in various countries. Blumstein and Schwartz (1983) examine which partner has more power in opposite-sex couples and in same-sex couples. Studies of factors that **predict** relationship commitment have generally focused on one relationship type in one culture. For example, using data from the Boston Couples Study, Bui, Peplau, and Hill (1996) tested Rusbult's Investment Model that commitment is a function of attraction to one's partner, investment in the relationship, and the lack of alternatives.

The present study is unique in comparing predictions of having a current partner and predictions of relationship satisfaction and relationship commitment across various relationship types and various cultural regions. The goal is to see whether the same factors make the same predictions, in spite of any differences in the average levels of those factors. For example, does the degree of love predict the degree of commitment, whether the degrees of love and commitment are low or high, across relationship types and cultural regions?

Hence, the distinction between predictions of factors and average levels of factors is crucial for understanding the findings reported in this book. This distinction is illustrated later in this chapter after statistical tools are introduced.

WHAT FACTORS ARE EXAMINED IN EACH CHAPTER OF THE BOOK?

Chapter 2 asks why people seek intimate relationships. Chapter 3 asks how partners are selected. Chapter 4 asks what is love and how is intimacy expressed. Chapter 5 asks about sexual attitudes and behaviors. Chapter 6 asks about the dynamics of exchange and power. Chapter 7 asks how couples cope with conflict. Chapter 8 asks how external factors matter in intimate relationships. Chapter 9 asks how intimate relationships relate to well-being.

Chapter 10 summarizes the predictions from previous chapters and combines them into a *Comprehensive Partner Model* and a *Comprehensive Commitment Model.* Chapter 11 explores how much the levels of factors vary. Chapter 12 discusses limitations of the study, and implications of the findings for self-reflection, couples' counseling, and well-being. Chapter 13 asks how the findings might apply to other social relationships and proposes a *Comprehensive Relationship Model.* The Epilogue identifies future research needed using the statistical tools and conceptual tools described in this book.

Included in most chapters are SPOTLIGHTS contributed by collaborators that focus on particular factors, relationship types, or cultures. They provide insights on how average levels of factors vary. Most chapters also include *SELF-REFLECTION* sections to encourage readers to apply the findings to their own lives.

WHY DO THESE FACTORS MATTER?

Theorizing about the importance of these factors occurs in each of the chapters and is summarized in Chapter 10. Included in this theorizing are key concepts from theories that view relationships from a **social exchange** perspective. These theories include Social Exchange Theory (Blau, 1964; Emerson, 1976), Incremental Exchange Theory (Huesmann & Levinger, 1976), Resource Theory (Foa & Foa, 1980), the Investment Model (Rusbult, 1980; Rusbult et al., 2012), and Interdependence Theory (Thibaut & Kelley, 1959; Berscheid & Reis, 1998; Dainton, 2015). Key concepts in these theories include rewards, costs, investments, alternatives, comparison levels, and commitment (Clark et al., 2015).

According to Social Exchange Theory (Blau, 1964), we exchange not only tangible things like goods and favors but also intangible things like advice and love. When one person gives a reward to another, the other is **obligated** to reciprocate in an appropriate manner. We are taught a norm of reciprocity, that we are supposed to give in return, but even more importantly, we must reciprocate if we want to receive future rewards. For example, if you receive a gift on a holiday, you feel obligated to give a gift in return; if you don't, you may feel embarrassed, and the other is less likely to give you a gift in the future.

In social exchange, what is given in return is generally unspecified, unlike **economic exchange** in which the obligations are always specified. This requires trust that the other will reciprocate. Hence, relationships usually begin with small rewards to minimize the risk that an offer of a reward might be refused, or accepted but not reciprocated. If the other person accepts and reciprocates, that builds trust. Hence, there often is **incremental exchange**, with increasing rewards as trust increases (Huesmann & Levinger, 1976). For example, on first meeting we disclose little personal information, but as the other person shares more, we also share more, keeping us equally vulnerable to the revelation of private information. But if the other person doesn't share equally private information, or reveals secrets to others, we share less in the future.

When deciding whether or not to continue a relationship, one considers not only the **current rewards and costs** but also the **investment costs** of time, money, and effort spent developing that relationship, as well as the **opportunity costs** of not having pursued other relationships, and whether there are suitable **alternative** relationships potentially available. Thus, one may stay in a less than satisfactory relationship with attempts to salvage one's investment, especially if one is less confident about finding an alternative with its uncertain outcome.

In evaluating rewards and costs, people also consider **comparison levels** of rewards and costs in their previous relationships, other people's relationships, and potential alternative relationships, as well as notions about relationships from fairy tales and the media. For example, as people learn about the relationships of their relatives and friends, they compare them to positive and negative aspects of their own relationships. And fairy tales and movies tell us that couples live happily ever after once they fall in love and are married, giving unrealistic expectations for relationships that actually require effort to succeed.

Additional theoretical concepts are introduced in chapters where relevant and summarized in Chapter 10. References for theoretical perspectives on relationships are included in a comprehensive bibliography by Le and Emery (2015) and are described in chapters in Simpson and Campbell (2013).

FOR WHOM DO THESE FACTORS MATTER?

The present study expands the Boston Couples Study and other existing research by investigating the following question: In what ways are intimate relationships similar, and in what ways are they different, across relationship types and cultures? The relationship types include the eight combinations of men or women, in opposite-sex or same-sex relationships, who are unmarried or married. Cultures are studied by comparing nine cultural regions around the world, which are described later in this chapter.

In previous research, cross-cultural comparisons have often been conceptualized in terms of individualist cultures, which emphasize independence and individual achievement, and collectivist cultures, which emphasize interdependence and group harmony (Argyle et al., 1986; Hofstede, 1980, 2011; Markus & Kitayama, 1991; Smith & Bond, 1993; Triandis, 1995). Western countries are generally more individualistic while Eastern countries are generally more collectivistic.

But there are differences between North American and Latin American countries, between Western and Eastern European countries, and between East Asian and other Asian countries. Hence the present study makes comparisons of cultural regions around the world, keeping in mind that there are cultural and individual variations within each of these regions. For example, each region usually has more than one religious tradition, and there often are individual differences in adherence to religious restrictions on intimate behavior.

To make sure that the questions would be appropriate for different relationship types and cultures, a draft of the questionnaire was reviewed by thirty colleagues of various social and cultural backgrounds for social inclusiveness and cultural appropriateness. Collaborators have translated the final questionnaire into multiple languages, which the author has used to create webpages that have been online at https://cf.whittier.edu/chill/ir. He met these collaborators by giving and attending research presentations at international psychology conferences around the world.

FROM WHERE HAVE PARTICIPANTS BEEN RECRUITED?

Hill and his collaborators have recruited students and non-students in countries in North America, Latin America, Western Europe, Eastern Europe, South Asia, East Asia, South East Asia, Africa, and Oceana. Participants have also responded from other countries in these regions, which further increases the diversity of the participants. Specific countries and numbers are listed later in this chapter.

In addition, Hill obtained addresses from marriage license records to recruit same-sex and opposite-sex newlyweds to provide unique comparisons of gay, lesbian, and heterosexual marriages. The marriage licenses were obtained from Los Angeles County in California and from Hennepin County in Minnesota, and they included licenses for newlyweds who came to those states from other states where same-sex marriage was not yet legal.

Hill attempted to obtain marriage license records from other states, but they had been made confidential. In addition to these newlyweds, other adults in opposite-sex and same-sex relationships, both marital and non-marital, were among the participants recruited elsewhere.

Hill also invited former participants of the Boston Couples Study to participate in the online study, by sending each an individual code number to enter online to provide a thirty-eight-year follow-up of their original responses. In spite of missing addresses, sixty-six of them are included in the analyses throughout this book. Key comparisons with their earlier responses in the Boston Couples Study are discussed in Chapter 9.

To supplement the online questionnaire, colleagues in Pakistan administered a printed shorter version in Urdu to both members of 125 married couples, of which 65 were parent-choice ("arranged") marriages and 60 own-choice ("love") marriages. They are included in analyses throughout the book, with comparisons of marriage types in a SPOTLIGHT in Chapter 8.

The couples in Pakistan are the only participants whose id numbers link them as partners. All others participated anonymously as individuals, even though their partners may have also participated in some cases. Being in the same couple reduces the independence of their responses, which slightly affects the statistical significance of statistical tests, but with the large sample sizes in this study that does not affect the conclusions.

HOW MANY PARTICIPANTS ARE ANALYZED IN THIS BOOK?

Among the 8839 participants in this study, 69% are women and 31% are men. It is common for women to volunteer more than men for psychological research (Hill, Rubin, Peplau, & Willard, 1979). Women and men are compared throughout this book. In addition, there were 40 persons who differed from the binary gender categories used to define relationship types in this book; they are discussed in Chapter 12.

The ages of the participants range from 18 to 84, with a median (half above and half below) age of 21, reflecting the fact that 75% are students. Chapter 12 documents that the *Comprehensive Commitment Model* developed in this book makes similar predictions for both students and non-students.

Among the 72% overall who report a current relationship, 84% describe an opposite-sex partner and 16% describe a same-sex partner, and 25% of all partners are married. Numbers in each category are reported in the next sections.

HOW MANY PARTICIPANTS HAVE A CURRENT PARTNER?

Combining gender and whether or not they Have a Current Partner results in the groups that are compared in Table 1.1.

TABLE 1.1 *Current partner groups*

• Females with current partner	(N=4395)
• Females without current partner	(N=1671)
• Males with current partner	(N=1974)
• Males without current partner	(N=799)

TABLE 1.2 *Relationship types*

• Female opposite-sex unmarried	(N=2727)
• Male opposite-sex unmarried	(N=1073)
• Female opposite-sex married	(N=728)
• Male opposite-sex married	(N=348)
• Female same-sex unmarried	(N=454)
• Male same-sex unmarried	(N=115)
• Female same-sex married	(N=137)
• Male same-sex married	(N=223)

HOW MANY PARTICIPANTS ARE IN EACH RELATIONSHIP TYPE?

Relationship types are defined in the book in terms of gender combinations and marital status. Among those with a current partner, combining gender, sex of partner, and marital status results in the eight relationship types that are compared in Table 1.2.

HOW ARE CULTURAL REGIONS DEFINED IN THIS BOOK?

Cultures develop to cope with environmental conditions, such as climate and availability of resources such as water, fish, game, grains, and minerals. They also change as a result of migrations, conquests, and trade (Diamond, 1997). Intercultural contact results in the diffusion of technologies, religions, languages, and customs. As a result, cultural groupings can be identified by language families and by religions. For example, the expansion of the Roman Empire brought Latin across southern Europe, which developed into Spanish, Portuguese, French, Italian, Romansh (in southeast Switzerland), and Romanian. European conquest of the Americas brought Spanish, Portuguese, and the Catholic religion to Latin America.

Hence geography, along with history, plays a major role in defining cultural regions. The broadest cultural regions are continents. The cultural regions used in this book are similar to those defined by Cole (1996). Note that Mexico is included in **Latin America** instead of with the rest of **North America**, due to its conquest by Spain. **Eastern Europe** is distinguished from **Western Europe** by its former domination by the USSR after World War II. **Central, West, and South Asia** had to be combined in this book due to low numbers of participants other than in Pakistan. **East Asia** includes China, Korea, and Japan due to the influence of Confucianism and Buddhism. **Southeast Asia, Africa,** and **Oceana** are the additional geographic regions.

HOW MANY PARTICIPANTS RESIDE IN EACH CULTURAL REGION?

Participants were asked to select the country in which they were born. If they currently reside in a different country, they were also asked to select that country. Based on these questions, the cultural regions and countries in which they reside are shown here. Those answering in Russian who were born in the former USSR are included with Russia:

- North America (N=3249)
  (Canada 422, United States 2827; Mexico is included in Latin America)
- Latin America (N=995)
  (Argentina 178, Brazil 622, Colombia 88, Cuba 1, Ecuador 1, Jamaica 1, Mexico 102, Nicaragua 1, Venezuela 1)
- Western Europe (N=1090)
  (Austria 9, Belgium 6, Denmark 3, Finland 6, France 8, Germany 85, Greece 78, Ireland 4, Italy 554, Luxemburg 5, Netherlands 7, Norway 2, Portugal 7, San Marino 1, Spain 233, Sweden 8, Switzerland 3, United Kingdom 71)
- Eastern Europe (N=1498)
  (Belarus 7, Bosnia and Herzegovina 1, Estonia 1, Hungary 319, Lithuania 102, Poland 281, Romania 294, Russia 487, Ukraine 6)
- Central, West, and South Asia (N=317)
  (Azerbaijan 1, Bangladesh 1, Georgia 5, India 45, Iraq 1, Israel 6, Kazakhstan 2, Kyrgyzstan 1, Oman 1, Pakistan 250, Turkey 1, United Arab Emirates 2, Uzbekistan 1)
- East Asia (N=987)
  (China Mainland 47, Hong Kong 254, Japan 482, South Korea 200, Taiwan 4)
- Southeast Asia (N=583)
  (Indonesia 576, Philippines 3, Singapore 3, Thailand 1)
- Africa (N=71)
  (Botswana 7, Burundi 2, Central African Republic 2, Nigeria 53, South Africa 4, Togo 1, Zimbabwe 2)
- Oceana (N=38)
  (Australia 32, Kiribati 1, New Zealand 3, Tonga 1, Tuvalu 1)

These nine cultural regions are used in comparisons throughout the book. Similarities found across the cultural regions occur in spite of the diversity among the countries within each cultural region.

HOW ARE THE FACTORS MEASURED?

In any study, researchers are concerned about reliability, validity, and generalizability. **Reliability** refers to the following issue: if you did the measurement again, would you get the same result? To address this issue, researchers typically ask more than one question to measure the same factor. That is why questionnaires are often long and appear repetitive.

Responses to the questions that are consistent with one another indicate reliability. Combining the questions into a scale provides a more reliable measure of the factor. In the present study, most questions have responses from 0=NOT AT ALL to 8=COMPLETELY, or 0=NOT AT ALL to 8=EXTREMELY. Scales are created by averaging the responses to the questions that have consistent responses. Scales to measure relationship satisfaction and relationship commitment are described later in this chapter, and other scales are described throughout this book.

In some cases, a question is worded in reverse, so the responses need to be reversed before averaging with the other questions. In this book, the reverse questions are identified with a minus in front of the questions, while a plus is used for the other questions. Since the goal of the study was to develop comprehensive models, it was not possible to have long scales for every variable; when shorter scales are used, they include items that best capture the conceptual components of the scale.

Validity refers to the following issue: are you measuring what you think you are measuring? To address this, researchers see if the measure relates to other measures that conceptually ought to be related. For example, to test the validity of his love scale, Zick Rubin had observers watch couple members' eye gazing at each other and found that his love scale predicted mutual eye gazing (Rubin, 1970). The fact that his "paper and pencil" love scale predicted an observable behavior indicated that his love scale had validity. That led the National Science Foundation to give Zick Rubin a grant that funded the initial data collection of the Boston Couples Study.

Generalizability refers to the following issue: can the results be applied beyond those in the particular study? In cross-cultural research, issues of validity and generalizability are expressed in concerns about equivalence of measures across cultures, called **measurement invariance** (He & van de Vijver, 2012).

In the present study, these measurement issues are addressed by seeing if the same questions combine in the same way into the same scales across relationship types and cultural regions, and whether the measures relate in the same ways to other measures across relationship types and cultural regions.

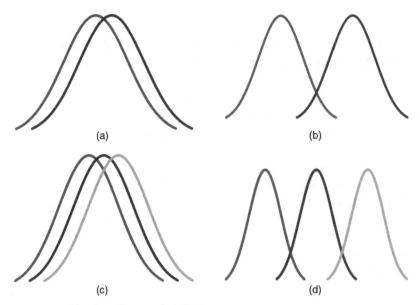

(a)   (b)

(c)   (d)

FIGURE 1.3   Overlap of group distributions

WHAT KINDS OF ELEMENTARY DATA ANALYSES ARE USED TO MAKE COMPARISONS?

Group averages, called **means**, are typically compared using t-tests for two groups, or using F-tests for multiple groups. These tests are based on how much the distributions of the groups overlap. In Figure 1.3, the curves represent the frequency distributions of scores in hypothetical groups, with the middle of each curve representing the mean of the group, and the width of each curve representing the individual variation within that group.

The variation (spread) in each group is measured by the **standard deviation (s.d.)**, which is the square root, of the sum of the squared difference, between each score and the group mean. The square of the standard deviation is called the **variance**.

T-tests determine how much the distributions of the two groups overlap by comparing the difference between the group means to the standard deviations within the groups. In (a), the distributions of two groups overlap so much that it is possible that the two groups could have come from populations that have the same mean, and the difference between the group means could be due to chance variations in sampling the two groups. In (b), the distributions overlap very little, so it is unlikely that they came from populations with the same mean. The difference between the group means is likely to be greater than might be expected due to chance variations in sampling the two groups.

Similarly, **F-tests** determine how much multiple groups overlap by comparing the variation among the group means to the variations within the groups, using calculations called **analysis of variance (ANOVA)**. When there are only two groups, F equals t-squared. To compare responses to different questions answered by the same group, **repeated measures ANOVA** is used.

In (c), the distributions of three groups overlap so much that it is possible that the three groups could have come from populations that have the same mean. In (d), the distributions overlap very little, so it is unlikely that they could have come from populations with the same mean. The differences among the group means is likely to be greater than might be expected due to chance variations in sampling the groups.

The logic of chance in these and other statistical tests is as follows. If you flip a coin ten times, it doesn't always turn up heads half of the time. But it is more likely that it would turn up heads four or six times than one or ten times. Similarly, if you had a population that had an equal number of males and females, and you randomly assigned them to either of two groups by flipping a coin, you wouldn't necessarily get equal numbers of males and females in each of the two groups. But you are more likely to get a small sex difference between groups than a large sex difference.

What a statistical test does is estimate how likely group differences of various sizes are to occur by chance. It compares the actual group difference to the estimated frequency distribution of all possible group differences, to determine the **probability** that a group difference that large could have occurred by chance. This is illustrated in Figure 1.4, in which the curve represents a **probability distribution** of all possible differences between the means of two sample groups randomly drawn from a population.

The curve reveals a high probability of getting a small difference between group means, and a low probability of getting a large difference. The right side represents a positive difference, and the left side a negative difference, with zero difference being the exact middle of the distribution. If the actual difference between group means is in one of the tails outside the vertical lines, that means that the probability of obtaining that large a difference either positively or negatively is less than 5%.

It is standard scientific practice to report a difference as **statistically significant** if the probability that the differences were due to chance is less than 5%, which is usually written $p<.05$. This means that there is one chance in 20 that the difference was due to chance. But how do we know if this isn't the one time in 20 when the result is due to chance? That is why **replication**, finding the same result again, is important. The probability of two studies both being due to chance is 1/20 times 1/20 = 1/400, and the probability of three is 1/20 times 1/20 times 1/20 = 1/8000, and so on.

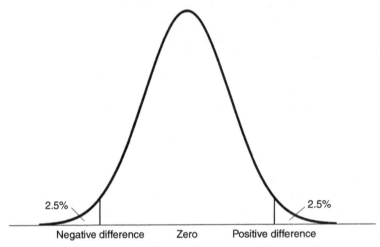

FIGURE 1.4   Probability distribution of difference between two groups

It doesn't take many studies to be confident that the result is not due to chance. But when reviews of the literature reveal conflicting findings, then researchers look for similarities and differences among the studies that might account for the conflicting findings, leading to new theories and studies of possible moderating variables, that is, variables that account for differing effects of other variables.

If the probability is higher than .05, it is reported as *ns* for not statistically significant. For ease of reading, in this book probability values will generally be reported using asterisks, which is common in research reports: * for $p<.05$, ** for $p<.01$, and *** for $p<.001$).

To analyze relationship dynamics, associations among variables are measured using Pearson **correlations** (r) and standardized regression coefficients based on them. Correlations can vary positively from 0 to 1, or negatively from 0 to −1. For example, in Chapter 5, we will see that there is a positive correlation between love and relationship commitment, which means that those with greater love tend to be more committed to their relationship. In Chapter 7, we will see that conflicts are negatively correlated with relationship satisfaction, which means that those with more conflicts tend to have less relationship satisfaction. Correlations are explained further later in this chapter.

When correlations are squared, their decimal value indicates the **explained variance**, in other words, the percentage of the variation in one variable that is predicted by the variation in the other variable. Hence a high correlation of r=.9 predicts .9 × .9=.81= 81%, a moderate correlation of r=.5 predicts 25%, and a slight correlation of r=.10 predicts only 1%. Correlations of r<.10, which predict less than 1%, will be called **trivial correlations** in this book, since they are not very theoretically significant, even if they are statistically significant due to large sample sizes. In this large study, correlations as small as r=.03, which explain .09 of 1% of the variance, can be statistically significant. Thus, r-squared is a useful measure of **effect size**, how much one variable predicts another. Due to the complexity of human behavior, effect sizes are often small in social science research. Hence, it is important to note when correlations and effect sizes are trivial.

When one of the variables has just two values, such as YES or NO, its correlation with another variable is called a **point-biserial correlation**. Its probability is statistically equivalent to that of a t-test comparing means on that variable, but it has the advantage of indicating the effect size when it is squared. For example, a t-test comparing those with and without a current partner on the importance of sexual activities as a reason for being in a committed relationship reveals that those with a partner rated sexual activities as more important than those without a partner. But the t-test doesn't indicate how strong the relationship is, while the point-biserial correlation does indicate the effect size when squared.

All of the predictions of Having a Current Partner in this book will be reported in terms of point-biserial correlations, instead of t-tests, to reveal the size of the effects. Additional information about elementary statistics is provided in textbooks such as Gravetter and Wallnau (2016), which has examples from the social sciences.

WHAT KINDS OF ADVANCED DATA ANALYSES ARE USED TO MAKE COMPARISONS?

Correlations are the bases of **factor analyses** that tell which items "load" on a factor, which means that they are correlated with each other, but not so much with other items that constitute other factors in that analysis. For example, ratings of the importance of physical attractiveness, height, and weight as mate selection criteria load on one factor, while ratings of social status, wealth, and education load on another factor, separate from each other and from other factors to be discussed in Chapter 3.

Items with factor loadings of .4 or above are considered part of the same factor, and those items can be averaged to create a **scale**, which is more reliable than any individual item. Correlations are also the bases of **reliability analyses** that tell how consistently the items are measuring the same concept. This is reported as Alpha (Cronbach, 1951) on a scale from 0 to 1, in which .6 is questionable, .7 is acceptable, .8 is good, and .9 is excellent.

In addition, correlations are the bases of **multiple regression** and similar analyses, which tell how well several variables together predict other variables in specified patterns. The multiple regression **R-squared** tells what percentage

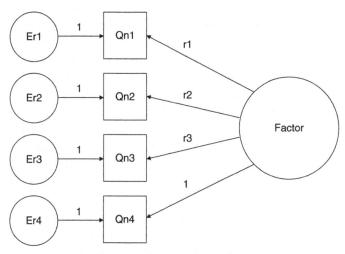

FIGURE 1.5 Illustration of SEM Measurement Models

of the variation in the predicted (dependent) variable is explained by all of the predictor (independent) variables together.

To assess whether findings are similar across groups, Structural Equation Modeling (SEM; Arbuckle, 2016) is used in this book. **SEM Measurement Models** are used for confirmative factor analysis to measure similarity in factor loadings across groups. An illustration of what these SEM models look like appears in Figure 1.5.

This model has questions labeled Qn1 to Qn4, which are assumed to reflect an underlying factor. For example, later in this chapter, four questions are used to measure the underlying factor Relationship Commitment. These questions do not measure the underlying factor perfectly, so they have measurement errors, which are labeled Er1 to Er4. The factor loadings are represented by regression coefficients labeled r1 to r3 and 1, which take on values that are compared across groups in the SEM analysis.

SEM Structural Models are used for **path analysis** to measure similarity in predictions across groups, such as relationship types and cultural regions in this book. An illustration of what these SEM models look like appears in Figure 1.6.

For example, in Chapter 4, SEM Structural Models are used to see if factors such as feelings of love, emotional closeness, and verbal and nonverbal expressions of affection predict relationship satisfaction. Factors like those are labeled Factor1 to Factor4 in Figure 1.6. The regression coefficients labeled r1 to r4 indicate how well the factors predict Relationship Satisfaction, which in turn predicts Relationship Commitment with regression coefficient r9. But in addition, regression coefficients r5 to r8 represent how well the factors predict Relationship Commitment independent of Relationship Satisfaction. These

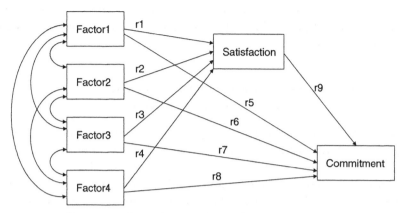

FIGURE 1.6   Illustration of SEM Structural Models

regression coefficients take on values that are compared across groups in the SEM analysis.

The SEM Structural Model illustrated in Figure 1.6 reflects the key feature of the *Comprehensive Commitment Model* that is developed in this book. It theorizes that certain factors, such as love and being invested in the relationship, will predict Relationship Satisfaction, and that Relationship Satisfaction will predict Relationship Commitment. But in addition, love and being invested in the relationship might increase Relationship Commitment whether Relationship Satisfaction is high or low. Sometimes people stay in unsatisfying and even abusive relationships due to love of the partner, or in hopes of holding onto their investment in the relationship by giving even more. These predictions about love and being invested in the relationship are tested in Chapters 4 and 6, respectively.

The Comparative Fit Index (CFI) and the Root Mean Squared Error of Approximation (RMSEA) are two measures that are commonly used to indicate how similar the findings are across groups. A CFI above .950 is one indicator of good fit (Hu & Bentler, 1999), and a RMSEA below .05 is another indicator of good fit (Arbuckle, 2016).

These and other analyses discussed previously are some of the types of data analyses recommended for cross-cultural research (van de Vijver & Leung, 1997). In the present study, data analyses are conducted using IBM SPSS AMOS for SEM analyses and IBM SPSS for all other analyses.

Most analyses in this book compare groups with each other as separate groups, but some analyses of the average levels of factors in Chapters 8 and 11 compare each group with the other groups combined, using point-biserial correlations to determine effect sizes. When multiple comparisons involve the same groups, the statistical tests are not independent, and smaller probability values are needed for the results to be statistically significant. With large sample sizes, and probabilities of $p<.001$, this is generally not a problem in the present study.

ARE THERE GROUP DIFFERENCES IN WHO HAS AN INTIMATE RELATIONSHIP?

Among those participating in the questionnaire, there is no statistically significant difference between the percentage of the women (72.5%) and the percentage of the men (71.2%) who describe Having a Current Partner. But there is a statistically significant variation ($p<.001$) among cultural regions in the percentage of participants describing Having a Current Partner, with the lowest rates of having a partner in the East Asia (53.7%) and Southeast Asia (45.6%) cultural regions. Reasons for these low rates are discussed in the SPOTLIGHT on Filial Piety and Intimate Relationships in East Asia, and in the SPOTLIGHT on Conflicting Views of Dating in Indonesia later in this chapter. Having a current partner risks engaging in premarital intercourse, which reflects poorly on parenting in cultures where premarital intercourse is prohibited.

Factors predicting having a current partner are discussed in various chapters. Those analyses exclude data from Pakistan since they include only married couples. The Pakistani data are included in analyses of relationship satisfaction and relationship commitment throughout the book.

HOW IS SATISFACTION WITH THE RELATIONSHIP MEASURED?

Relationship Satisfaction is measured in this study using answers to the following items, with possible responses from 0=NOT AT ALL to 8=COMPLETELY, where CP refers to the Current Partner.

- All in all, how satisfied would you say you are with your relationship with CP?
- CP and I have a good relationship.
- Currently, how satisfied are you with each of the following aspects of your life? – Your relationship with your spouse or partner

These three items, from different parts of the questionnaire, "load" highly on a single dimension in factor analyses, with a good overall reliability measure of Alpha=.88. SEM Measurement Models indicate high consistency in the factor loadings across the eight relationship types (CFI=.994, RMSEA=.025), and across the nine cultural regions (CFI=.991, RMSEA=.024). Hence, they are averaged to measure Relationship Satisfaction. Three items are an efficient number for a reliable measure, in the sense of how much more reliability is contributed by each additional item.

HOW IS COMMITMENT TO THE RELATIONSHIP MEASURED?

Relationship Commitment is measured in this study using answers to the following items, with possible responses from 0=NOT AT ALL to 8=COMPLETELY for the first three items, and from 0=NOT AT ALL to 8=EXTREMELY for the last item.

- To what extent do you consider yourself to be in a committed relationship with CP?
- I cannot imagine ending my relationship with CP.
- I view my relationship with CP as permanent.
- To what extent do you feel *committed* to remain in a relationship with CP?

The first item was written specifically for this study. The second and third items are from the commitment subscale of Sternberg's (1986) Triangular Theory of Love, which is discussed in Chapter 4. The fourth item is part of a set of items written specifically for this study to explore Rusbult's (1980) Investment Model, which was supported using data from the Boston Couples Study by Bui, Peplau, and Hill (1996) and will be discussed more in Chapter 6.

These four items, from different parts of the questionnaire, load highly on a single dimension in factor analyses, with a good overall reliability measure of Alpha=.85. SEM Measurement Models indicate consistency in the factor loadings across the eight relationship types (CFI=.962, RMSEA=.043) and across the nine cultural regions (CFI=.961, RMSEA=.035). Hence, they are averaged to measure Relationship Commitment.

What Does Relationship Commitment Mean?

Relationship Commitment has multiple meanings, levels, and stages. It can mean an agreement and promise to remain in a relationship, an expectation that one will remain in a relationship, and an obligation to remain in a relationship. It can refer to these at the personal level, the couple level, and the social level. The first stage is a **personal commitment** to the relationship, which may be followed by a mutual **couple commitment** that is initially private, but which may become a **social commitment** as others become aware of the relationship and treat the partners as a couple.

A social commitment can become a **legal commitment** if there is a marriage license or domestic partner registration. It can also become a **religious commitment** if a ceremony is held in a church, temple, or mosque. Marriages or other commitment ceremonies create increased personal, couple, and social commitment as the couple and others plan for, are invited to, attend, or are informed about a public ceremony. Smaller repeated private or public rituals affect commitment as well (Campbell & Ponzetti, 2007).

Marriage rituals vary across cultures but have similar effects on these various types of commitment. Depending on who is involved in the ritual, it expresses approval of the relationship by parents, friends, co-workers, religious authorities, and the state through the issuance of a marriage license. Illegal marriages indicate disapproval of the relationship, such as same-sex marriages in certain cultural contexts.

As expected, an F-test comparing relationship commitment among relationship types found that the four groups that are married (male and female opposite sex, and male and female same sex) all reported higher average levels of relationship commitment than the four groups that are unmarried, with an overall mean of 6.83 for those married versus 5.75 for those unmarried, for possible responses from 0 to 8 ($p<.001$).

HOW WELL DOES RELATIONSHIP SATISFACTION PREDICT RELATIONSHIP COMMITMENT?

Overall, the correlation between the measure of Relationship Satisfaction and the measure of Relationship Commitment is r=.73. SEM Structural Models reveal consistency in the regression coefficient of this link across relationship types (CFI=.978, RMSEA=.044) and across cultural regions (CFI=.967, RMSEA=.041). In other words, Relationship Satisfaction makes similar predictions of Relationship Commitment across eight relationship types and nine cultural regions, in spite of any variations in average levels of relationship satisfaction and relationship commitment. Why predictions are independent of means is illustrated in the SPOTLIGHT on Correlations Are Independent of Group Averages later in this chapter.

Consistency in regression coefficients across groups indicates that the factors make similar predictions, even if the average levels of the factors vary across the groups. For example, the average levels of love and commitment are higher in married relationships than in unmarried relationships ($p<.05$). But the effect of love in predicting commitment might be similar across relationship types, which will be tested in Chapter 5. Equal power is more likely in Western Europe than in cultural regions in Asia ($p<.05$), yet the effect of equal power in predicting relationship satisfaction might be similar across cultural regions as will be tested in Chapter 6.

Lalonde, Cila, Lou, and Cribbie (2015) argue that cross-cultural research has placed too much emphasis on differences, and not enough emphasis on similarities. The present study places more emphasis on similarities by using SEM models to test for similarity in predictions across relationship types and cultural regions, and by using effect sizes to determine when differences are trivial.

WHAT ELSE BESIDES RELATIONSHIP SATISFACTION PREDICTS RELATIONSHIP COMMITMENT?

Since the correlation between Relationship Satisfaction and Relationship Commitment is .73, and the square of that is .53, only 53 percent of Relationship Commitment is predicted by Relationship Satisfaction. This indicates that other factors besides relationship satisfaction also matter for relationship commitment. Some people feel committed to their relationship even if they are not completely satisfied with the relationship, for various reasons that will be identified in SEM Structural Models throughout this book.

In each chapter, correlations will be used to identify factors that predict Relationship Satisfaction and Relationship Commitment. The factors with nontrivial correlations will then be combined in SEM Structural Models to see their **indirect predictions** of relationship commitment through relationship satisfaction, and their **direct predictions** of relationship commitment independent of relationship satisfaction. In other words, the models will reveal which factors predict relationship satisfaction and which factors predict relationship commitment whether relationship satisfaction is high or low.

In SEM Models, effects are reported as **standardized regression coefficients** called gamma (γ), which can vary from 0 to 1 or from 0 to −1, similar to correlations. When γ<.10, they add less than 1 percent to the explained variance in the model. In other words, they add only a trivial amount to the predictive power of the combined predictors. The factors that have nontrivial standardized regression coefficients will be called central factors in this book.

What Are Central Factors?

When several factors, called **independent variables**, are combined to predict another factor, called the **dependent variable**, their combined effect is measured by Multiple R-Squared. This measure indicates the percentage of variation in the dependent variable that is predicted by the independent variables together. If the independent variables are correlated with one another, which is called multicollinearity, what they predict *in common* may be accounted for by the factor with the strongest effect, leaving little additional variance to be accounted for by other factors correlated with it. This may be reflected in low standardized regression coefficients for the other factors correlated with it, even if they have sizable correlations with the dependent variable, unless they have additional effects independent of what they have in common.

For example, Chapter 5 indicates that sexual frequency, ideal sexual frequency, equal interest in having sex, and sexual satisfaction are all positively correlated with relationship satisfaction, while frequency of having sex when you don't want to is negatively correlated with relationship satisfaction. But when these predictors are combined in an SEM Structural Model predicting relationship satisfaction, sexual satisfaction accounts for the predictions of all of these other factors since they are correlated with it. When sexual satisfaction is taken into account, these other factors add only trivial explained variance in relationship satisfaction.

The strongest predictor factors that are correlated with other predictor factors and capture what they predict in common, or have additional predictions beyond what they have in common, are called **central factors** in this book. Hence sexual satisfaction is a central factor in predicting relationship satisfaction in Chapter 5.

Central Factors are analogous to **central traits** in person perception research (Asch, 1946). Central traits are traits that are highly correlated with other traits, such that knowing one trait can predict other traits. "Warm" is a central trait, since it may predict being friendly, kind, generous, etc., while "being polite" is not a central trait since it predicts little else.

Central factors are identified in each of Chapters 2–9, then combined in a *Comprehensive Partner Model* and a *Comprehensive Commitment Model* in Chapter 10. These models test whether **predictions** are similar across eight relationship types and nine cultural regions, in spite of any differences in **average levels** of factors. Reasons for possible variations in central factors in other research are discussed in Chapter 12.

Differences in average levels of factors are discussed in Chapter 11 and in SPOTLIGHTS in various chapters. Statistical terms that are described in this chapter and that are used throughout the book to identify predictors and average differences are summarized in a Glossary of Statistical Terms at the end of the book.

SPOTLIGHT ON FILIAL PIETY AND INTIMATE RELATIONSHIPS IN EAST ASIA

ALGAE K. Y. AU AND SYLVIA XIAOHUA CHEN

Over the past five decades, there has been a global trend toward later and fewer marriages, especially in East Asia (Raymo, Park, Xie, & Yeung, 2015). Once characterized by universal marriage with a low unmarried rate (Jones, 2017), East Asia is now home to single and sexless populations. At first glance, single-hood and sexlessness are not necessary consequences of later and fewer marriages. However, East Asians tend to take courtship seriously and consider dating as a means to marriage rather than an end in itself. Therefore, casual dating that does not lead to commitment is discouraged, and premarital sex is strictly forbidden.

East Asians' conservative view on premarital sex can be seen from the findings of a global survey (Pew Research Center, 2014), in which 35% of respondents from South Korea and 58% from China found premarital sex unacceptable, in contrast to less than 10% disapproval from European respondents in Spain, Germany, and France. Previous research argued that premarital sex rises with economic development (Wellings et al., 2006); however, it is not the case in the second-largest economy in the world, China. The proportion of those engaging in premarital sex among young Chinese remains low, despite the country's skyrocketing economic growth in the past two decades. A national survey in China revealed that only 28% of male and 15% of female Chinese college students are sexually experienced (Chinanews.com, 2016), contrary to the findings of the National Survey of Family Growth 2011–2015 that more than 40% of American teenagers had premarital sex (Abma & Martinez, 2017).

However, sexual abstinence and singleness always go hand in hand. Virginity puts off potential partners by reducing an individual's desirability for a relationship (Gesselman, Webster, & Garcia, 2017), making those sexually inexperienced even more undateable. For example, in Japan, more than 40% of young adults remain chaste, while more than 60% are not in any kind of romantic relationship (NIPSSR, 2017). One possible explanation for the prevailing singleness and sexlessness across East Asian societies is their shared Confucian culture, which restricts courtship and discourages premarital sex through the behavioral guidance of filial piety.

CONFUCIAN FILIAL PIETY AND THE PARENT-CHILD RELATIONSHIP

To fully understand how an ancient Oriental wisdom affects present-day romantic relationships and sexual behavior, we will start by examining the historical underpinnings and major features of Confucianism, especially the relationship between filial piety and parental obedience and control.

Confucianism

Developed by the great scholar Confucius and his disciples, Confucianism is more than just an ancient Oriental school of thought, but a way of life that is still impacting Chinese and East Asian societies today (Zuo et al., 2012). Over the past 2500 years, Confucian values have penetrated every stratum of the societies, via both the model-based imperial examination system among elites dated back to the Han dynasty, and the frequency-based everyday life practices among lay-people throughout the generations (Nichols, 2013). Key virtues of Confucianism, including *ren* (benevolence), *yi* (righteousness), and *xiao* (filial piety), continue to be the guiding principles of appropriate behaviors for communal life in modern Confucian societies. Among all, filial piety is regarded as the cardinal virtue of Confucian ethics, which affects most teaching (Yan, 2017).

Filial Piety

Filial piety refers to one's affective, behavioral, and cognitive obligations to parents and familial elders, and obedience to absolute parental control (Ho, 1996; Nichols, 2013; Yeh & Bedford, 2003). The rationale behind the hierarch-ical, obliged, and obedient nature of filial piety is that children are forever indebted to their parents, a debt that can never be fully repaid. Everything children have, including food, clothes, education, and their very precious lives, all come from their parents. Although this debt can never be fully repaid, children should nevertheless try to do so by exhibiting filial piety through daily practices such as taking care of elderly parents and making them happy.

However, the bottom line of filial piety is not to disgrace the family by one's own behavior. In Confucian culture, a person is defined not by the individual one is, but the relations one is in. The most important and most irrevocable relation is the family relation, into which one is born (Rosemont, 1991). This interconnected relationality implies that every move a person makes will inevi-tably influence everyone else in these delicate familial relational networks. Hence one's inappropriate behavior not only damages the reputation of the self but also that of the family, as the whole family will share the consequential disgrace.

An empirical study in Hong Kong and Beijing, China, shows that the value of conservation predicted filial behavior over and above filial attitudes, and that interdependent self-construal (viewing the self as interdependent with others) moderated the relation between cultural group and filial behavior, with stronger effect in Hong Kong than Mainland China (Chen, Bond, & Tang, 2007).

The Filial Parent-Child Relationship

Nevertheless, not to disgrace the family is just a necessary but insufficient requirement for filial piety. Filial piety is such an important concept that different Confucian doctrines have different interpretations of it. According to *Mencius*, the most important filial obligation is to continue the family lineage (Mooney & Williams, 2016), which involves making a good mate choice and having a good marriage. While in the *Classic of Filial Piety*, the ultimate goal of filial piety is to glorify one's parents by following the Way, establishing oneself and making one's name famous (Yan, 2017).

On the other hand, parental obligation is also outlined in some Confucian doctrines. For example, according to the *Three Character Classic*, a Confucian book for young readers, it is the father's fault if a child is raised but not taught (Chinasage, 2017). One interesting point is that teaching, in the unique sense of Confucianism, usually refers to an authoritarian parenting style that involves strict discipline and firm control to enforce children's compliance. All in all, the three Confucian classics have summed up several key behavioral guidelines for parent-child relationships. Filial children should be cautious in mate-related issues, appropriate in behavior, diligent in study, and ambitious in their careers, while parents have to discipline and control their offspring to ensure they are on the right track of filial endeavors. A cross-cultural study in Taiwan and the United States found that the Taiwanese were more likely than European Americans to prioritize parental relationships over marital relationships, and obligation accounted for the cultural differences in hypothetical life-or-death and everyday situations (Wu, Cross, Wu, Cho, & Tey, 2016).

FILIAL PARENT-CHILD CONFLICT IN OFFSPRING MATE SELECTION

Conflict is an inevitable part of all relationships, and the filial parent-child relationship is no exception. The conflict is most intense over offspring mate selection, and clashes between parents' and children's preferences can usually put filial piety to the test (Nichols, 2013).

When it comes to mate selection, parents and children often have differing opinions (Buunk, Park, & Dubbs, 2008). Parents generally focus on parental investment (expenditure of time and resources) potential in their offspring's mates, while offspring usually emphasize heritable fitness (positive genetic characteristics) in their mates (Buunk et al., 2008). In Western cultures, children's choice always triumphs over that of the parents. In Confucian societies, however, parents are always the winner of this parent-child tug-of-war, as filial children are obliged to fulfill parents' expectations rather than their own.

If children ever insist on their own decision, they will be heavily condemned as unfilial (To, 2015b). Empirical findings also indicate that East Asian parents are more empowered than Western parents to have control over their offspring's mate selection (Dubbs, Buunk, & Taniguchi, 2013). For example, a cross-cultural study revealed that East Asian university students in

Canada are more willing than their Western counterparts to accept parental influence on their mate choice (Buunk, Park, & Duncan, 2010).

Confucian parents see offspring mate selection as one of the most important decisions they have to make for their children. In Confucian belief systems, marriage is not merely a union between two loving persons but a joint venture between two families, an all-important decision that brings either honor or disgrace to both parties and their future generations (To, 2015b). A common sought-after trait for potential sons- and daughters-in-law is filial piety, which is highly valued as a good indicator for future parental investment. The underlying logic is that if a person is filial to one's own parents and respects the elderly, the person must be a good spouse and parent in the future as well (Guo, Feng, & Wang, 2017).

Parental Obedience in Restricting Courtship and Discouraging Premarital Sex

As marriage has huge collective influences over a family's economic and social wellness, Confucian parents tend to keep a tight grip not only on selecting whom their offspring would marry but also on controlling premarital behavior before the knot is tied.

As mentioned, two important behavioral guidelines for filial children are caution in mate-related issues and appropriateness in behavior. Therefore, filial children are only allowed to engage in long and committed relationships, rather than short and casual ones. Behavioral indicators of short-term mating strategies such as hasty courtship and premarital sex are socially rejected (Guo et al., 2017). Confucian parents, as official moral gatekeepers of their offspring, are authorized to restrict courtship and discourage premarital sex among their young adults, who, according to filial piety principle, are also expected to restrain themselves and succumb to parental control (To, 2015a).

Restricting Courtship

Restricting courtship is closely related to two behavioral guidelines for filial children: being diligent in study and ambitious in one's chosen career. Over the past few decades, there has been a growing trend toward extended schooling and delayed career (Furstenberg, 2000). Nowadays, it is not uncommon to see people who are still studying in their late 20s and have not yet started their first job. With this extended adolescence and delayed adulthood (Buchmann, 1989), many grown-up offspring are still striving for higher education or a better career.

Such a lengthy time gap between sexual maturity and social maturity is especially torturing for East Asian offspring. In the eyes of Confucian parents, marriage is the ultimate goal of courtship; if the grown-ups are not yet ready for spousal and parental responsibilities, they are unqualified for intimate relationships altogether. In Confucian tradition, courtship is generally restricted until the offspring have fulfilled their filial duty in their academic and career pursuits.

Discouraging Premarital Sex

While courtship is generally restricted, marital sex is simply out of the question. The main reason for prohibiting premarital sex is chastity, a highly praised Confucian feminine ideal for preserving virginity until marriage. Discouragement of premarital sex is mainly related to two behavioral guidelines for filial children: caution in mate-related issues and appropriateness in behavior. Along with the global trend of delayed marriage, premarital sex has become increasingly common in Western culture (Barber, 2018), yet it continues to be a taboo in modern Confucian societies. For example, Japan and Korea still hold a conservative attitude toward premarital sex, where cohabitation is discouraged and pregnancy before marriage is socially rejected (Koh & Matsuo, 2016).

Although it takes two to have a relationship, guarding one's chastity is still deemed to be the sole responsibility of the woman herself, and the stigma of premarital sex is more on the female than on the male. Therefore, Confucian parents would be furious and shamed if a daughter were found to have premarital sex (To, 2015a). As chastity is proxy for parental influence on the daughter, the mere act of premarital sex itself is an indicator of failed parental control and poor filial teaching. Therefore, Confucian parents are particularly stringent about their daughters' premarital behavior, while premarital sex is also largely discouraged across Confucian societies.

CONCLUSION

Prevailing singleness and sexlessness across East Asian societies can be explained by their shared Confucian culture of filial piety that restricts courtship and discourages premarital sex. As the cardinal virtue of Confucian ethics, filial piety provides the essential behavioral guidance for the parent-child relationship, a relationship built upon a power structure of parental obedience and control, legitimized by the reciprocity of indebtedness and repayment. Although the Confucian authoritarian parenting style seems to be effective in controlling offspring's mating behavior, it is unclear whether a relationship that is largely based on obligation and guilt, rather than love and warmth, would truly benefit both parents and offspring in the long run.

Author Note: The contribution of the Hong Kong team was supported in part by the Departmental General Research Grant (#G-UB63) from the Hong Kong Polytechnic University.

SPOTLIGHT ON CONFLICTING VIEWS OF DATING IN INDONESIA

JENNY LUKITO SETIAWAN

For Indonesians, it is uncommon for an unmarried person to mention having a current partner. The term "current partner" connotes a sex partner. Mentioning having a sex partner before marriage is a sensitive issue. This is related to social pressures, which to some degree are based on cultural norms and religious values. Therefore, even if some young people have a sex partner, they tend to hide this and not disclose it to the public.

The Muslim religion prohibits premarital sex, yet some are engaged in it or are conflicted about it. To explore this, interviews were conducted to identify pressures not to have premarital sex and pressures to engage in sex before marriage. A total of eight Moslem undergraduate students were interviewed to learn their views of dating, premarital sex, the influence of parents, and the influence of friends. The students included three Hijabi females (those who wear an Islamic female's scarf on a daily basis), two non-Hijabi females, and three males.

DATING

Dating is a romantic relationship between two persons that does not necessarily involve intercourse. Some students view dating as a preparation toward marriage, an opportunity for couple members to get to know each other in a deeper way before they carry their relationship on to marriage. But other students view dating as something prohibited.

Explanations for prohibiting dating include viewing dating as a distraction from the main duty as students. In addition, some Moslem students viewed dating as *zina*, an unlawful relation in religious law. Normally in dating, the couple has its private space and does not involve others, which can lead to sins such as premarital intercourse. Hence, being alone with an unlawful partner without the presence of other people is forbidden in Islam.

It was reported in an interview that Islam does provide a method to get to know each other, which is called Taaruf. Contrary to dating, in Taaruf a man and woman get to know each other through the mediation of a family member. When they meet, they can discuss critical issues to know whether or not they are compatible to build a marital relationship. There is no opportunity to have a private space as they have the chaperone, which reduces the risks of *zina*.

Some other students mentioned that dating is allowed. Two reasons underlie this view. First, they believe that the culture of Taaruf is not effective in getting to know the potential spouse. There may be concerns about the family's honesty in providing information about the person. Dating is viewed as a way to get a deeper understanding of the potential spouse. Second, dating is viewed as friendship, as a way to get social support and gain positive affective experience from significant others besides the parents.

However, it was also emphasized that dating should be accompanied by good self-control and awareness of social limitations. When one decides to have a dating relationship, one should maintain self-control and sensitivity toward social limitations that view premarital sex as a disgrace. In spite of those concerns, six out of the eight interview participants had experience in a dating relationship. The majority of the interviewees view premarital sex as something unacceptable, although sometimes it does occur. Premarital sex is taboo in Indonesian culture; having sex before marriage strongly violates a social norm. Sexual intercourse is viewed as appropriate if and only if it is done with one's married partner. Having sex before marriage involves losing one's virginity and a risk of pregnancy. Virginity is socially believed to be a precious thing to preserve until marriage. Losing one's virginity and becoming pregnant will lead to pressure on the female, especially when the male partner does not take responsibility and marry her. Premarital pregnancy will bring disgrace to the whole family. Accordingly, it is common for a family to cover up an unwed pregnancy by isolating the family member from society.

Having sex before marriage is not approved by religion; it is considered as *zina*, an unlawful relation, which is a great sin. Therefore pre-marital sex is considered *haram*, which means forbidden by God. It was explained in the interview that in Islam even shaking hands or gazing at someone of the opposite sex who is not a *mahram* (a family member) is forbidden. In Islam, intentionally touching the skin of non-*muhrim* (non-family members) is already clearly prohibited, and there is a consequence for each such wrongdoing. For these reasons, dating is also not acceptable, as dating usually involves the couple without the presence of others, and this will bring the risks of gazing and touching the skin of the partner. It was mentioned that in dating, there are many things related to *maksiat* (act of breaking religious law).

THE INFLUENCE OF PARENTS

According to the interviews, parents take various positions regarding dating, including prohibiting dating, not clearly stating the regulations, and allowing dating. The reasons involved in prohibiting dating were worries that dating would interfere with studies and beliefs that prohibiting dating would protect their daughter. However, for those allowing dating, the parents are still involved in the process of partner selection. In Indonesian culture, parents' or family's approval of the chosen partner has a significant impact. Parents' protection can be manifested through actions contributing to selecting their children's partner.

All female participants reported that their parents prohibit them from having premarital sex. However, interestingly, one of the male participants reported that his parents emphasize the using of a contraceptive method if he does have sexual intercourse.

Parents use several methods to teach their daughters or sons regarding topics of dating and premarital sex. Parents emphasize that premarital sex is religiously forbidden; therefore, they expect their children to avoid any related actions. Additionally, they also show the negative consequences of premarital sex by pointing to examples that children can see from their surroundings and emphasize that children should prevent themselves from making the same mistake of having premarital sex.

Having premarital sex especially leading to unwed pregnancy will lead to shame and fear and will bring shame not only for themselves but also for the whole family. Those who engage in premarital sexual intercourse are forced to lawfully marry the partner as a form of responsibility, especially when it causes unwanted unwed pregnancy. Usually premarital sex will invite strong anger from parents, and this also leads to the children's feelings of fear.

FRIENDS

There are several functions of dating that participants see from their friends, including having a source of affective and motivational support, having fun, raising social prestige, making preparations for future marriages, and having a sexual partner to channel sexual drive. Participants also reported that they knew some friends who were fine with having sexual intercourse. They saw that their friends whose relationship with their partners' family was already really close were less hesitant to continue to the level of sexual intercourse. One of the participants mentioned that having premarital sexual intercourse was already considered a common thing. These reports show that premarital sex does occur among students.

CONCLUSIONS

It is interesting that when participants were asked about their friends in terms of premarital sex, they reported that some of their friends did have premarital sexual intercourse. They also reported that premarital sex was common among their friends. However, when the participants were asked about their own perception of premarital sex, they tended to say that premarital sex was prohibited. These contradictory phenomena imply that premarital sex brings conflicting attitudes among them. In addition to religious law, it seems that social judgment is very prominent. This was shown by the use of several terms in the interviews such as "social norms," "people's criticism," "family disgrace," "moral responsibility," and "social shaming." Fear of not being able to fulfill social expectation is apparently salient.

Therefore, it can be understood that talking about premarital sex brings uneasiness, especially talking to the public or to someone who is not very close in relationship. Having premarital sex leads to guilt feelings of breaking religious law and social expectations. This may also influence their openness in talking about premarital sex behavior to others.

It seems that parents are more protective and strict toward their daughters than toward their sons. Social expectations are higher for females than males. Parents are more permissive toward their sons than toward their daughters. This different treatment is possibly caused by the perceptions that females are more prone than males to be victimized by negative consequences of premarital sex, such as losing virginity, becoming pregnant, and having no guarantee that the sexual partner would marry her.

SPOTLIGHT ON CORRELATIONS ARE INDEPENDENT OF GROUP AVERAGES

CHARLES T. HILL

When a correlation is calculated, the variables are converted to **standard scores** (i.e., "normalized") by subtracting the average (called the mean) and dividing by the standard deviation of each variable. This indicates that correlations, and standardized regression coefficients based on them in SEM models, are independent of the means and standard deviations of the variables being correlated. To illustrate this, consider the hypothetical groups illustrated in Figure 1.7, comparing the ages of women and men in couples.

In group (a), the men and women have the same ages, and there is a correlation of r=1 between their ages because the oldest woman is paired with the oldest man, the next oldest woman with the next oldest man, and so on down to the youngest woman with the youngest man. In other words, the women's ages are in the same order as the men's ages in the pairing across couples.

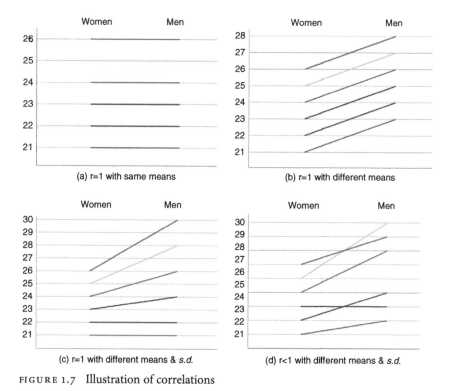

(a) r=1 with same means

(b) r=1 with different means

(c) r=1 with different means & *s.d.*

(d) r<1 with different means & *s.d.*

FIGURE 1.7   Illustration of correlations

In group (b), the man is two years older than the woman in every couple, so there is a mean difference of two years between the men and the women. But the correlation is still r=1, because the oldest woman is still paired with the oldest man, and so on. In other words, the women's ages are still in the same order as the men's ages in the pairing across couples.

In group (c), the mean of the men is higher than the mean of the women, and the standard deviation (variation) of the men is higher than the standard deviation (variation) of the women. But the correlation is still r=1, because the oldest woman is still paired with the oldest man, and so on. The women's ages are still in the same order as the men's ages in the pairing across couples.

In group (d), the mean of the men is higher than the mean of the women, and the standard deviation (variation) of the men is higher than the standard deviation (variation) of the women. But the correlation is less than 1, because the pairing is no longer such that the oldest woman is paired with the oldest man, and so on for every couple. The women's ages are no longer completely in the same order as the men's ages in the pairing across couples. However, the correlation is greater than zero because the women's ages are partly in the same order as the men's ages in the pairing across couples.

Because correlations are independent of the means and standard deviations of the variables being correlated, *correlations can be the same* across groups, even if the means and standard deviations vary across the groups. The same is true for standardized regression coefficients based on correlations. Therefore, predictions measured by correlations, or by standard regression coefficients in SEM models, can be the same across groups, even if the means and standard deviations vary across those groups.

2

Why Do People Seek Intimate Relationships?

Predictions of having a current partner, as well as relationship satisfaction and relationship commitment, are explored in terms of the following:

- Reasons for wanting a committed relationship
- Goals in life
- Values
- Attitudes about intimate relationships

HOW HAVE REASONS FOR INTIMATE RELATIONSHIPS BEEN STUDIED IN THE PAST?

Maslow (1943) argued that humans have a **hierarchy of needs**, which are usually displayed as a pyramid with the following layers from the top to the bottom:

- Self-actualization – achieving your full potential
- Cognitive and aesthetic – the arts, education, religion, or philosophy
- Esteem – respect, self-esteem, social approval, recognition, social status
- Social – acceptance, belonging, love, sex
- Safety and security – physical safety and psychological security
- Physiological – air, water, food, sunlight, sleep, exercise, clothing, shelter

Maslow originally listed sex as a physiological need, but others consider it a social need (Kenrick et al., 2010), since it is not essential for an individual's physiological survival. In later years, Maslow (1971) added self-transcendence to self-actualization, referring to altruism and relating to others and nature beyond oneself.

Maslow argued that the set of needs listed on the bottom must be met first; then when each set is met, the next higher set emerges. While it is true that the bottom level is necessary for survival, the answers to the cognitive and aesthetic needs teach us how to meet all of the other needs. And meeting social needs provides social support to cope with the stresses involved in meeting needs. Hence, the hierarchical nature of the needs can be questioned.

Social and other needs provide reasons and goals for seeking intimate relationships. Baumeister and Leary (1995) argued that humans have a fundamental need for belonging, and this is included as relatedness along with autonomy and competence as three primary motivations in Self-Determination Theory (Ryan & Deci, 2017). A lack of interpersonal relationships can lead to loneliness (Peplau & Perlman, 1982). Weiss (1974) distinguished between two types of loneliness: emotional (due to lack of intimate relationships) and social (due to lack of a social network). DiTommaso and Spinner (1997) further distinguished between romantic emotional loneliness and family emotional loneliness. Hence, avoiding loneliness is a major reason for seeking an intimate relationship. In the Boston Couples Study, those who broke up reported feeling lonely and depressed (Hill, Rubin, & Peplau, 1976). In addition, loneliness is a major risk factor for mortality, as important as physical factors (Holt-Lunstad et al., 2015).

WHAT ARE THE BIOLOGICAL REASONS FOR INTIMATE RELATIONSHIPS?

Human babies are dependent upon others for survival. To promote maternal care, oxytocin is released during ovulation, pregnancy, and nursing (Moberg, 2003). Oxytocin promotes emotional bonding not only to babies but also to children and adults (Moberg, 2013). It is released during orgasm in both women and men, and it is released in response to touch in both men and women, facilitating emotional bonding to others of both sexes.

There is an African saying that it takes a village to raise a child. It is helpful to keep the father around to help raise the child. Oxytocin promotes this. So does human females being sexually receptive even when they are not ovulating and cannot get pregnant, which is unusual in the animal kingdom. It is also helpful to keep other relatives and friends around to help raise the child and to meet other human needs. Thus, it is important to have emotional bonding of both women and men with others of both sexes. Sports teams promote emotional bonding to work together but call it "team spirit." And the military promotes emotional bonding to defend and even die for others in one's unit but call it *esprit de corps.*

Needs motivate us to set goals and engage in behaviors to meet those needs. And cultures develop ways of meeting needs in the midst of social and physical environments, such as how to hunt, fish, survive the cold, and get along in small villages and in dense urban settings. These ways of meeting needs are expressed in terms of values, attitudes, and norms for appropriate behaviors, which are passed down across generations, through contacts with

TABLE 2.1 *Reasons for being in a committed relationship*

	Mean	(s.d.)
• Emotional closeness	7.15	(1.24)
• Commitment to stay together	6.91	(1.68)
• Exclusivity (monogamy)	6.39	(2.31)
• Sexual activities	6.15	(1.85)
• Financial security	5.23	(2.33)
• Having a child	5.11	(2.76)
• Someone to cook and clean for you	3.23	(2.59)

peers and others, and through books and other media. Thus, culture is created, modified, and transmitted through social relationships.

HOW HAVE VALUES BEEN STUDIED IN THE PAST?

Schwartz (2012) identified values that vary across and within cultures. Factor analyses of measures of these values indicate that they can be grouped into the following four High-Order Values:

- **Self-Transcendence:** *universalism, benevolence*
- **Conservation:** *security, tradition, conformity*
- **Self-Enhancement:** *achievement, power, hedonism*
- **Openness to Change:** *stimulation, self-direction, hedonism*

These can be arranged in a circle with Self-Transcendence opposite Self-Enhancement, and Conservation opposite Openness to Change. Self-Transcendence is especially relevant for the intimate relationships studied in this book, since it involves concern about others. And Conservatism is relevant for cultural restrictions on whom to marry and avoiding premarital sex.

WHAT ARE THE MOST IMPORTANT REASONS FOR BEING IN A COMMITTED RELATIONSHIP?

To measure **relationship reasons** in this study, participants are asked "How important to you are each of the following as reasons for being in a marriage or other committed relationship?" The overall means and standard deviations for all 8839 participants in the study are listed in Table 2.1.

The items are ordered in Table 2.1 according to their overall mean rating, for possible responses from 0=NOT AT ALL to 8=EXTREMELY. Each mean is statistically significantly different from the mean below it in a repeated measures analysis of variance, due to the large sample size.

Note that ratings of emotional closeness and commitment to stay together are very high, with not a great deal of individual variation reflected in their standard deviations (*s.d.*). An example of what young people are seeking in intimate relationships, and what their relationships are like, is provided in the SPOTLIGHT on Intimate Relationships of Youth in Russia later in this chapter.

HOW ARE THESE REASONS CORRELATED WITH HAVING A CURRENT PARTNER?

Having a Current Partner is correlated overall with more desire for sexual activities (r=.15***) and less desire for financial security (r=−.11***) or having someone to cook and clean for you (r=−.13***). In other words, those desiring sex are slightly more likely to have a partner, while those seeking financial security or someone to cook and clean for them are slightly less likely to have a partner. Correlations with the other reasons are trivial (r<.10), meaning that those without a partner are just as desirous of emotional closeness, commitment, exclusivity, and having a child as those with a partner.

HOW ARE THESE REASONS CORRELATED WITH RELATIONSHIP SATISFACTION AND COMMITMENT?

Relationship Satisfaction is correlated overall with more desire for emotional closeness (r=.18***) and for commitment to stay together (r=.17***), and less desire for someone to cook and clean (r=−.12***). Correlations with the other reasons are trivial (r<.10), meaning they did not matter for Relationship Satisfaction.

Similarly, Relationship Commitment is correlated overall with more desire for emotional closeness (r=.17***) and for commitment to stay together (r=.26***), plus desire for exclusivity (r=.11***). Correlations with the other reasons are trivial (r<.10), meaning that they do not matter for relationship commitment. These relationship reasons are combined with life goals in SEM Structural Models after life goals are introduced.

HOW DO GOALS FOR INTIMATE RELATIONSHIPS COMPARE WITH OTHER LIFE GOALS?

To measure **life goals** in this study, all participants are asked "How important to you is each of the following as a goal in your life?" See Table 2.2.

The items are ordered in Table 2.2 according to their overall mean rating for possible responses from 0=NOT AT ALL to 8=EXTREMELY. Note that the means for all of the goals except the last three are quite high, and that the most individual variability reflected in the standard deviations is in having a biological child and in raising children.

TABLE 2.2 *Importance of life goals*

	Mean	(*s.d.*)
• Being financially self-supporting	7.22	1.26
• Having time for leisure activities	6.93	1.34
• Spending time with family	6.91	1.59
• Having a committed relationship	6.89	1.69
• Supporting a family	6.73	1.86
• Having a romantic or sexual partner	6.69	1.77
• Having a career	6.59	1.79
• Spending time with friends	6.55	1.54
• Helping others	6.30	1.61
• Raising children	6.11	2.53
• Taking care of a home	6.06	1.92
• Having my own biological child	5.78	2.75
• Making as much money as possible	5.40	2.18
• Participating in community cultural events	4.95	2.07

HOW ARE THESE LIFE GOALS CORRELATED WITH HAVING A CURRENT PARTNER?

Having a Current Partner is correlated overall with the goals of having a romantic or sexual partner ($r=.17^{***}$) and having a committed relationship ($r=.14^{***}$). Correlations for the other goals are trivial ($r<.10$), meaning they do not matter much for having a partner. In other words, those who have the goals of having a partner or having a committed relationship are actually more likely to have them. This is not surprising but indicates the importance of being motivated to have a partner.

HOW ARE THESE LIFE GOALS CORRELATED WITH RELATIONSHIP SATISFACTION AND COMMITMENT?

Similarly, Relationship Satisfaction is correlated with the goal of having a romantic or sexual partner ($r=.14^{***}$) and with the goal of having a committed relationship ($r=.26^{***}$), plus the goals of spending time with family ($r=.15^{***}$) and taking care of a home ($r=.13^{***}$).

Relationship Commitment is also correlated with the goal of having a romantic or sexual partner ($r=.17^{***}$), and especially with the goal of having a committed relationship ($r=.35^{***}$), plus the goals of spending time with family ($r=.17^{***}$), taking care of a home ($r=.17^{***}$), and supporting a family ($r=.11^{***}$).

HOW DO RELATIONSHIP REASONS AND LIFE GOALS COMBINE IN SEM MODELS?

Structural Equation Modeling (SEM) was introduced in Chapter 1. SEM Structural Models combining relationship reasons and life goals to predict Having a Current Partner reveal that Desiring Sexual Activities is a Central Factor, but with only a slight effect, with standardized regression coefficient $\gamma=.11$. The other relationship reasons and life goals add only trivial explained variance when they are taken into account. These models are similar across gender (CFI=.999, RMSEA=.013) and across nine cultural regions (CFI=.997, RMSEA=.010).

SEM models combining relationship reasons and life goals are also used to predict Relationship Satisfaction, as well as direct predictions of Relationship Commitment independent of Relationship Satisfaction. These models are similar across eight relationship types (CFI=.976, RMSEA=.021) and nine cultural regions (CFI=.989, RMSEA=.014).

These models reveal that the goal of Having a Committed Relationship is a Central Factor in predicting Relationship Satisfaction. Other relationship reasons and life goals add only trivial explained variance after the goal of Having a Committed Partner is taken into account. Its standardized regression coefficient with relationship satisfaction is $\gamma=.20$. It also has a direct prediction of Relationship Commitment with $\gamma=.13$. In other words, having a goal of a committed relationship increases Relationship Satisfaction and also increases Relationship Commitment slightly independently of Relationship Satisfaction.

SELF-REFLECTION

What are your goals in life? How important is having a committed relationship, and how important are various reasons for having one? If you are not in a committed relationship, when do you think you would be ready to be in a committed relationship and why then?

HOW DO VALUES PREDICT INTIMATE RELATIONSHIPS?

To measure **values**, the short 21-item version of the Portrait Values Questionnaire (PVQ; Schwartz, 2012) employed in the European Social Survey is used. Only Self-Transcendence and Conservation are predictive of Having a Current Partner or Relationship Satisfaction or Relationship Commitment in this study, so only they are discussed. See the SPOTLIGHT on Self-Transcendent Values later in this chapter.

Previous research had questioned the measurement invariance of the 21-item PVQ – that is, whether the factor loadings are similar across cultural groups (e.g., Cieciuch & Davidov, 2012). In the present study, measurement invariance is achieved by omitting the items in italics in the lists that follow.

Self-Transcendence is measured using the following items, which are rated from 0=NOT AT ALL LIKE ME to 8=VERY MUCH LIKE ME in response to the following prompt, which uses female or male pronouns depending on the gender identity of the study participants:

"Here we briefly describe some people. Please read each description and think about how much each person is or is not like you. Click on the number that shows how much the person in the description is like you."

- He thinks it is important that every person in the world be treated equally. He believes everyone should have equal opportunities in life.
- It is important to him to listen to people who are different from him. Even when he disagrees with them, he still wants to understand them.
- It's very important to him to help the people around him. He wants to care for their well-being.
- It is important to him to be loyal to his friends. He wants to devote himself to people close to him.
- *He strongly believes that people should care for nature. Looking after the environment is important to him.*

All of the items except the last one concern people, so it is not surprising that they load together in a study of intimate relationships. Without the item about nature, the other items load on a single factor, with consistency in factor loadings across eight relationship types (CFI=.959, RMSEA=.024) and nine cultural regions (CFI=.961, RMSEA=.022).

Self-Transcendence is correlated overall with Relationship Satisfaction (r=.13***), but only trivially (r<.10) with Having a Current Partner and with Relationship Commitment. In other words, values embodying concern about others matter in Relationship Satisfaction.

Conservation is measured using the items that follow, under the same prompt with the previous items:

- She believes that people should do what they're told. She thinks people should follow rules at all times, even when no-one is watching.
- It is important to her always to behave properly. She wants to avoid doing anything people would say is wrong.
- It is important to her that the government ensure her safety against all threats. She wants the state to be strong so it can defend its citizens.
- *It is important to her to be humble and modest. She tries not to draw attention to herself.*

- *Tradition is important to her. She tries to follow the customs handed down by her religion or her family.*
- *It is important to her to live in secure surroundings. She avoids anything that might endanger her safety.*

The first three items load on a single factor, with high consistency in factor loadings across eight relationship types (CFI=.998, RMSEA=.008) and nine cultural regions (CFI=.996, RMSEA=.010). Conservation is slightly negatively correlated with Having a Current Partner (r=−.10***). In other words, participants with conservation values are slightly less successful in having a partner. But Conservation is positively correlated with Relationship Commitment (r=.13***), and only trivially correlated with Relationship Satisfaction (r<.10). In other words, participants who value obedience to rules are more prone to keep a commitment to their relationship.

HOW DO SELF-TRANSCENDENCE AND CONSERVATION COMBINE IN SEM MODELS?

In SEM Structural Models combining Self-Transcendence and Conservation to predict Having a Current Partner, Conservation is a Central Factor, with a slight negative effect (γ=−.11). These models are similar across gender (CFI=.990, RMSEA=.016) and across nine cultural regions (CFI=.973, RMSEA=.013).

Self-Transcendence and Conservation are also combined in SEM Structural Models testing indirect predictions of Relationship Commitment through Relationship Satisfaction, and direct predictions of Relationship Commitment independent of Relationship Satisfaction. These models are similar across the eight relationship types (CFI=.965, RMSEA=.026) and nine cultural regions (CFI=.968, RMSEA=.020).

These models reveal that Self-Transcendence is a Central Factor, while Conservation adds only trivial explained variance after it is taken into account. Self-Transcendence's standardized regression coefficient with Relationship Satisfaction is a slight γ=.10. It has only a trivial coefficient with Relationship Commitment (γ<.10), meaning that it primarily affected Relationship Commitment through Relationship Satisfaction. In other words, participants with values embodying concern about others have slightly more satisfying intimate relationships, similarly across eight relationship types and nine cultural regions.

WHAT ATTITUDES ABOUT INTIMATE RELATIONSHIPS MATTER IN INTIMATE RELATIONSHIPS?

Participants are asked "To what extent does each of the following statements describe your feelings about relationships?"

- To be truly in love is to be in love forever.
- As long as they at least love each other, spouses or partners should have no trouble getting along together.
- One should not marry against the serious advice of one's parents.
- It is easy for me to become emotionally close to others.
- I want to be completely emotionally intimate with others, but I find that others are reluctant to get as close as I would like.
- I am uncomfortable getting close to others. I find it difficult to trust others completely or to depend on them.

They are also asked the following questions:

- Have you ever had a romantic or sexual relationship that ended? ____No ____Yes
- To what extent have you been concerned about possible rejection if you approach others with whom you might be interested in engaging in romantic or sexual activities?
- To what extent are you currently interested in finding a partner for a committed relationship?
- Throughout your life, how difficult has it been to find an appropriate partner for a committed relationship?

The first three items are from the Romanticism Scale used in the Boston Couples Study, although they do not load on a single factor in the present study. The next three items measure Secure Attachment, Anxious Attachment, and Avoidant Attachment as conceptualized by Hazen and Shaver (1987); an update of research on attachment is provided by Mikulincer and Shaver (2017). The remaining four items were written specifically for this study. Since these ten attitude items do not form consistent scales, they are all analyzed separately.

Having a Current Partner is positively correlated with having had a previous partner ($r=.23^{***}$), suggesting that success in finding a partner in the past indicates competence and confidence in being able to find another partner. But Having a Current Partner is negatively correlated with concern about parental advice ($r=-.14^{***}$), Anxious Attachment ($r=-.13^{***}$), Avoidant Attachment ($r=-.13^{***}$), looking for a partner ($r=-.17^{***}$), and difficulty finding a partner ($r=-.22^{***}$). It may be that anxiety about relationships makes it difficult to establish relationships, or it may be that difficulty establishing relationships increases relationship anxiety. It is likely that both effects can occur.

Relationship Satisfaction is positively correlated with feeling that true love lasts forever ($r=.14^{***}$), and love guarantees getting along ($r=.11^{***}$). But it is negatively correlated with Anxious Attachment ($r=-.18^{***}$), Avoidant Attachment ($r=-.13^{***}$), concern about rejection ($r=-.14^{***}$), concern about losing friendship (r=−.12***), looking for a partner (r=−.17***), and difficulty finding a partner (r=−.19***). Romantic beliefs about love may lead respondents to perceive their relationship more positively or act in more positive ways. On the other hand, having a satisfying relationship may lead one to believe that love lasts and overcomes obstacles. Anxiety about intimate relationships may result in less Relationship Satisfaction, or less Relationship Satisfaction may lead to more relationship anxiety. The causal directions may go either way.

Similarly, Relationship Commitment is correlated with believing that true love lasts forever (r=.21***) and love guarantees getting along (r=.14***). It is negatively correlated with Avoidant Attachment (r=−.10***), concern about rejection (r=−.14***), concern about losing friendship (r=−.14***), having a previous relationship that ended (r=−.11***), looking for a partner (r=−.22***), and difficulty finding a partner (r=−.17***). Again, these concerns can lead to less commitment, or less commitment can lead to these concerns, or both. Note that difficulty finding a partner may reflect availability of alternatives, which predicts commitment in Rusbult's Investment Model (Rusbult, 1980; Rusbult, Agnew, & Arriaga, 2012).

HOW DO ATTITUDES ABOUT RELATIONSHIPS COMBINE IN SEM MODELS?

SEM Structural Models combining relationship attitudes to predict Having a Current Partner reveal that having had a previous relationship is a positive Central Factor (γ=.19), while interest in finding a partner (γ=−.12) and difficulty in finding a partner (γ=−.16) are negative Central Factors. The other attitudes add only trivial explained variance when these are taken into account. These models are similar across gender (CFI=1.00, RMSEA=.008) and across nine cultural regions (CFI=.992, RMSEA=.012). In other words, those who have a current partner are more likely to have had a previous partner, are less interested in finding partner, and believe they have less difficulty finding a partner. While this is not surprising, it is noteworthy that it is consistent across gender and the nine cultural regions.

These attitudes about relationships are also combined in SEM Structural Models testing indirect predictions of Relationship Commitment through Relationship Satisfaction, and direct predictions of Relationship Commitment independent of Relationship Satisfaction. These models are consistent across the eight relationship types (CFI=.981) and nine cultural regions (CFI=.997, RMSEA=.012).

These models reveal that believing that True Love Lasts Forever is a positive Central Factor for Relationship Satisfaction (γ=.10), while

Anxious Attachment ($\gamma=-.14$) and Interest in Finding a Partner ($\gamma=-.12$) are negative Central Factors. Other factors add only trivial explained variance after these are taken into account. In other words, those with the romantic belief that true love lasts forever are slightly more satisfied with their current relationship, while those anxious about attachment to others and those looking for another partner are less satisfied with their current relationship. Note that Anxious Attachment may represent the effect of alternatives on commitment, which are important in Rusbult's Investment Model (Rusbult, 1980; Rusbult, Agnew, & Arriaga, 2012).

All of the direct predictions of these factors on relationship commitment are trivial ($\gamma<.10$), meaning that they predict relationship commitment primarily through relationship satisfaction.

IN SUMMARY, WHAT CENTRAL FACTORS ARE IDENTIFIED IN THIS CHAPTER?

For Having a Current Partner, desiring sexual activities and having had a previous partner are positive Central Factors. Conservation values, interest in finding another partner, and difficulty finding a partner are negative Central Factors. SEM models reveal that these Central Factors make similar predictions across gender and nine cultural regions.

For relationship satisfaction and relationship commitment, the goal of having a committed relationship, Self-Transcendent values embodying concern for others, and believing true love lasts forever are positive Central Factors. Anxious Attachment and interest in finding another partner are negative Central Factors. SEM models reveal that these Central Factors make similar predictions, across eight relationship types and nine cultural regions.

The predictions of these Central Factors are similar even though the levels of these factors may vary. These Central Factors will be combined with Central Factors from other chapters in a *Comprehensive Partner Model* and in a *Comprehensive Commitment Model* in Chapter 10. Variations in levels of factors will be discussed in Chapter 11.

SPOTLIGHT ON INTIMATE RELATIONSHIPS OF YOUTH IN RUSSIA

VICTORIA V. ILCHENKO, VALERY L. SITNIKOV, NATALIA V. PARNYUK, AND FATIMA G. SANAKOEVA

Romantic relationships are recognized as being the most important sphere of interpersonal interaction influencing a person's emotional well-being. Various studies have demonstrated that romantic relationships represent a significant resource for personal development in youth, whereas poor intimate relationships are the source of conflicts and destructive behavior (Bochevar, 2012; Hill & Peplau, 2001; Ilchenko, 2010). And many studies have found attitudes about intimate relationships to have an impact on sexual behavior of youth (e.g., Ilchenko & Sanakoeva, 2015; Markova, 2014; Sitnikov & Ilchenko, 2016).

This research explores romantic relationships and intimate attitudes of Russian males and females aged 18–25, who were students of higher educational institutions and working youth from Vladikavkaz, Russia (N=129; 56 males and 73 females). Our findings demonstrate that love feelings appear to be the main motive to start intimate relations for more than half of Russian males and females (males – 78.1%, females – 67.9%). In addition, the majority of male respondents engage in intimate relationships to obtain premarital sexual experience (28.6% – "agree," 28.6% – "strongly agree"). On the contrary, most female respondents indicated that they are less likely to gain such experience (54.8% – "disagree," 26.1% – "strongly disagree") (t=4.43 $p \leq 0.001$). Men are more likely than women to seek sex due to physical wants (males – 50%, females – 13.7%) and sexual desire (males –51.8%, females – 21.9%). Other reasons for women to have sexual intercourse are to start a family (males – 41.1%, females – 67.1%) and conceive (males – 30.4%, females – 37.0%).

The study reveals that the female respondents focus most, and slightly more than males, on such qualities in their partners as firmness of purpose (males – 7.4, females – 8.1) (t=2.39 $p \leq .05$) and responsibility (males – 7.4, females – 8.3) (t=3.6 $p \leq 0.01$). Women also have more preference for a partner's height (males – 5.3, females – 6.7) (t=2.9 $p \leq .001$), his social status (males – 3.6, females – 5.11) (t=3.7 $p \leq 0.001$) and material welfare (males – 4.3, females – 5.6) (t=3.4 $p \leq .001$). On the other hand, partner's physical attraction appears to be a somewhat more important factor for men than for women (7.6 vs. 6.9) (t=2.39 $p \leq .05$).

The study reveals that males gain dating experience earlier than females (males – mean age 14.9; females – mean age 16.5) (t=–4.07 $p \leq .001$). Male respondents are more likely to be involved in ongoing romantic relationships earlier (mean age 15.6) than females (mean age 17.2). They also have more romantic partners (males – 4.1, females – 2.1) (t=5.33 $p \leq .001$). And males are more satisfied with their romantic relationships more than females (males – 7.6, females – 6.6) (t=2.3 $p \leq .05$).

The analysis shows that the males have the experience of the first kiss (mean age 15.4 vs. 16.6) and sexual relations (mean age 16 vs. 18.4) earlier than the females (t=−2.73 $p \leq .001$). Males have twice as many partners as females (4 vs. 2). The research reveals that women are more likely than men to be sexually inexperienced (15.8% vs. 73.8%).

However, a great number of the respondents have relationships based on romantic affection, including kissing and embracing without any sexual relations (males – 46.7%, females – 62.8%). One-third of the male respondents and 23.3% of the females are engaged in intimate relationships with their romantic partner. The rest of the respondents (males – 23.4% and females – 23.3%) have been involved only in platonic relationships.

Most respondents say that the most common place to get acquainted and meet a partner is an educational institution (males – 35.8%, females – 36.9%); the respondents also meet at their friends' homes (males – 28.6%, females – 26.1%) and through the internet (males – 21.4%, females – 26.1%). The study reveals that men are more likely than women to meet in clubs, bars, cafes, and restaurants (males – 8.9% vs. females – 0%) (t=2.65 $p \leq .01$).

The data show that the majority of both men and women having romantic relationships meet their partners regularly (every day or more than three times a week) (males – 56.7%, females – 51.2%). One-third of the survey respondents say that they see their partners once/twice a week (males – 30.0%, females – 30.2%), less than once a week (males – 6.7%, females – 7.0%. The rest have meetings less than once a week (males – 6.7%, females – 11.6%).

The respondents say that jealousy (males – 41.1%, females – 45.2%), quarrels (males – 35.8%, females – 49.3%), and misunderstanding (males – 39.3%, females – 39.7%) cause relationship problems. To overcome these difficulties in romantic relationships, the male respondents spend time with friends (males – 46.4%, females – 32.9%) (t=2.18 $p \leq .05$) and go in for sports (males – 39.3%, females – 12.3%) (t=3.7 $p \leq .001$). The female respondents are more likely than males to express needs for support seeking help of their friends (males – 0%, females – 16.4%) (t=−3.8 $p \leq .05$). Women have a tendency to cry and shout, so they respond emotionally to the problems in romantic relationships (males – 3.6%, females – 17.8%) (t=2.8 $p \leq .05$). The data indicate that to release tension during romantic relationships men are likely to use physical methods while women appear to resort to emotional ones.

Both males and females are likely to initiate the break-up of romantic relationships (males: "strongly my initiative" – 28.3%, "my initiative" – 30.4%; females: "strongly my initiative" – 29.3%, "my initiative" – 27.6%).

Our research also reveals correlations between the aspects of romantic relationships and the respondents' personality characteristics, using measures from McCrae and Costa (1987). Russian men having intimate intercourse with their romantic partner are more dominant (r=.37 $p \leq$.01), active (r=.30 $p \leq$.05), extroverted (r=.32 $p \leq$.05), communicative (r=.28 $p \leq$.05), curious (r=.27 $p \leq$.05), self-reliant (r=−.29 $p \leq$.05) and emotionally stable (r=−0.38 $p \leq$.01), while women having intimate intercourse with their romantic partner are more emotionally labile (r=.29 $p \leq$.05), emotionally unstable (r=.32 $p \leq$.01), self-critical (r=.27 $p \leq$.05), and strained (r=.28 $p \leq$.05). Our results suggest that these female respondents are less likely to control their emotions than female participants not having sexual intercourse. The latter seem to be more self-reliant (r=−.35 for $p \leq$.01), emotionally stable (r=−.27 $p \leq$.05) and communicative (r=.24 $p \leq$.05) (Ilchenko & Sanakoeva, 2017).

SPOTLIGHT ON SELF-TRANSCENDENCE VALUES

CLÁUDIO V. TORRES

The concept of "values" is central to the field of psychology. As noted by Rokeach (1973), the value concept can "unify the apparently diverse interests of all the sciences concerned with human behavior." In his seminal work, Shalom Schwartz (1992) presented a perspective on human values that is undoubtedly one of the most influential in psychology, especially in cross-cultural psychology. In the *Journal of Cross-Cultural Psychology*, about 20 per-cent of the articles published between the years 2007 and 2009 referred to values (Knafo, Roccas, & Sagiv, 2011).

Values are shared conceptions of what is socially considered to be right or wrong. Hence values motivate behavior. Values Theory, proposed by Schwartz (1992) is motivationally oriented because it proposes a way of organizing the different needs and goals proposed by previous theories and states that a primary aspect of a value is the type of motivational goal it expresses. Among the ten motivationally distinct value orientations suggested by the Values Theory (Schwartz, 1992), as well as the nineteen value orienta-tions of the Refined Values Theory (Schwartz et al., 2012), data analyses reveal that the values are grouped into four High Order Values (HOV). They are Conservation vs. Openness to Change and Self-Enhancement vs. Self-Transcendence. These four HOV include all of the core values recognized in different cultures.

Of particular importance here, Self-Transcendence values include Universalism and Benevolence, which serve collective interests. These values share a common motivational goal, concerned with the enhancement of others and transcendence of selfish interests. Benevolence and Universalism refer explicitly to others with whom the person has proximity and identifica-tion as an in-group. They involve the commitment to fair treatment, accep-tance, and harmony with all people and with nature (Torres, Schwartz, & Nascimento, 2017). Simply stated, Benevolence is concerned with the welfare of those with whom one is in close personal contact in everyday interactions, whereas Universalism refers to tolerance, appreciation, and respect for the welfare of all people and for nature.

Thus, Benevolence can be viewed as a prosocial value type focused on close others, while Universalism has a broader focus, associated with the survival needs of all groups, outside the extended primary group (Schwartz, 1992). Together, the compatibility of their motivations promotes supportive social relations and acceptance of others. Being adjacent as proposed by the theory, however, also suggests that individuals distinguish between these two values (Schwartz, 1990), making it possible to hypothesize their differences. Schwartz (1992) suggests that that "secularism, individualism, and education are correlated with giving priority to universalism ... whereas conventional religiosity and collectivism are correlated with giving priority to benevolence" (p. 39).

Some evidence suggests the relationship of Self-Transcendence values with different demographic aspects. For instance, women from societies where gender stereotypes are common tend to endorse benevolence values, while also pursuing power (Schwartz, 2012). As women also tend to affiliate more with others when compared to men, who in turn tend to be more autonomous, it is only natural to expect that men are more attached to status and power, whereas the former are more concerned with caring for the welfare of in-group members (Gilligan, 1982). Caring for the welfare of close ones is the essence of Benevolence, an important part of Self-Transcendence values. Hence, these differences in women's and men's social orientations find a reflection in the expression of values priorities, leading to the hypotheses that women give more importance to Self-Transcendence values (Schwartz, 2012). Schwartz and Rubel (2005) reported that men attribute consistently more importance than women do to power, stimulation, hedonism, achievement, and self-direction values, with the reverse being true for benevolence and universalism values.

Finally, it should be noticed that cross-cultural studies do suggest that women tend to display different values when compared to men, resulting in a pattern of gender differences in value priorities that holds true across a number of countries (Hofstede, 2011; Schwartz & Rubel, 2005). In the cultural level of analyses, men's culture differs greatly from women's culture in such a way that cultures could be categorized into either those exhibiting compassion, solidarity, collectivism, and universalism or competition, autonomy, merit, results, and responsibility (Hofstede, 2002).

Yet, we should remember that values, by their nature, are transsituational goals, hence, transcending specific actions and situations. As a result, we should expect that values would guide the selection or evaluation of actions, policies, people, and events in different cultures equally and can simultaneously operate throughout concrete instances. Values predict relevant behavioral intentions independently of attitudes. As suggested by Maio (2017), "discrepancies between personally held values and the perceived values of one own's culture predict feelings of estrangement from the culture over and above discrepancies between personally held attitudes toward ... culturally relevant items" (p. 276) such as relationships.

3

How Are Intimate Partners Selected?

Predictions of having a current partner, as well as relationship satisfaction and relationship commitment, are explored in terms of the following:

- What characteristics people are seeking in a partner
- Their confidence in attracting a partner
- Their opportunities for meeting a partner
- Their readiness for having a partner

HOW HAS MATE SELECTION BEEN STUDIED IN THE PAST?

Research on **mate selection** has taken two approaches. One approach is to study mate selection criteria, asking people how important various characteristics are in selecting a mate. The other approach is to study matching between spouses in married couples.

From an **evolutionary psychology** perspective, it has been argued that men are seeking women who are physically attractive, as an indicator of fertility, while women are seeking men of high status, to support themselves and their offspring (Buss, 1989). Yet the mean ratings in Buss's data indicate that both physical attractiveness and social status were rated only moderately important for both men and women across thirty-seven countries, even though there were gender differences.

In research on marriage, it has been argued that there are social pressures for **homogamy** (same mating), which is marrying someone similar to oneself, especially in ethnicity, religion, and social status. Research has found that spouses tend to be similar on various social and personal characteristics, as Buss (1985) pointed out. **Filter Theory** (Murstein, 1976) argues that dating couples are first sorted on physical attractiveness, then social characteristics, and then values, with couples breaking up sequentially in that order. But there were no data to support the sequential aspect of the theory.

The Boston Couples Study explored these theories by examining similarity between couple members, and by seeing whether similarity predicted staying together and eventual marriage (Hill & Peplau, 1998; Hill, Rubin, & Peplau, 1976). At the beginning of the study, there was some matching on physical attractiveness, based on ratings of their separate color photos by panels of four undergraduate men and four undergraduate women. But the correlation was only r=.24, which squared indicated that only 6 percent of partner selection was based on physical attractiveness.

There was also some matching on age (r=.19), SAT verbal scores (r=.24), SAT math scores (r=.22), sex role attitudes (r=.47), religiosity (r=.37), number of children wanted (r=.51), and height (r=.21). But matching on father's educational level, an indicator of social status, had r=.11, which was not statistically different from zero. On the two-year follow-up, couples who had stayed together tended to be more similar on age, SAT scores, and physical attractiveness than those who broke up, but the differences were not statistically significant. Hence, there was little support for Filter Theory.

But women who rated themselves *low* on physical attractiveness were more likely to marry their college boyfriend. This was true even though the boyfriend's and photo ratings of the women's attractiveness did not predict marrying. Women's low self-ratings on intelligence and desirability as a dating partner also predicted marrying their college boyfriend. They apparently had less confidence that they could attract someone else. Similar effects were not found for men. In other words, physical attractiveness played a role in initial meeting but only mattered in the long run when women underestimated their attractiveness.

WHAT CHARACTERISTICS ARE PEOPLE SEEKING IN A PARTNER?

In the present study, respondents rate the importance of each of twenty-one items. Factor analysis indicates that among these items, four factors have consistent loadings (Table 3.1).

Structural Equation Modeling (SEM) is introduced in Chapter 1. SEM Measurement Models reveal that the factor loadings for each of these factors are similar across the eight relationship types and nine cultural regions as indicated in Table 3.2.

For each factor, the items are averaged to form a Scale. The overall mean ratings, and standard deviations (*s.d.*), of these Scales are as shown in Table 3.3, with possible ranges of importance from 0=NOT AT ALL to 8=EXTREMELY.

Each mean is statistically significantly different from the mean below it in a repeated measures analysis of variance, due to the large sample size. Note that the Personality Important Scale is rated most important. The Attractiveness Important Scale and the Social Status Important Scale are

TABLE 3.1 *Mate selection factors*

- Personality Important: Personality, Attitudes and Values, Sense of Humor
- Attractiveness Important: Physical Attractiveness, Height, Weight
- Social Status Important: Social Status, Wealth, Education
- Ethnicity Important: Ethnicity, Race, Cultural Background

TABLE 3.2 *Mate selection SEM measures*

	Relationship Types	Cultural Regions
• Personality Important	CFI=.992, RMSEA=.015	CFI=.990, RMSEA=.018
• Attractiveness Important	CFI=.992, RMSEA=.022	CFI=.994, RMSEA=.016
• Social Status Important	CFI=1.00, RMSEA=.000	CFI=.984, RMSEA=.034
• Ethnicity Important	CFI=1.00, RMSEA=.000	CFI=.995, RMSEA=.023

TABLE 3.3 *Mate selection scale means*

	Mean	*(s.d.)*
• Personality Important	7.07	*(1.02)*
• Attractiveness Important	4.96	*(1.71)*
• Social Status Important	4.51	*(1.85)*
• Ethnicity Important	3.19	*(2.45)*

rated only moderately important. The Ethnicity Important Scale is rated least important but varied the most, suggesting that parents of some participants emphasize marrying within their own ethnic group more than do others.

Having a Current Partner is negatively correlated with the Social Status Important Scale ($r=-.10$***) and the Ethnicity Important Scale ($r=-.12$***). In other words, persons who consider social status and ethnicity more important are slightly less likely to be successful in having an intimate relationship. Correlations with the Personality Important Scale and the Attractiveness Important Scale are trivial ($r<.10$), which means that they are considered just as important by those without a partner as by those with a partner. These Scales are combined with ratings of partner similarity in SEM models that are described after partner similarity ratings are introduced.

Relationship Satisfaction is positively correlated with the Personality Important Scale ($r=.15$**) and slightly negatively correlated with the Social Status Important Scale ($r=-.10$***). The Attractiveness Important Scale and the Ethnicity Important Scales have trivial correlations with Relationship Satisfaction ($r<.10$). In other words, those who value personality are somewhat

TABLE 3.4 *Partner similarity SEM measures*

	Relationship Types	Cultural Regions
• Personality Similarity	CFI=.987, RMSEA=.021	CFI=.995, RMSEA=.010
• Attractiveness Similarity	CFI=.992, RMSEA=.022	CFI=.988, RMSEA=.016
• Social Status Similarity	CFI=1.00, RMSEA=.000	CFI=.987, RMSEA=.018
• Ethnicity Similarity	CFI=1.00, RMSEA=.004	CFI=.991, RMSEA=.024

TABLE 3.5 *Partner similarity Scale means*

	Mean	(s.d.)
• Ethnicity Similarity	6.19	(2.32)
• Personality Similarity	6.06	(1.32)
• Social Status Similarity	5.58	(1.64)
• Attractiveness Similarity	5.21	(1.65)

more likely to be satisfied with their relationship, while those who value social status are somewhat less likely to be satisfied.

Relationship Commitment is positively correlated with the Personality Important Scale ($r=.13^{***}$) and trivially correlated ($r<.10$) with the other three Scales. In other words, personality matters most as a mate selection criterion for relationship commitment.

HOW SIMILAR ARE PARTNERS ON THESE CHARACTERISTICS?

The same twenty-one items are used to ask how similar the respondent is to the current partner. For the same four factors, SEM Measurement Models revealed that the factor loadings are similar across the eight relationship types and nine cultural regions, as indicated in Table 3.4.

For each factor, the items are averaged to form a Scale. Overall mean ratings and standard deviations for these four Scales appear in Table 3.5. The first three means are statistically significantly different from each other, but the fourth mean does not differ statistically significantly from the third mean, in repeated measures analyses of variance.

Note that the Personality Similarity Scale is rated higher than the Attractiveness Similarity and Social Status Similarity Scales, while the Ethnicity Similarity Scale is rated highest of all. Ethnicity Similarity may partly reflect pressures to court and marry partners within one's ethnic group, but it may also reflect restricted opportunities to meet partners and to develop relationships in socially segregated neighbor-hoods and schools. The degree of similarity between partners is generally affected by the social contexts in which they meet (Mollenhorts, Völker, & Flap, 2008).

Partner Similarity ratings only apply to those Having a Current Partner, so they are not included in SEM Structural Models predicting Having a Current Partner discussed later in this chapter.

Relationship Satisfaction is positively correlated with the Personality Similarity Scale (r=.43***), the Social Status Similarity Scale (r=.25***), the Attractiveness Similarity Scale (r=.17***), and the Ethnicity Similarity Scale (r=.10***). In other words, partner similarity in general matters for relationship satisfaction, but especially partner similarity on personality.

Similarly, Relationship Commitment is positively correlated with the Personality Similarity Scale (r=.31***), the Social Status Similarity Scale (r=.20***), the Attractiveness Similarity Scale (r=.13***), and the Ethnicity Similarity Scale (r=.10***). Again, partner similarity in general matters for relationship commitment, but especially similarity on personality.

In addition to these partner similarity Scales, two individual items matter. Rating the partner Similar on Intelligence is correlated with Relationship Satisfaction (r=.32***) and Relationship Commitment (r=.26**). And rating the partner Similar on Willingness to Have Children is correlated with Relationship Satisfaction (r=.33***) and Relationship Commitment (r=.37***).

An example of partner similarity is provided in the SPOTLIGHT on Partner Similarities in Romania. In contrast, partner dissimilarity is discussed in the SPOTLIGHT on Cross-Cultural Marriages in India.

SEM Structural Models combine the mate selection Scales to predict Having a Current Partner. These models are similar across gender (CFI=.999, RMSEA=.014) and nine cultural regions (CFI=.996, RMSEA=.009). These models reveal that the Personality Important Scale is a Central Factor, with a standardized regression coefficient γ=.10. The other factors add trivial explained variance when the Personality Important Scale is taken into account.

SEM Structural Models combine the mate selection Scales and the partner similarity Scales plus two items to test indirect predictions of Relationship Commitment through Relationship Satisfaction, and direct predictions of Relationship Commitment independent of Relationship Satisfaction. These

TABLE 3.6 *Self and partner mean ratings*

	SELF	CP	r=
• Intelligent	6.39	6.82	.29***
• Creative	5.87	6.18	.25***
• Talented	5.71	6.49	.31***
• Self-confident	5.42	6.01	.13***
• Socially out-going	5.63	6.14	.13***
• Physically attractive	5.43	6.62	.25***
• Cute	5.53	6.76	.29***
• Sexy	4.94	6.40	.32***
• Athletic	4.56	5.42	.31***
• Desirable as a partner in a committed relationship	6.16	6.90	.23***

models are similar across eight relationship types (CFI=.967, RMSEA=.024) and nine cultural regions (CFI=.982, RMSEA=.014).

These models reveal that the Personality Similarity Scale is a Central Factor (γ=.29) predicting Relationship Satisfaction. So are partner Similarity on Intelligence (γ=.13) and Similarity on Willingness to Have Children (γ=.21). The other factors add trivial explained variance when these are taken into account. In addition to their indirect predictions of Relationship Commitment through Relationship Satisfaction, there is a direct prediction of partner Similarity on Willingness to Have Children for Relationship Commitment (γ=.15). In other words, partner similarity on willingness to have children can increase relationship commitment whether relationship satisfaction is high or low.

HOW SIMILAR ARE RATINGS OF SELF AND PARTNER CHARACTERISTICS?

Respondents are asked to rate themselves and their current partner on various characteristics, which are compared to measure similarity. For those with a current partner, mean ratings of self and partner and the correlation between them are shown in Table 3.6.

Note that there is some similarity between ratings of the self and partner on every characteristic. Paired t-tests reveal that the partner is rated higher than the self on every characteristic (all $p<.001$). A similar difference between partner ratings and self-ratings was previously found in the Boston Couples Study (Hill, Peplau, & Rubin, 2008) and in other research (Murray, Holmes, & Griffin, 1996).

WHAT ARE THE DIMENSIONS OF PHYSICAL ATTRACTIVENESS?

In this study, Cute, Sexy, and Athletic were added to the ratings previously used in the Boston Couples Study, in an attempt to add more dimensions of attractiveness. Physical attractiveness has at least four dimensions. One dimension is cognitive, based on responses to symmetry of facial features that are average rather than pronounced, which would be called "aesthetic." However, while average faces are attractive, they may not be the most attractive (Alley & Cunningham, 1991).

A second dimension is emotional, based on responses to neonatal (newborn) features, which would be called "cute." Mammals are programmed to respond emotionally to neonatal features, which promotes caretaking. And a third dimension is sexual, based on responses to sexual maturity cues, such as women's breasts and figure, or men's muscles and facial hair (traditionally beards and moustaches but now beard stubble in advertising), which would be called "sexy." Both of these dimensions are found in cross-cultural research (Cunningham et al., 1995).

A fourth dimension is behavioral, based on nonverbal behaviors such as smiling, eye gazing, gestures, posture, and voice that includes "flirting," as well as grooming and personality more generally. Judgments of someone's attractiveness may also be influenced by situational and personal factors, such as being drunk, which is called wearing "beer goggles"; a recent breakup, which is called being "on the rebound"; testosterone levels in men and women, which promote ease of sexual arousal, called being "horny"; and the fertile time of a woman's ovulatory cycle, which may be related to "sexual receptivity" in humans as it is in other organisms.

HOW DO SELF AND PARTNER RATINGS COMBINE INTO FACTORS?

Factor analyses indicate that certain self-ratings load on an Attractiveness Factor and others load on an Intelligence Factor. The partner ratings also load on an Attractiveness Factor and on an Intelligence Factor. The individual items on each factor follow:

- Attractiveness Factor – Physically Attractive, Cute, Sexy
- Intelligence Factor – Intelligent, Creative, Talented

So even though cute and sexy are conceptually separate aspects, they load on the same factor with physically attractive in this study, similarly across relationship types (CFI=.996, RMSEA=.022) and cultural regions (CFI=.998, RMSEA=.014) for self-ratings, and across relationship types (CFI=.988,

RMSEA=.032) and cultural regions (CFI=.995, RMSEA=.015) for partner ratings. In addition, the Intelligence Factor loadings are similar across relationship types (CFI=.994, RMSEA=.019) and cultural regions (CFI=.976, RMSEA=.035) for self-ratings, and across relationship types (CFI=.993, RMSEA=.021) and cultural regions (CFI=.987, RMSEA=.021) for partner ratings.

For each factor, the items were averaged to form a Rating Self Attractive Scale and a Rating Partner Attractive Scale, as well as a Rating Self Intelligent Scale and a Rating Partner Intelligent Scale.

HOW ARE SELF AND PARTNER RATINGS CORRELATED WITH RELATIONSHIP SATISFACTION AND COMMITMENT?

Having a Current Partner is correlated with rating the Rating Self Attractive Scale (r=.23***), the Rating Self Intelligent Scale (r=.14***), and the Rating Self as a Desirable as a Partner in a Committed Relationship item (r=.25***). High self-ratings can promote success in having an intimate relationship; at the same time, success in having an intimate relationship can promote high self-ratings.

Relationship Satisfaction is correlated with the Rating Partner Attractive Scale (r=.34***), the Rating Partner Intelligent Scale (r=.38***), the Rating Self Attractive Scale (r=.15***), and the Rating Self Intelligent Scale (r=.19***). In addition, it is strongly correlated with Rating Partner as a Desirable Partner in a Committed Relationship (r=.58***), and Rating Self as a Desirable Partner in a Committed Relationship (r=.24***). Rating the partner highly can lead to relationship satisfaction, but the reverse causal direction may also occur: relationship satisfaction can lead to rating the partner highly. Similarly, rating the self highly can lead to relationship satisfaction, but it may also be that relationship satisfaction leads to rating the self highly for being successful in having a satisfying relationship.

Relationship Commitment is similarly correlated with the Rating Partner Attractive Scale (r=.28***), the Rating Partner Intelligent Scale (r=.28***), and the Rating Self Intelligent Scale (r=.12***), but only trivially with the Rating Self Attractive Scale (r<.10). It is also strongly correlated with Rating Partner as a Desirable Partner (r=.60***) and Rating Self as a Desirable Partner (r=.21***). It is likely that the same dual direction of effects applies as well.

HOW DO RATINGS OF SELF AND PARTNER COMBINE IN SEM MODELS?

SEM Structural Models combine the Rating Self measures to predict Having a Current Partner. These models were similar across gender (CFI=.999, RMSEA=.013) and nine cultural regions (CFI=.992, RMSEA=.015). They reveal that Rating Self Desirable as a Partner is a Central Factor, with $\gamma=.19$. When it is taken into account, the Rating Self Attractive Scale and the Rating Self Intelligent Scale add trivial explained variance.

SEM Structural Models combine the Rating Self and Rating Partner Scales, and the self and partner Desirable as a Partner ratings, to test indirect predictions of Relationship Commitment through Relationship Satisfaction and direct predictions of Relationship Commitment independent of Relationship Satisfaction. These models are similar across eight relationship types (CFI=.982, RMSEA=.022) and nine cultural regions (CFI=.987, RMSEA=.020).

These models reveal that Rating Partner as a Desirable Partner in a Committed Relationship is a Central Factor ($\gamma=.46$) in predicting Relationship Satisfaction. So are Rating Self as a Desirable Partner ($\gamma=.12$) and the Rating Partner Intelligence Scale ($\gamma=.12$). In addition, Rating Partner Desirable directly predicts Relationship Commitment ($\gamma=.27$), meaning that rating the partner desirable increases commitment whether relationship satisfaction is high or low.

HOW DO SELF-RATINGS RELATE TO HAVING A PARTNER IN THE BOSTON COUPLES STUDY?

Previously reported results of the Boston Couples Study were based on both members of 231 dating couples recruited from four colleges in the Boston area (Hill, Rubin, Peplau, & Willard, 1979). In addition, there were unpublished data from 100 persons who were not "going with" anyone (having an on-going exclusive relationship) when the study began, who were recruited from the largest school in the study. These 58 women and 42 men were compared with the 103 women and 103 men recruited as couples from that same school.

Both women and men in couples rated themselves higher than those not in couples on desirable as a dating partner (r=.24, $p<.01$ for women and r=.31, $p<.001$ for men), and higher on desirable as a marriage partner (r=.30, $p<.001$ for women and r=.18, $p<.05$ for men). They also tended to rate themselves as more physically attractive (r=.15, $p<.06$ for women and r=.22, $p<.05$ for men). In other words, those not in a couple had somewhat less confidence that they could attract a committed partner.

SELF-REFLECTION

Think about the friends and relatives you care about. They come in all shapes and sizes. Why do you like or love them? Is it because they look like models in the media, or is it because of their personality and how they treat you?

HOW DID PARTNERS MEET IN THE BOSTON COUPLES STUDY?

In the Boston Couples Study, unpublished findings indicated that college students typically met in informal settings, both academic and social, where they could be themselves. In a follow-up interview with a couple who had married, the man said that it was fate. He gave her a ride when she was hitchhiking. If she had not been standing there when he drove by, they might never have met and eventually married. But what he called fate, was actually **chance** that was **socially structured**. He picked her up in front of her school, Boston College, where he also attended. They got along well because they had similar backgrounds, both being Catholic. He was at ease because he wasn't trying to impress her, since he was dating someone else. When that relationship ended, he remembered the encounter and wanted to date her but couldn't remember her name. Fortunately, he recalled that she knew his cousin, and that enabled him to contact her.

Someone else introduced about half of the partners in the Boston Couples Study. Parks and Eggert (1991) similarly found that half of those in their study who were dating were introduced by someone else and also found that two-thirds knew someone in their partner's network before meeting their partner.

It is easier to trust someone who is known by someone you trust. In a "meat market" situation like a singles bar, you cannot be sure that you can trust strangers you meet. The same is true meeting people online today. Hence, it is best to first meet in person in a safe public place, and it is wise to introduce the person to friends to get their judgments of the person's trustworthiness and suitability.

In the Boston Couples Study, rarely were the meetings exotic or romantic. The most exotic place was London where one couple unromantically met when he retrieved a stranded Frisbee for her. The most interesting setting was in band practice, where a tuba player bumped into a xylophone player. One woman thought her future boyfriend must be studious since she kept seeing him in the library. But he said that he happened to see her in the library one day and he kept returning in hopes of seeing her again, and it worked!

HOW DO PARTNERS MEET IN THE PRESENT STUDY?

Participants with a current partner were asked the questions in Table 3.7, with the percentages reporting each item ordered from highest to lowest.

"Through mutual friends" is the most common way of meeting. This way has the following advantage: you often share values and interests with your friends, and your friends can help judge a potential partner's personality and character. Next most common is in a class or other academic setting. Schools

TABLE 3.7 *How partners meet*
• How did you and CP first meet (select all that apply)?

44% ____Through mutual friends
25%____In a class or other academic setting (e.g., in a library)
21%____At a social gathering (such as a dance, mixer, or party)
17%____Through some other activity or interest (e.g., hobby, sports, political, or cultural)
14%____Through interaction on the Internet
11%____Through work
10%____Through a club or organization
8%____In a nightclub or bar
7%____Other (Describe:_____)
6%____We were neighbors (e.g., in our hometowns or in a dormitory)
4%____On a date arranged by someone else
3%____Through a commercial dating service
3%____Introduction by parents
1%____Through a newspaper ad

generally have the widest pool of potential partners who are unattached and similar in intelligence and education. Hence, the last time one attends school is the best time to find a partner for a committed relationship, whether that is high school, college, or graduate school. In the Boston Couples Study, women who planned to attend graduate school were less likely to marry their undergraduate dating partner and waited to marry someone met during graduate school.

Dating someone after finishing school is harder since co-workers and others are generally older and less likely to be unattached. And dating at work risks awkwardness if the relationship ends since the ex-partner may still be a co-worker. In a bar, a person might find a one-night stand but may be less likely to find a person who is compatible and interested in a committed relationship. The internet widens the pool of potential partners, but people may misrepresent themselves and pose other risks.

DOES IT MATTER HOW PARTNERS MEET?

In the Boston Couples Study, one meeting setting stood out. Unpublished data indicated that those who had met in a bar were more likely to break up than those who met in other settings. Other than drinking alcohol, and perhaps wanting a one-night stand, those who met in a bar may have had little else in common.

In the present study, all of the methods of meeting had trivial correlations ($r<.10$) with Relationship Satisfaction and Relationship Commitment. Other factors mattered more.

HOW IS READINESS FOR COMMITMENT MEASURED IN THE PRESENT STUDY?

There has been little research on commitment readiness, as noted by Hadden, Agnew, and Tan (2018), who measure courtship readiness as an attitude. In the present study, it was hypothesized that people would be more likely to be ready for commitment when they are older, have finished school, and have full-time employment. These are measured by asking the following questions:

- When were you born? Month_____ Year_____
- Are you currently a student? ____NO ____YES, PART-TIME ____YES, FULL-TIME
- Are you currently employed (by others or self-employed) for pay? ____NO ____YES, PART-TIME ____YES, FULL-TIME

Age is calculated by subtracting the birth year from the year of participation in the study, adjusting for the relative months. Having a Current Partner is positively correlated with Age (r=.16***) and Employment status (r=.14***) and negatively correlated with Student status (r=−.14**). Relationship Satisfaction is trivially correlated with all three measures. But there are direct predictions of Age (r=.19***), Employment Status (r=.11***), and Student Status (r=−.18***) for Relationship Commitment. In other words, participants are more likely to be in a committed relationship when they are older, employed, and no longer students.

HOW DO READINESS MEASURES COMBINE IN SES MODELS?

SEM Structural Models combine Age, Employment Status, and Student Status to predict Having a Current Partner. These models are consistent across gender (CFI=.999, RMSEA=.016) and nine cultural regions (CFI=.996, RMSEA=.011). They reveal that Age is a Central Factor (γ=.16). Employment Status and Student Status add trivial explained variance when Age is taken into account, since younger persons are more likely to be students and have less employment.

SEM Structural Models combine Age, Employment Status, and Student Status to test indirect predictions of Relationship Commitment through Relationship Satisfaction and direct predictions of Relationship Commitment independent of Relationship Satisfaction. These models are similar across eight relationship types (CFI=.982, RMSEA=.021) and nine cultural regions (CFI=.982, RMSEA=.020). These models reveal that Age is a Central Factor in making a direct prediction of Relationship Commitment across cultural regions (γ=.13), but not across relationship types (γ=.03).

In particular, age does not predict commitment among just those unmarried or among just those married. But age does predict commitment when unmarried and married are combined, since those married are more likely to be older and more committed. Hence, age is not among the Central Factors included in the *Comprehensive Commitment Model* in Chapter 10 but is included in the *Comprehensive Partner Model* in Chapter 10.

IN SUMMARY, WHAT CENTRAL FACTORS ARE IDENTIFIED IN THIS CHAPTER?

For Having a Current Partner, the Central Factors are the mate selection Personality Important Scale, Rating Self as a Desirable Partner in a Committed Relationship, and Age. SEM models reveal that the same Central Factors make similar predictions across gender and nine cultural regions.

For Relationship Satisfaction and Relationship Commitment, the Central Factors are the mate selection Personality Important Scale, the Rating Partner Intelligent Scale, the Intelligence Similarity Scale, Rating Partner as a Desirable Partner, and Rating Self as a Desirable Partner. SEM models reveal that these Central Factors make similar predictions across eight relationship types and nine cultural regions.

The predictions of these Central Factors are similar, even though the levels of these factors may vary. These Central Factors will be combined with Central Factors from other chapters in a *Comprehensive Partner Model* and in a *Comprehensive Commitment Model* in Chapter 10. Variations in levels of factors will be discussed in Chapter 11.

SPOTLIGHT ON PARTNER SIMILARITIES IN ROMANIA

LOREDANA IVAN

The family system in Romania is very similar to the "strong family ties" system found in Southern European countries (Castiglioni et al., 2016): (1) A high percentage of young adults live at their parental homes until they marry, although the age of leaving the parental home is lower compared with other countries from Southern Europe. (2) A small percentage of young people live alone, primarily those leaving the parental home to pursue a college degree. (3) There is a low, but increasing level of non-marital cohabitation. (4) A relatively high percentage of older people live with their children or with other relatives, and a quite low percentage of older people live in retirement homes or nursing homes.

The co-residence of married couples and their parents is more frequent than in Southern Europe, but such differences are normally explained in terms of economic struggle, housing difficulties in large cities, and the low level of wages for young people entering the labor market. In this context, partners' similarities in terms of family background and prior living arrangements could be important and might interfere with couples' stability and marital satisfaction.

THE ROMANIAN CONTEXT – SOME PARADOXES

The rate of marriages in Romania is among the highest in Europe: 8.78 per 1000 inhabitants (Popescu, 2010). Also, the average age at first marriage is one of the lowest in Europe (25.2 for women and 28.5 for men). Subsequently, the average age of mothers at the birth of their first child is rather low. Three-quarters of Romanian households are formed of married couples, showing again one of the largest percentages in Europe. Moreover, satisfaction with family life, as depicted from large-Scale surveys, has remained constant over the time, with more than 85 percent of the Romanian population declaring they are "satisfied" and "very satisfied" with their family life, again a larger percentage compared to other countries in Europe.

Still, the divorce rate is close to the European mean, 1.5 divorces per 1000 inhabitants (a constant value for the past years), and the marriage duration for divorced couples is 2 years lower than the European mean. Also the number of single-parent families in Romania is close to the European mean. The fertility rate in Romania is one of the lowest in Europe, at levels comparable with other countries from the Socialist group. Half of the families have only one child, and the single-child model seems to be quite common. Even the percentage of multigenerational families living together had always been higher compared to other countries in Europe (7.5 percent of the total households), and it has increased during the past ten years up to 9.5 percent, increasing the context of potential conflict and difficulties for couples' satisfaction.

THE IMPORTANCE OF PARTNER SIMILARITY

Studies conducted using national representative surveys (see Popescu, 2010, for a review) show that most people from the rural areas (more than 50 percent) met their partners in close proximity (in the area in which they live), whereas in the urban areas 20 percent met their partners in close proximity and 25 percent through their friends. Approximately 20 percent of the people (from both urban and rural areas) met their partners at work or in school. These data show that similarity in background, region, and education plays an important role in partner selection, even more than people themselves actually think: when interviewing people about criteria that mater for a happy marriage, they would mention love, reciprocal trust, good housing conditions, mutual respect and support, fidelity, and available financial resources.

In contrast, partners' actual similarities (social status, education, ethnicity, common preferences, closeness in age, common religious beliefs) were not considered important aspects of a successful marriage by the respondents. Even when financial resources were mentioned as a condition of a successful relationship, this was considered the least important factor among the ones listed here. Also, having an independent household and not living with parents was considered less important in couple marital satisfaction, compared with love, trust, and fidelity.

A study conducted in Bucharest (Ghebrea, 1999) investigated the role of similarities in couple duration by comparing two samples: one of divorced couples and another of couples who have continued their relationship for more than seven years and have shown high marital satisfaction. Note that the capital city, Bucharest, holds the highest divorce rate in the country, 2 per 1000 inhabitants. The results show that similarity in age between the two spouses was not a discriminant factor between the two samples. Still, when the wife was older than the husband, the marriage had more stability. In 72 percent of the investigated situations, the level of education for the spouses was the same, so there was not enough variation in the samples to investigate whether similarity in educational background has an important role in marital satisfaction. The same happened for the family economic background of the two spouses: in 91 percent of the cases, the spouses were coming from families with similar economic backgrounds.

Still this study shows that the risk of divorce increases when the wife earns more than the husband (26 percent of the divorced wives had salaries that exceeded those of their husbands). Another factor that was an important predictor was the socialization in the family of origin – with those having divorced parents being more at risk to become divorcees themselves. Also the presence of love in the family of origin (being loved) was an important factor predicting couple success. In this respect, having conflicts with one's father was an important predictor for one's own marital failure to a higher extent than having a conflict with one's mother for both husbands and wives. In general, the lack of support from the family of origin was an important predictor associated with divorce, as well as the disapproval of the relationship from the family of one spouse.

The study also explains the role of intergenerational families living together in the same household in the success of the marriage. The study found that when both partners agree with co-residence of intergenerational families, and had a positive attitude toward it, this factor was not a predictor for divorce. Whereas, when one of the spouses or both hold negative attitudes toward intergenerational co-residence, the risk of divorce increased.

Similarities in friends (common friends) and in activities outside the family duties were also important factors that differentiated the two samples. The age of the partners when they got married did not make any difference between those who divorced and those who did not. When both partners preferred to spend their free time with family and to a lesser extent with others, the chances of a successful marriage increased.

CONCLUSIONS

Partner similarity in Romania seems to be more important in the way couples are formed and maintained than people might actually think. As the Romanian family system is very similar to the strong family ties system found in Southern European countries, we expect partner similarity to be key for marital success. This is also what studies conducted on couples (married versus divorced) show: similarity in family background and family support and approval are important for couple stability, and also spouses coming from more stable families have better chances and are more likely to continue to stay together. As Romania has also, a certain level of traditionalism in values (particularly values associated with gender roles – see, for example, Voicu & Telegdy, 2016), dissimilarities in employment income are sources of couple dissolution, particularly when women earn more than their spouses. Also, living with other family members from different generations might be a source of dissolution, particularly when the two partners hold different values in this respect.

SPOTLIGHT ON CROSS-CULTURAL MARRIAGES IN INDIA

SUHAS SHETGOVEKAR

"Marriages are made in Heaven" is a common phrase used in India, in Hindi movies, in jewelry advertisements, on online marriage sites, and so on. People quite easily buy in to this idea of marriage and are in a quest to meet their soul mates and have a happily ever after. However, the phrase does come with "conditions," as most often families arrange the marriages in India by taking into consideration religion, caste, even subcaste, status, and sometimes after matching horoscopes.

In India, marriages are endogamous (marrying within one's own group) in nature and are often seen as necessary and as serious affairs. They are also linked to the honor and status of the family in society. Thus, the adult children are often expected to settle down with a person seen as suitable and a right match for them by their families. But, despite social norms that promote endogamous marriages, there are a number of cross-cultural marriages in India. The phenomenon of cross-cultural marriages is not new, and Indian history is full of such instances of marriages between diverse groups like Indo Aryans, Dravidians, Iranian, Austro-Asian, and Tibeto Burban persons (Singh & Goli, 2011).

Hofstede (2011) defined culture as "the collective programming of the mind that distinguishes the members of one group or category of people from others." Cross-cultural marriages can be descried as marriages between partners belonging to different cultures. These could be marriages between individuals belonging to different faiths, races, religions, and geographical regions.

When two persons decide to enter a committed relationship, their diverse cultural backgrounds can have an influence on their adjustment and relationship. These influences can be positive or negative. Any marriage requires adjustment as well as acceptance and respect (especially because there will be some difference or another in the families of the couple); however, in cross-cultural marriages, much more adjustment, open-mindedness, acceptance, and respect are required and in certain cases the couple may be on its own without the support of their families (because they were against such an alliance).

Cross-cultural marriages can be somewhat attributed to the rapid cultural, social, and economic changes in Indian society. Such marriages could be arranged or based on love. In the case of love marriages, the family of the couple may or may not support the idea of marriage. In the case of arranged cross-cultural marriages, the marriages could be between individuals who may come from different regions of India and may speak different languages, but they belong to same religion, caste, and subcaste (e.g., a Punjabi girl belonging to a certain religion and caste is married to a boy from Uttarakhand who belongs to same religion and caste. Punjab and Uttarakhand are states in India that differ in terms of culture, language spoken, and even practices and rituals followed). Cross-cultural marriages may cause some turmoil or conflict in the family and community. A study by Dhar (2013) indicated that the caste system is still prevalent in rural areas of India, where intercaste marriages are prohibited and condemned and couples who defy this norm often face dire consequences. Thus, couples who marry across cultures may be criticized and risk judgment from family, extended family, significant others, and in some cases even the community.

There are situations where the choice of life partner (who may belong to a different culture, religion, and caste) is seen as a violation of community norms and as a threat or attack on the family's and community's reputation, status, and honor. This can also be linked to the culture of honor in which individuals, especially males, are very protective about their reputation and very sensitive to any humiliations, insults, and threats to their honor (Barrett, 2017). Thus, when an individual defies the norms related to marriages as laid down in certain communities, the family and community feels insulted and humiliated and could engage in a display of aggressive behavior directed toward the couple breaking the norms.

Deol (2014) studied honor killings in India, specifically Punjab, and found that the root cause of honor killings was the intolerance displayed by the family members with regard to the premarital relationships and matrimonial choices, especially with reference to intercaste marriages. However, honor killings are not only prevalent in the northern states in India but also in other parts as well. For example, honor killings were also reported in Tamil Nadu (Kumar, 2016).

However, cross-cultural marriages have come to be more accepted in Indian society and even celebrated. An article in the *Hindustan Times* titled "When love conquers all: Scenes from cross-cultural weddings" by Singh et al. (2015) highlights cross-cultural weddings and the celebrations involved. There are also cases where the families of the couple wholeheartedly support the decision taken by the couple and participate in the wedding preparation and celebration.

Thus, there is a sort of continuum in this regard, where on the one hand, there are extreme cases where there is complete intolerance toward cross-cultural marriages (mainly intercaste and interreligious) and on the other hand there are a number of couples who engage in cross-cultural marriages and are accepted (and celebrated) by their families.

The main issue that emerges and is of concern in cross-cultural marriages is that of the rituals and practices the couple will follow. In India, when two individuals get married, it is just not the coming together of two people, but of two families. And when two families belonging to different cultures are brought together due to marriage, numerous cultural differences emerge that can give rise to conflict, problems, and issues. And as the families come to terms with these differences and issues, conflicts and problems, it is important to focus on the impact of such marriages and the reaction of significant others to such marriages.

To explore the marital adjustment and interpersonal relationship among cross-cultural couples, seventeen cross-cultural couples in India were studied. The Marital Adjustment Questionnaire by Pramod Kumar and Kanchana Rohtagi, which is standardized to the Indian population, was used to measure marital adjustment. The Marital Adjustment Questionnaire consists of twenty-five highly discriminating "Yes – No" items. The questionnaire covers sexual, social, and emotional marital adjustment. The marital adjustment score was obtained separately for husbands and wives (a couple score was not obtained).

A structured questionnaire with both closed and open-ended questions was also used to study the interpersonal relationship. Informed consent was taken and confidentiality was ensured. The data were analyzed quantitatively and qualitatively.

DESCRIPTION OF THE SAMPLE

The couples had medium or high socioeconomic status. They were at least college graduates and held good jobs. All the participants were presently residing in urban areas. The mean age difference between the couple was 3.18, with a minimum of approximately one year and a maximum of eight years. All the couples were Indians. Ten of the seventeen were interreligious marriages; the others were either intercaste or interstate (belonging to different states in India that vary in terms of culture, language, practices, and rituals). With reference to the age of the wives, 29.4% belonged to age group 24–27 years, 35.3% belonged to age group 28–31 years, 23.5% belonged to age group 32–35 years, and 11.8 % belonged to age group 36–39 or older. With reference to age of husbands, 5.9% belonged to age group 24–27 years, 29.4% belonged to age group 28–31 years, 41.17% belonged to 32–35 years, and 23.52% belonged to age group 36–39 or older.

With regard to years of marriage, 58.82% of couples were married for 1–5 years, 35.29% for 6–10 years, and 5.9% for 11–15 years; 23.53% belonged to joint families (families where individuals belonging to multiple generations stay together), and 76.47% belonged to nuclear families (constituting couple and any children). A total of 17.6% had no children, 58.8% had one child, 17.6% had two children, and 5.9% had three children. Of the couples, 11.76% had a court marriage, 76.48% had a traditional wedding, and 11.76% had a traditional wedding but without the presence of their families. A total of 88.24% married with consent of parents and 11.76 married without consent of parents.

RESULTS AND DISCUSSION

The mean marital adjustment score for wives was 19.94 with a standard deviation of 2.21. The mean marital adjustment score for husbands was 21.0 with a standard deviation of 1.77, although the difference was not statistically significant. The wife often has to make many more adjustments compared to husbands. This is especially true of cross-cultural marriages, as the wife may have to make adjustments with regard to cultural practices and rituals as well. This is even more prevalent when the wives have to reside in a joint family post wedding.

The correlation between the marital adjustment scores of the wives and the husbands was r=.55 (p<.01). In India, most of the cross-cultural marriages are also love marriages, indicating that the couple had a courtship period during which they were able to get to know each other. This could be one reason for a positive correlation between the marital adjustment of the wives and the husbands.

The couples were also asked various open-ended questions and some of the responses were as follows: how they met was through friends, working or studying together, social gatherings, and social networking; 58.85% of the participants had a love marriage and 11.8% had an arranged marriage, that is, they met through their parents. Couples who had an arranged marriage came from different states or geographical regions of India but belonged to the same religion and caste. A total of 29.4% of the couples reported that they had a "love cum arranged marriage," a term largely used to indicate that they did not meet their spouse through an arrangement by parents or significant others. It was a love marriage, but the marriage was arranged by consent and participation of their parents and family.

The couples were also asked about similarities and differences between them. Similarities reported by them were being on the same wavelength in terms of thinking and perspective toward the world, social status, education, and open mindedness. With regard to differences, the responses that emerged were culture, language, food, personality, interests, and hobbies.

The couples were also asked about the issues that they faced before and after their wedding. Opposition from parents and other relatives and a feeling of apprehension were the main issues the couples reported facing before they got married. After their wedding, the main issues were adjusting to marital life and adjustment regarding lifestyle, specifically food. This was true especially of couples with interreligious marriages. Another issue faced by the couples post wedding was interference from the in-laws who insisted that the couple follow certain cultural practices and rituals.

The couples were also asked what they believed are advantages and disadvantages of a cross-cultural marriage. Advantages included becoming more aware about new cultures/practices/rituals and getting to learn a new language. The majority believed that there were no disadvantages as such. One of the couples termed it as an "adventure worth trying." However, they thought that it takes some time for the close and extended family members to accept the marriage. The majority also believed that there were no other significant issues, except those that are the same in any other marital relationship.

The couples were also asked to report about some of the conflicts that they face in their marital life. Responses included differences over household activities, decision making, interference from relatives regarding following certain rituals and religious practices, naming the children, and child-rearing practices. The couples also reported that communication-related issues could also emerge especially while communicating with one's in-laws (also due to language). However, the conflicts highlighted by spouses differed to some extent. The wives reported issues related to following certain rituals and practices that they did not believe in. One of the wives reported being asked to fast for her husband's long life and safety on "Karva chauth," that is, a festival celebrated by married women where they fast from sunrise till the moon rises. Since she refused to do so, her mother-in-law did not speak to her for a considerable period of time. An issue related to naming their children was also raised by some of the wives, where they had to name the child according to their husband's religion.

The couples were also asked about aspects they thought are important for successful cross-cultural marriages. The responses included adjustment and willingness to adjust, awareness about one's spouse's beliefs and practices, respect and acceptance of each other's culture and cultural differences, understanding and trust, flexibility and an open-minded approach, and open communication. The couples also reported that the support they received from family and friends was also important.

The majority (88.23%) believed that courtship was important to develop understanding. They also reported that some of them had extended their courtship before getting married, as they had to convince their parents. Premarital counseling was also indicated as important by majority of the couples (76.47%).

CONCLUSIONS

Both spouses reported that they had to make adjustment with regard to their lifestyle. The wives reported making greater adjustments with regard to food and clothing. The couples displayed overall effective interpersonal relationships. The majority reported enjoying the best of both of their cultures. And they believed that they had in fact developed a mixed third culture at home. The couples thought that close relatives especially parents and in-laws do play an important role and that if the family was supportive, there were fewer reactions from society. Willingness to adjust, acceptance, and respect were found be important. The couples reported that conflicts were not necessarily related to the cultural differences, although minor arguments related to naming of the children, child-rearing practices, and following certain practices were reported.

4

What Is Love and How Is Intimacy Expressed?

Predictions of having a current partner, as well as relationship satisfaction and relationship commitment, are explored in terms of the following:

- Components of love
- Expressions of affection
- Self-disclosure
- Honesty
- Knowing the partner

HOW HAS LOVE PREVIOUSLY BEEN CONCEPTUALIZED AND MEASURED?

William James and Carl Lange proposed in the 1880s that every emotion has a unique pattern of physiological responses (Cannon, 1927), but when researchers studied emotional responses, they found overlapping responses, such as increased heart rate for anger, fear, and surprise. So Schachter and Singer (1962) proposed that all emotions have the same physiological arousal, and what differentiates them is labeling based on cognitive cues. For example, my heart is racing and I look around and see that I am in a street and a car is approaching me; therefore, I must be afraid.

But while physiological responses often overlap among emotions, they are not always the same. For example, blood rushes to the face when angry but away from the face when frightened, and heart rate slows when sad. And in most cases, the cue comes before the arousal and indeed causes the arousal, e.g., my heart is racing because I saw the approaching car. Hence, researchers thought it was impossible to measure emotions, including love.

But Rubin (1970) took a different approach. He decided to measure love as an attitude. Social psychologists think of attitudes as having three components:

- **Cognitive** – beliefs about the attitude, object, or person
- **Affective** – feelings toward the attitude, object, or person
- **Behavioral** – dispositions to act toward the object or person in certain ways

Love certainly involves all three. The advantage of this approach is that we think we know how to measure attitudes, since we have been doing this for decades. So Rubin developed a Love Scale, by asking degree of agreement with items thought to be related to love. The love items measure **caring, attachment,** and **intimacy.**

At the same time, Rubin developed a Liking Scale, to demonstrate that love can be distinguished from other positive emotions. The liking items relate mainly to respect, which isn't quite the same as liking. You may respect someone you don't like, or not totally respect someone, such as a relative, whom you do like. But the Liking Scale does show that love can be distinguished from another positive emotion.

As noted in Chapter 1 of this book, to assess the validity of his Love Scale, Rubin recruited dating couples to participate in a study of eye gazing. After completing a questionnaire including the Love Scale, he had partners sit across from each other, with an observer holding a stop watch for each of them to record looking at the partner, and a third stop watch to record when they were both looking at each other at the same time. He found that couples with higher Love Scale scores engaged in more mutual eye gazing.

The fact that his paper-and-pencil measure of love predicted an observable behavior was impressive. The American Psychological Association gave him an award for the best doctoral dissertation of 1969, and the National Science Foundation gave him a grant to study the development of love over time, which became the Boston Couples Study.

Berscheid and Walster (1969, 1978) made a distinction between **passionate love** and **companionate love**. Schachter and Singer's (1962) theory of emotion inspired their conceptualization of passionate love. People experience arousal during early stages of a relationship, which becomes labeled as passionate love. For example, one might become excited to see the other, feel sexual arousal, or be anxious about whether the other reciprocates one's interest and desire. In contrast, companionate love is a bond that occurs when people feel comfortable with each other. Later research found that passionate love was the strongest predictor of marital satisfaction (Contreras, Hendrick, & Hendrick, 1996).

Sternberg (1986) proposed a Triangular Theory of Love with three components: intimacy, passion, and commitment and studied the extent to which relationships involve each of these three. Lee (1973) argued that there are a variety of **love styles**, and different combinations of them: eros (erotic), ludus (fun), storge (familial), pragma (practical), mania (obsessive), and

TABLE 4.1 *Four components of Love Scale items*

• **Caring:**	One of my primary concerns is CP's welfare. (Rubin, 1970)
• **Attachment:**	It would be hard for me to get along without CP. (Rubin, 1970)
• **Intimacy:**	I have a relationship of mutual understanding with CP. (Sternberg, 2986)
	I give considerable emotional support to CP. (Sternberg, 1986)
• **Passion:**	My relationship with CP is very romantic. (Sternberg, 1986)

TABLE 4.2 *Measures of Lee's Love Styles*

• **Eros:**	I feel that CP and I were meant for each other.
• **Ludus:**	I have sometimes had to keep CP from finding out about other lovers.
• **Storge:**	Our friendship merged gradually into love over time.
• **Pragma:**	One consideration in choosing CP was how CP would help me in my career.
• **Mania:**	When CP doesn't pay attention to me, I feel miserable.
• **Agape:**	I am usually willing to sacrifice my own wishes to let CP achieve CP's wishes.

agape (altruistic). Hendrick and Hendrick (1986) developed measures of these items in a Love Attitudes Scale.

More recently, Karandashev (2015) provided a historical, psychological, sociological, and anthropological review of cultural perspectives on love. He concluded that the emotion of love is universal, although how it is conceptualized and experienced is influenced by culture.

HOW ARE THE COMPONENTS OF LOVE MEASURED IN THE PRESENT STUDY?

In the present study, the measurement of love is built upon the previous theorizing. Factor analyses indicate that items in Table 4.1 representing those four components of love load on a single factor, with an overall reliability of Alpha=.83. SEM Measurement Models reveal similarity in the factor loadings across eight relationship types (CFI=.961, RMSEA=.032) and across nine cultural regions (CFI=.962, RMSEA=.025) (CP refers to Current Partner).

These five items are averaged to create the Four Component Love Scale used in further data analyses. Commitment is excluded from the Four Component Love Scale since relationship commitment is conceptualized as distinct from love in this study. As expected, the items from Hendrick and Hendrick (1986) used in this study to measure the six components identified by Lee (1973) are not consistently correlated with these Love Scale items or each other and, hence, are analyzed separately (see Table 4.2). In regard to Agape, recent research has explored the role of sacrifice in opposite-sex relationships (Stanley et al., 2006; Whitton, Stanley, & Markman, 2002, 2007).

Participants are also asked the following two questions from the Boston Couples Study:

- To what extent would you say that you and CP are in love?
- How emotionally close would you say your relationship with CP is right now?

TO WHAT EXTENT DOES LOVE MATTER?

In the Boston Couples Study, both women's and men's initial Rubin Love Scale scores predicted dating satisfaction, staying together during the first two years of the study, and eventually marrying that partner (Hill & Peplau, 1998). Initially saying they were both in love also predicted dating satisfaction, staying together, and eventually marrying that partner. However, love was not a guarantee of staying together: among those who stayed together on the two-year follow-up, 81 percent had initially said they were both in love; among those who broke up, 57 percent had also said that they were both in love (Hill, Rubin, & Peplau, 1976).

In the present study, the Four Component Love Scale is strongly correlated with Relationship Satisfaction ($r=.72^{***}$) and Relationship Commitment ($r=.77^{***}$). Similarly, saying that you and CP are in love is strongly correlated with Relationship Satisfaction ($r=.73^{***}$) and Relationship Commitment ($r=.79^{***}$). Emotional Closeness is also strongly correlated with Relationship Satisfaction ($r=.75^{***}$) and Relationship Commitment ($r=.70^{***}$). These and other measures of emotional intimacy are combined in SEM Structural Models later in this chapter. As expected, the six Love Styles items used in this study have varying overall correlations with Relationship Satisfaction and Commitment, as shown in Table 4.3.

HOW WERE EXPRESSIONS OF AFFECTION MEASURED?

Besides sexual activity, which is discussed in the next chapter, intimacy can be achieved through expressions of affection and through self-disclosure. **Expressions of affection** are measured in this study using a set of items to measure own expressions of affection, and a set of items to measure perceptions of partner's expressions of affection:

- I often express affection to CP verbally.
- I often express affection to CP nonverbally.
- CP is certain that I have affection for CP.
- CP often expresses affection to me verbally.
- CP often expresses affection to me nonverbally.
- I am certain that CP has affection for me.

TABLE 4.3 *Correlates of Lee's Love Styles*

	Satisfaction	Commitment
• Eros (we were meant for each other)	.62***	.90***
• Storge (our friendship merged into love)	.22***	.24***
• Mania (I am miserable when CP ignores me)	.10***	.25***
• Agape (I sacrifice my own wishes)	.28***	.42***
• Ludus (I kept other lovers secret)	−.17***	−.12***
• Pragma (CP would help my career)	−.02	.02

Note that the Eros, Storge, Mania, and Agape items are positively correlated with Relationship Satisfaction and Relationship Commitment, while the Ludus item is negatively correlated, and the Pragma item is not correlated at all.

The three items for own expression of affection load on a single factor, with similar factor loadings across relationship types (CFI=.977, RMSEA=.038) and across cultural regions (CFI=.996, RMSEA=.013). In addition, the three items for perceptions of partner's expression of affection load on a single factor, with similar factor loadings across relationship types (CFI=.971, RMSEA=.041) and across cultural regions (CFI=.995, RMSEA=.013). Hence, each set is averaged to create a scale.

The Own Expression of Affection scale is moderately correlated with Relationship Satisfaction (r=.59***) and Relationship Commitment (r=.49***). Similarly, the Perception of Partner's Expression of Emotion Scale is moderately correlated with Relationship Satisfaction (r=.61***) and Relationship Commitment (r=.59***).

HOW DO THE MEASURES OF LOVE AND EXPRESSIONS OF AFFECTION COMBINE IN SEM MODELS?

Structural Equation Modeling (SEM) is introduced in Chapter 1. SEM Structural Models combine the measures of love and expressions of affection to test indirect predictions of relationship commitment through relationship satisfaction, and direct predictions of relationship commitment independent of relationship satisfaction. These models are similar across eight relationship types (CFI=.984, RMSEA=.026) and nine cultural regions (CFI=.987, RMSEA=.019).

The standardized regression coefficients in these models reveal that the Four Component Love Scale (γ=.21), Emotional Closeness (γ=.30), Saying Both Are in Love (γ=.14), and Own Expression of Affection scale (γ=.12) are all Central Factors in predicting Relationship Satisfaction. That means that each of these Central Factors predicts satisfaction beyond what they have in common. But Perception of Partner's Expression of Affection and the Love Styles items add trivial explained variance (γ<.10) when these Central Factors are taken into account.

In addition, the Four Component Love Scale (γ=.25), Saying Both Are in Love (γ=.29), and the Love Style Eros item (we were meant for each other, γ=.20) have direct predictions of Relationship Commitment independent of Relationship Satisfaction. In other words, loving the partner can lead to commitment whether relationship satisfaction is high or low, sometimes remaining even in abusive relationships. And believing that you were meant for each other reflects a destiny belief about intimate relationships as opposed to a growth belief that relationships take work (Knee & Petty, 2013).

HOW DO PUBLIC DISPLAYS OF AFFECTION MATTER?

A question that was not asked in the present study was how comfortable partners were expressing affection publically. Public Displays of Affection (PDAs) let others know about the intimate relationship, which can support having a couple identity that is recognized by others. But it can also lead to jealousy by friends and potential alternative partners about time spent with the partner, and to harassment by others who disapprove of the relationship. This is especially likely to be a problem for those in same-sex relationships, due to homophobia and religious prohibitions against same-sex intimacy.

But even in opposite-sex relationships, a man expressing "too much" affection in front of male friends can lead them to accuse him of being "whipped." That is, his emotional involvement in the relationship may make him vulnerable to being dominated by his partner, indicating weakness on his part. Disagreement on public displays of affection is one of the sources of conflict that is discussed in Chapter 7.

SELF-REFLECTION

How comfortable are you expressing affection in public – to relatives, to friends of the opposite sex, to friends of the same sex, to a romantic or sexual partner? In what ways do you express affection or acknowledge your relationship to them – a simple greeting, a bow, shaking hands, a hug, a kiss? There are cross-cultural differences in expectations for appropriate greetings (Morrison & Conaway, 2006).

Cross-cultural differences in expressions of affection are discussed in the SPOTLIGHT on Intimacy and Relational Mobility later in this chapter. When there is more choice about potential partners, there is more need for expressions of affection and commitment to keep partners in relationships.

HOW DID SELF-DISCLOSURE MATTER IN PREVIOUS RESEARCH?

In the Boston Couples Study, participants were asked the extent to which they had disclosed to their partner on a variety of topics, and responses were summed to obtain a total disclosure scale. The scale was correlated with satisfaction with the dating relationship but did not predict eventual marriage (Hill & Peplau, 1998). Similarly, Sprecher and Hendrick (2004) found that self-disclosure was correlated with relationship satisfaction but did not predict whether the couple stayed together over time. And Hendrick (1981) found that self-disclosure was correlated with marital satisfaction.

HOW IS SELF-DISCLOSURE MEASURED IN THE PRESENT STUDY?

Self-disclosure is measured in this study using a set of items to measure own disclosure and a set of items to measure partner's disclosure:

• To what extent have you revealed each of the following to CP?
  a. Your cultural and social background
  b. Your attitudes and values
  c. Your goals in life
  d. Your feelings about CP

• To what extent has CP revealed each of the following to you?
  a. CP's cultural and social background
  b. CP's attitudes and values
  c. CP's goals in life
  d. CP's feelings about you

The four items for own disclosure load on a single scale with similar factor loadings across relationship types (CFI=.969, RMSEA=.038) and cultural regions (CFI=.971, RMSEA=.027). Similarly, the items for partner's disclosure load on a single factor with similar factor loadings across relationship types (CFI=.966, RMSEA=.040) and cultural regions (CFI=.965, RMSEA=.31). Hence, each set is averaged to create a scale.

The Own Disclosure Scale is correlated with Relationship Satisfaction (r=.54***) and Relationship Commitment (r=.59***). Similarly, the Partner Disclosure Scale is correlated with Relationship Satisfaction (r=.54***) and Relationship Commitment (r=.54***).

Omitted from these scales is an additional item about revealing prior romantic or sexual activities, which does not have consistent factor loadings across relationship types. Own disclosure about prior sexual romantic or sexual activities has stronger positive correlations with Relationship Satisfaction for men in same-sex relationships ($r=.53^{***}$) than for men and women in the other relationship types ($r=.27^{***}$). Similar predictions are found for partner's disclosure on this item ($r=.46^{***}$ vs. $r=.29^{***}$). In other words, revealing prior romantic or sexual activities matters more for men in same-sex relationships. Hence, these items are not included in SEM Structural Models in the next section. Variations across relationship types in correlates of having had prior sexual partners are discussed in Chapter 5.

To measure **honesty** in self-disclosure, the following two items are asked, which do not load consistently on a single factor and hence are entered as individual items in SEM Structural Models following the next section:

- I trust CP not to lie to me.
- I never lie to CP.

Trusting the Partner Not to Lie is correlated overall with Relationship Satisfaction ($r=.58^{***}$) and Relationship Commitment ($r=.52^{***}$). Similarly, Never Lying to the Partner is correlated with Relationship Satisfaction ($r=.46^{***}$) and Relationship Commitment ($r=.41^{***}$).

HOW IS KNOWING THE PARTNER MEASURED?

In addition, the questions in Table 4.4 are asked, which also do not load consistently on a single factor and hence are entered as individual items in SEM Structural Models that follow. Their correlations with Relationship Satisfaction and Relationship Commitment are also listed in Table 4.4.

HOW DO SELF-DISCLOSURE, HONESTY, AND KNOWING THE PARTNER COMBINE IN SEM MODELS?

SEM Structural Models combine the disclosure scales, honesty, and knowing the partner to test indirect predictions of Relationship Commitment through Relationship Satisfaction, and direct predictions of Relationship Commitment independent of Relationship Satisfaction. These models are similar across eight relationship types (CFI=.988, RMSEA=.022) and nine cultural regions (CFI=.982, RMSEA=.021).

These models reveal that the Own Disclosure Scale ($\gamma=.13$), Trusting Partner ($\gamma=.21$), Never Lying to Partner ($\gamma=.12$), How Well Know Partner ($\gamma=.12$), and especially How Often Partners Communicate ($\gamma=.45$) are all Central Factors in predicting Relationship Satisfaction.

TABLE 4.4 *Correlates of knowing the partner*

	Satisfaction	Commitment
• How well would you say that you know CP?	.55***	.55***
• How well would you say that CP knows you?	.56***	.55***
• About how often do you and CP currently see each other in person?	.31***	.37***
• About how often do you and CP currently communicate with each other (in person or by telephone, text messages, email, instant messaging, letters, etc.)	.47***	.47***

In addition, Own Disclosure Scale (γ=.35), how often partners see each other (γ=.20), and how often partners communicate (γ=.29) have direct predictions of Relationship Commitment independent of Relationship Satisfaction. In other words, communication is important in relationship satisfaction, and those who are committed to their relationship communicate more.

IN SUMMARY, WHAT CENTRAL FACTORS ARE IDENTIFIED IN THIS CHAPTER?

For Relationship Satisfaction and Relationship Commitment, the Central Factors are the Four Component Love Scale, Emotional Closeness, Saying Both in Love, Own Expression of Emotion, the Love Style Eros Item (we were meant for each other), How Often Partners Communicate, Trusting the Partner, Never Lying to the Partner, Knowing the Partner, the Own Disclosure Scale, and How Often See the Partner. Each of these Central Factors has additional predictions beyond those they have in common. SEM models reveal that these same Central Factors make similar predictions across eight relationship types and nine cultural regions.

The predictions of these Central Factors are similar, even though their levels may vary. These Central Factors will be combined with Central Factors from other chapters in a *Comprehensive Commitment Model* in Chapter 10. Variations in levels of factors will be discussed in Chapter 11.

SPOTLIGHT ON INTIMACY AND RELATIONAL MOBILITY

MIE KITO

Romantic relationships and friendships are usually referred as *intimate relationships*. Both the general public and relationship researchers use this term. You may not doubt that romantic relationships and friendships are *intimate*, but is this similar around the world? The answer seems to be "No." As you will see, your cultural background or characteristics of the society where you live play a role in how intimate you feel and act toward your romantic partner or friends. (See Adams, Anderson, & Adonu, 2004, for discussions on how the concept of *intimacy* is culturally grounded.)

Imagine that you were back home from a month-long summer trip you took by yourself. When you got out from the gate at an airport, your romantic partner was longing to see you. What would you and your partner do when you finally got to each other? If you are from North America or Western Europe, you are likely to first give each other a hug and/or kiss. What happens if you are from Asia? Would you respond in the same way? Probably not. You might calmly talk to your partner, and your partner would ask how your trip was, without hugs or kisses. Of course, these are somewhat overgeneralized examples, and your reactions may depend on other factors than your cultural background. But, you get the idea. These examples show cultural differences in *expressions of intimacy.*

In fact, previous research found that one's cultural background is related to how intimate people feel toward their close others. For instance, European Canadians reported that they felt greater intimacy toward their romantic partner compared to Chinese Canadians (Marshall, 2008). In friendships, the level of intimacy is higher among Americans than among Poles (Rybak & McAndrew, 2006). My colleagues and I (Yamada, Kito, & Yuki, 2015) attempted to replicate this cross-cultural difference in intimacy between Canadians and Japanese and found the expected cross-societal differences in the level of intimacy; Canadians experience greater intimacy toward their closest friend and romantic partner compared to Japanese.

Why do Canadians feel greater intimacy than Japanese? What factors predict this cultural difference? Another purpose of our study (Yamada et al., 2015) was to answer this question. We specifically focused on a socioecological factor, called *relational mobility*. It refers to the number of opportunities in a given society that are available to choose relational partners based on their personal preferences (Kito, Yuki, & Thomson, 2017; Yuki & Schug, 2012).

In societies high in relational mobility (e.g., North America), there are abundant opportunities to meet, and form relationships with, new potential partners and to voluntarily end a relationship if it is no longer necessary or satisfying. In such societies, both you and your partner have relational options. Thus, at the same time that you can end the relationship with your partner, your partner can leave for another person to replace you if alternatives are available.

One of the necessary tasks in such high–relational mobility societies is to retain current relational partners. Intimacy may function as a psychological mechanism that leads to behaviors adaptive for partner retention. In fact, previous research suggests that high intimacy is related to greater social support (e.g., Reis & Franks, 1994; Sternberg, 1986). Thus, higher intimacy may elicit investing behaviors toward relational partners (e.g., social support), and these behaviors are especially adaptive in high–relational mobility societies where relationships are relatively fragile (Kito et al, 2017).

In contrast, societies low in relational mobility (e.g., East Asia) are characterized with a closed network of relational ties. There are few opportunities to choose relational partners, and their relationships tend to be prescribed by circumstance and stable once formed. Since there is low risk that one's partner will leave for an alternative partner, active effort to retain the partner is unnecessary. Thus, intimacy, a psychological process contributing to partner-retention behaviors, is less needed in low–relational mobility societies (Kito et al., 2017).

Turning back to our cross-cultural study on intimacy (Yamada et al., 2015), what did we find in terms of relational mobility as an explaining factor? Well, we found the results consistent with the previous arguments. That is, the results indicated that cross-societal differences in intimacy toward closest friends between Canadians and Japanese are partly due to differences in relational mobility of the surrounding society (the effect was not statistically significant for romantic relationships). That is, relational mobility was higher in Canada than Japan, and higher relational mobility in turn predicted greater intimacy felt toward one's closest friends.

Other research has shown that relational mobility explains a variety of cross-cultural differences in behaviors and psychological processes, such as self-disclosure (Schug, Yuki, & Maddux, 2010), similarity between friends (Schug, Yuki, Horikawa, & Takemura, 2009), passion toward romantic partners (Yamada, Kito, & Yuki, 2017), general trust (Thomson, Yuki, & Ito, 2015), and caution toward friends (Li, Adams, Kurtis, & Hamamura, 2015). For comprehensive reviews of relational mobility, see Kito et al. (2017) and Schug and Yuki (2012). Cross-cultural differences in the present study are described in Chapter 11.

Taken together, even such commonly used terms as *intimate relationships* are open to various interpretations and experiences in societies around the world. How intimate people feel toward their relational partners (or at least, closest friends) depends on characteristics of the society that surrounds them (e.g., relational mobility).

5

How Do Sexual Attitudes and Behaviors Matter?

Predictions of having a current partner, as well as relationship satisfaction and relationship commitment, are explored in terms of the following:

- Sexual attitudes
- Sexual behaviors
- Sexual satisfaction
- Sex outside the relationship

HOW DID SEXUAL ATTITUDES MATTER IN THE BOSTON COUPLES STUDY?

In the Boston Couples Study, whether or not the couple had sexual intercourse did not predict whether the couple stayed together during the two years of the original study (Hill, Rubin, & Peplau, 1976), nor did it predict eventual marriage and staying married on the fifteen-year follow-up (Hill & Peplau, 1998).

Interviews revealed that there were three attitudes about love and sex (Peplau, Rubin, & Hill, 1977). Those who were called **sexual traditionalists** believed that premarital sex was wrong. One man said in an interview that he wanted to have sex with his girlfriend, but she believed it was wrong, so out of love and respect for her he did not pressure her to have sex. Those who were called **sexual moderates** believed that casual sex was wrong, but that sex was okay when a relationship reached a certain level of love and commitment. And those who were called **sexual liberals** believed that sex was okay even if you were not in love, and they often found that physical intimacy increased emotional intimacy. It is now understood why that occurs: orgasm releases oxytocin, which promotes emotional bonding (Crenshaw, 1996).

Thus, some couples were having sex because they were in love, other couples were having sex even though they were not in love, and still others

TABLE 5.1 *Approval of sex for unmarried partners*

	Mean	(s.d.)
• A man who is in love with his sexual partner?	6.30	(2.61)
• A man who is *not* in love with his sexual partner?	3.75	(3.03)
• A woman who is in love with her sexual partner?	6.23	(2.68)
• A woman who is *not* in love with her sexual partner?	3.69	(3.05)

were not having sex even though they were in love. The net effect of combining them all together was that having sex did not predict staying together, even though love did predict staying together. However, other research has found a correlation between sexual satisfaction and relationship satisfaction (Sprecher et al., 2018).

HOW ARE SEXUAL ATTITUDES MEASURED IN THE PRESENT STUDY?

To measure **sexual approval** of non-marital sex, the present study asks the following question from the Boston Couples Study (the results appear in Table 5.1):
• To what extent do you approve of sexual intercourse for each of the following unmarried persons?

The overall mean scores in Table 5.1 indicate more approval for an unmarried man or woman who is in love than for an unmarried man or woman not in love, but little evidence of a double standard indicting more approval for a man than for a woman. The standard deviations for all four questions indicate quite a bit of overall variation in approval. While responses to these questions are generally correlated, the correlations vary, so that these four items do not have consistent factor loadings on a single factor. Hence, they are analyzed separately.

Having a Current Partner is somewhat correlated with approval for each of the four situations: a man in love ($r=.18^{***}$), a man not in love ($r=.16^{***}$), a woman in love ($r=.16^{***}$), and a woman not in love ($r=.15^{***}$). This is consistent with the finding reported in Chapter 2 that Having a Current Partner is somewhat correlated with the importance of sexual activities as a reason for being in a marriage or other committed relationship.

Structural Equation Modeling (SEM) is introduced in Chapter 1. SEM Structural Models combining these sexual attitudes to predict Having a Current Partner reveal that approval of sex for an unmarried man in love with his sexual partner is a Central Factor, since it had the strongest

TABLE 5.2 *Physical activities with CP*

		UNMARRIED	MARRIED
a Kissing on the lips	No Yes	94%	98%
b. Affectionate touching	No Yes	94%	99%
c. Sexual intercourse	No Yes	79%	97%
d. Other sexual activities	No Yes	72%	86%

association, but it had only a slight effect (γ=.12). The other attitudes add only trivial explained variance after it was taken into account, due to their generally being correlated with it. These SEM models are consistent across gender (CFI=1.00, RMSEA=.000) and nine cultural regions (CFI=.999, RMSEA=.010).

In addition, these sexual attitude measures have only trivial correlations (r<.10) with Relationship Satisfaction and Relationship Commitment, which is consistent across eight relationship types (CFI=.988, RMSEA=.031) and nine cultural regions (CFI=.996, RMSEA=.015). Thus, they are not included in SEM Structural Models described later in this chapter.

HOW WERE SEXUAL BEHAVIORS MEASURED?

To measure physical activities with the current partner (CP), the following question was asked, with the percentage saying yes listed separately for unmarried and for married participants (as shown in Table 5.2):

• Which of the following activities have you engaged in with CP?

Partners may engage in a variety of sexual behaviors besides or instead of sexual intercourse, and the meaning of "sexual intercourse" may differ for male and female same-sex partners, and even for opposite-sex partners. In the Boston Couples Study, one woman said that she and her dating partner had had sexual intercourse, while he said they had not. They had initiated intercourse, and she had been penetrated, so she considered it intercourse; however, he had not achieved orgasm, so he believed that it didn't count.

In the present study then, answering YES for either "sexual intercourse" or "other sexual activities" is combined in a variable called Sexual Activities, which had 85% YES for those unmarried and 98% YES for those married. Participants were also asked the following question (with results in Table 5.3):

• How frequently do you engage in sexual activities with CP?

TABLE 5.3 *Frequency of sexual activities with CP*

Every day	04%
Three or more times a week	22%
Once or twice a week	35%
Less than once a week	21%
Less than once a month	18%

Note that the most common frequency was once or twice a week. Reporting less frequent sexual activities was correlated overall with less Relationship Satisfaction (r=.23***) and with less Relationship Commitment (r=.14***). This measure is combined with other measures in SEM models later in this chapter. Other research on sexual behaviors is reported in the SPOTLIGHT on Sexual Behaviors in Hungary later in this chapter.

HOW IS SEXUAL SATISFACTION MEASURED?

To measure **sexual satisfaction**, the following questions are asked, which load on a single factor across relationship types (CFI=.999, RMSEA=.009) and across cultural regions (CFI=.975, RMSEA=.013):

- Overall, how personally satisfying to you are your sexual activities with CP?
- How satisfied are you with the frequency of your sexual activities with CP?
- How satisfied are you with the specific kinds of your sexual activities with CP?

These items are averaged to form a Sexual Satisfaction Scale, which had an overall reliability of Alpha=.78, and a mean value of 6.04 (*s.d.*=1.66), with possible responses from 0=NOT AT ALL to 8=COMPLETELY. Sexual Satisfaction is moderately correlated with Relationship Satisfaction (r=.44***) and somewhat correlated with Relationship Commitment (r=.24***).

HOW IS ENGAGING IN UNWANTED SEX MEASURED?

The following question is asked to measure compliance with **unwanted sex:**

- How often have you engaged in sexual activities with CP even though you did not want to?

The overall mean is 2.04 and the standard deviation is 2.29. While the mean is relatively low, the standard deviation indicates that there is a fair amount of variation in the responses. Its correlation with Relationship Satisfaction is r=−.13***, which means that those who engage in unwanted sex are slightly less likely to be satisfied with their relationship. But its correlation with Relationship Commitment is r=−.01,

TABLE 5.4 *Frequency of desired sex with CP*

Every day	19%
Three or more times a week	36%
Once or twice a week	28%
Less than once a week	8%
Less than once a month	5%
Not at all	5%

TABLE 5.5 *Who is more interested in sexual activities*

	WOMEN	MEN
CP is much more interested	18%	5%
CP is somewhat more interested	25%	11%
We are both interested to the same degree	43%	43%
I am somewhat more interested	10%	26%
I am much more interested	4%	15%

which means that those who engage in unwanted sex are just as committed as those who do not, which is presumably why they are willing engage in it. Impett and Pelau (2002) reported that women who were anxiously attached were the most willing to consent to unwanted sex, fearing that their partner would lose interest in them.

HOW IS DESIRED SEX WITH THE PARTNER MEASURED?

Participants are asked the following question (see Table 5.4):

- How frequently would you ideally like to engage in sexual activities with CP?

The gender difference on ideal frequency of sex was trivial ($r<.10$). Note that these responses indicate that the ideal frequency of sex with the partner was generally higher than the actual frequency reported earlier, which was confirmed by paired t-tests ($p<.001$). Answers to the following question are shown in Table 5.5:

- Who is more interested in engaging in sexual activities – CP or you?

There was a moderate gender difference with men more likely than women to say that they were more interested in sex than their partners ($r=.32^{***}$). Note that this gender difference in their perceived comparison of their own versus their partner's interest in sex is much larger than the gender difference in ideal frequency of sex reported earlier, which was trivial (r<.10). The compatibility of one's own and one's partner's interest in sex at a given moment may differ from idealized notions of sexual frequency.

This question is recoded to indicate the extent of Equal Interest in Sex (1=either one much more, 2=one somewhat more, 3=both to the same degree). The recoded measure is slightly correlated with Relationship Satisfaction (r=.14***) but not Relationship Commitment (r=.01). In other words, those who report unequal interest in sex are slightly less likely to be satisfied with their relationship, but not less likely to be committed to it. Other factors that keep people in committed relationships regardless of their relationship satisfaction are identified throughout this book.

HOW DO THE PREVIOUS MEASURES COMBINE IN SEM STRUCTURAL MODELS?

SEM Structural Models combined measures of sexual behaviors, sexual satisfaction, unwanted sex, ideal frequency of sex, and equal interest in sex to test indirect predictions of Relationship Commitment through Relationship Satisfaction, and direct predictions of Relationship Commitment independent of Relationship Satisfaction. These models are consistent across relationship types (CFI=.950, RMSEA=.030) and cultural regions (CFI=.965, RMSEA=.0198).

These models reveal that Sexual Satisfaction is a Central Factor in predicting Relationship Satisfaction (γ=.44). The other measures add trivial explained variance after it is taken into account, since their predictions are captured by it. But Sexual Satisfaction has only a trivial direct prediction of Relationship Commitment, which means that its impact on Relationship Commitment was primarily through Relationship Satisfaction.

SELF-REFLECTION

If you have a partner, do you discuss your sexual attitudes? Do you discuss your desired sexual frequency, and the sexual behaviors that you would like, or not like, to engage in with your partner? How satisfied are you with your sexual activities or your lack of sexual activities?

HOW COMMON IS SEX OUTSIDE THE CURRENT RELATIONSHIP?

To measure sex with others, the following questions are asked:

- *Before* your current relationship with CP, with how many females had you engaged in sexual activities?

TABLE 5.6 *Sex with others before relationship with CP*

	Sex with Females	Sex with Males
• Female opposite-sex unmarried	9%	58%
• Male opposite-sex unmarried	63%	4%
• Female opposite-sex married	9%	67%
• Male opposite-sex married	76%	7%
• Female same-sex unmarried	58%	58%
• Male same-sex unmarried	35%	74%
• Female same-sex married	70%	68%
• Male same-sex married	52%	95%

- *Before* your current relationship with CP, with how many males had you engaged in sexual activities?
- *During* your current relationship with CP, with how many females have you engaged in sexual activities?
- *During* your current relationship with CP, with how many males have you engaged in sexual activities?

The percentage having had sex with one or more females or males *before* the Current Partner are indicated in Table 5.6 for all eight relationship types.

Before the current relationship, few of those with an opposite-sex current partner had sex with someone of the same sex, highlighted in bold in the table. But many of those with a same-sex current partner had sex with an opposite-sex partner prior to the current partner, highlighted in bold in the table. This is not surprising since people have generally been expected to have opposite-sex partners, and some who end up with same-sex partners had previously presumed that they were heterosexual, or they were uncertain about their sexuality until exploring opposite-sex and same-sex partners.

Having had sex with both females and males was especially true for women with same-sex partners, who had opposite-sex prior partners about as frequently as same-sex prior partners. Previous research has found women's sexuality to have greater fluidity in regard to opposite-sex and same-sex partners (Peplau & Garnets, 2000).

In addition, some with same-sex or opposite-sex current partners may consider themselves bisexual in varying degrees (Kinsey, Pomeroy, & Martin, 1948). Sexuality has many dimensions, including sexual identities; aesthetic,

TABLE 5.7 *Sex with others during relationship with CP*

	Sex with Females	Sex with Males
• Female opposite-sex unmarried	3%	13%
• Male opposite-sex unmarried	21%	2%
• Female opposite-sex married	3%	13%
• Male opposite-sex married	27%	3%
• Female same-sex unmarried	18%	6%
• Male same-sex unmarried	6%	31%
• Female same-sex married	12%	5%
• Male same-sex married	3%	55%

emotional, and sexual attraction; arousal; behaviors; and lifestyles (Hill, 2001b).

However, having had sex with anyone before the current partner had no overall impact on Relationship Satisfaction (r=.02) or Relationship Commitment (r=.00).

The percentages having had sex with one or more females or males other than the current partner *during* the current relationship are indicated in Table 5.7, for all eight relationship types.

During the current relationship, few had sex with others who were *not* of the current partner's sex, highlighted in bold in the table. However, quite a few had sex with someone else, including those married, although some of those married may have had sex with someone else while dating the current partner before they were married. The men had more sex with others than did the women, especially men in same-sex relationships whether unmarried (31%) or married (55%). The latter parallels approval of sex outside the relationship, which is discussed in the next section.

Measures of having had sex with females and having had sex with males were recoded into a single measure of Outside Sex, having had sex with anyone else, during the current relationship. Outside Sex had a slight overall negative correlation with Relationship Satisfaction (r=−.12***) and Relationship Commitment (r=−.11***), but its impact varied somewhat in SEM models, which are discussed after the next section.

To measure **approval of outside sex**, the following questions are asked:

- To what extent does (or would) CP approve of your engaging in sexual activities with anyone else?
- To what extent do (or would) you approve of CP engaging in sexual activities with anyone else?

TABLE 5.8 *Approval of outside sex*

	CP's Approval	Own Approval
• Female opposite-sex unmarried	1.00	0.91
• Male opposite-sex unmarried	1.22	1.24
• Female opposite-sex married	0.68	0.54
• Male opposite-sex married	0.61	0.76
• Female same-sex unmarried	1.89	2.12
• Male same-sex unmarried	2.05	2.73
• Female same-sex married	0.66	0.78
• Male same-sex married	2.79	3.50

The mean ratings of CP's Approval of Outside Sex and Own Approval of Outside Sex, for the eight relationship types are shown in Table 5.8, with possible responses from 0=NOT AT ALL to 8=COMPLETELY.

In general, the approval ratings are very low for those in opposite-sex relationships, especially those married. The approval ratings are somewhat higher for men and women in unmarried same-sex relationships, and especially for men in same-sex marriages, but not for women in same-sex marriages. The higher approval ratings for men in same-sex relationships are consistent with their higher reports of having had sex outside the relationship. In other words, they are more likely to have an "open relationship" in which outside sex is allowed. This has been found in previous research (Diamond & Blair, 2018).

Participants are also asked the following question, with possible responses from 0=NOT AT ALL to 8=COMPLETELY:

• To what extent do you believe that CP has engaged in sexual activities with anyone else during your relationship with CP?

Responses to this question paralleled responses to the approval questions, with the highest means for men in same-sex relationships who were unmarried (3.10) or married (3.42). Overall among all participants, responses to this question were negatively correlated with relationship satisfaction ($r=-.26***$) and with relationship commitment ($r=-.24***$). Previous research had found a negative correlation between outside sex and relationship satisfaction in opposite-sex unmarried relationships (Maddox Shaw et al., 2013). Among those in opposite-sex couples engaging in outside sex, those with greater commitment to their partner were more likely to use a condom in outside sex (Buunk & Bakker, 1997).

HOW DOES SEX OUTSIDE THE RELATIONSHIP MATTER?

SEM Structural Models combine self or partner having Outside Sex during the current relationship, and the measures of approval of Outside Sex, to test indirect predictions of Relationship Commitment through Relationship Satisfaction, and direct predictions of Relationship Commitment independent of Relationship Satisfaction. These models are generally consistent across cultural regions (CFI=.967, RMSEA=.021), but somewhat inconsistent across relationship types (CFI=.943, although RMSEA=.036). The biggest differences in predictions were for men and women in same-sex marriages. Hence, SEM Structural Models are created separately for those two relationship types and for the other six relationship types.

For the other six relationship types, the SEM models reveal that perception of partner's Outside Sex is a Central Factor in predicting less Relationship Satisfaction ($\gamma=-.24$). Own approval of Outside Sex is a Central Factor in predicting slightly less Relationship Commitment ($\gamma =-.12$). In other words, partner's outside sex indicates less relationship satisfaction, and approving partner's outside sex reflects less commitment. These findings are consistent across the six relationship types (CFI=.973, RMSEA=.028).

For the two relationship types of male and female same-sex marriage, similar SEM Structural Models reveal that perception of partner's Outside Sex is again a Central Factor in predicting less Relationship Satisfaction ($\gamma =-.15$). But own approval of partner's Outside Sex did not predict less Relationship Commitment ($\gamma=.01$). In other words, approval of outside sex by the partner does not necessarily reflect a lack of relationship commitment in same-sex marriages as it does in other relationship types. Same-sex spouses were more likely to agree to an "open marriage" when they were committed enough to get married. But it still indicates somewhat less relationship satisfaction.

This slight difference in the impact of approval of partner's outside sex on one's own commitment, between same-sex marriages ($\gamma=.01$) and other relationship types ($\gamma =-.12$), is the main difference found among all of the SEM Structural Models of Relationship Satisfaction and Relationship Commitment throughout this entire book.

IN SUMMARY, WHAT CENTRAL FACTORS ARE IDENTIFIED IN THIS CHAPTER?

For Having a Current Partner, the Central Factor is approval of sex for an unmarried man in love with his partner. This captures the predictions in common for all four of the sexual attitude questions, which were generally correlated with one another. SEM models reveal that this Central Factor makes the same predictions across gender and nine cultural regions.

For Relationship Satisfaction and Relationship Commitment, Sexual Satisfaction is a positive Central Factor, and partner's Outside Sex during the relationship is a negative Central Factor. SEM models reveal that these same Central Factors make similar predictions for relationship satisfaction across eight relationship types and nine cultural regions, but slightly different predictions for relationship commitment in same-sex marriage relationships.

The predictions of these Central Factors are similar, even though the levels of these factors may vary. These Central Factors will be combined with Central Factors from other chapters in a *Comprehensive Partner Model* and in a *Comprehensive Commitment Model* in Chapter 10. Variations in levels of factors will be discussed in Chapter 11.

SPOTLIGHT ON SEXUAL BEHAVIORS IN HUNGARY

ZSUZSA F. LASSÚ

Hungarian society is quite conservative in its norms and values, and the conservatism and sexual double standard seem to have increased in the past eight years as right-wing parties rule the country. Women are victims of discrimination in workplaces and homes as well (see Eurobarometer 2009[1], or UN Working Group report 2016[2]), and sexism is a part of both the private and public spheres. Almost all countries in Central and Eastern Europe are in the same backlash situation where traditions seem to overtake equality (see collected papers on this issue in "Anti-Gender Movements in the Rise?"[3]).

As a result of these conservative norms, it is not surprising that there are only a few national representative studies of sexual behaviors. In this SPOTLIGHT we discuss three large sample studies of sexual behavior in Hungary. Two of them were conducted by a public opinion research company (Medián Ltd. in 1996 and 2007), and their results were published only on the company's website.[4] The latest one was administered by a research group of the Eötvös Loránd University (ELTE) in 2016, with more than 15,000 participants. From this study, only the results related to problematic pornography use have been published in scientific papers (Bőthe, Tóth-Király, Zsila, Griffiths, Demetrovics, & Orosz 2017; Bőthe, Tóth-Király, Demetrovics, & Orosz, 2017). However, a brief summary of the most important data was published online,[5] so we can draw a rough picture about the latest trends in Hungarian sexual life too.

Age of first intercourse is decreasing worldwide, including in Hungary. In 2007, the average age of first intercourse was 18 for the full population, but there were generational differences: the oldest generation was about 19 at the time of first intercourse, and if they were married (or widow/widower) 39% of them were a virgin at the time of marriage (Medián, 2007). Participants from the 18- to 29-year-old group were 17 at the time of the first intercourse; if married, only 17% of them married as a virgin. This number is even lower among the 30- to 50-year-old people among whom only 10% were virgins at the time of marriage. More women than men married as a virgin (25% and 11%, respectively), and people from small villages were more likely to keep

---

[1] http://ec.europa.eu/commfrontoffice/publicopinion/archives/ebs/ebs_317_en.pdf
[2] www.ohchr.org/EN/NewsEvents/Pages/DisplayNews.aspx?NewsID=20027&LangID=E
[3] www.boell.de/en/2015/04/21/anti-gender-movements-rise
[4] www.median.hu/object.27b47266-b3c1-4520-a710-db51f2d25b50.ivy
[5] https://444.hu/2017/03/19/itt-vannak-az-elte-eddigi-legnagyobb-online-szexkutatasanak-eredmenyei

their virginity until marriage than citizens of Budapest (20% and 6%, respectively), according to the Medián (2007) study.

An International HBSC study[6] also investigated sexual behavior among teens and found that in 2013–2014 in Hungary, 29% of boys and 27% of girls had their first intercourse by the age of 15. With these results, Hungary is above the European average, but in Eastern Europe Hungarian boys are under the average, whereas girls are above the average, and the gender difference is quite small, as in Sweden, Finland, or Iceland, compared to the other Eastern European countries (Romania, Bulgaria, Macedonia) where the gender gap is larger (and boys always start their sex lives earlier than girls) (Inchley et al., 2016).

According to the ELTE study in 2016, the respondents said they started their solitary sexual activity, on average, at age 13 and their partnered sex at age 17 (ELTE, 2016). These data also support the general impression that teenagers start sexual activity at a younger and younger age and highlight the importance of sexual education programs in Hungary. It appears that "there is neither a general overall policy, nor a unified practice regarding sex education for adolescents in Hungary," according to the official report of the European Parliament about Policies for Sexuality Education in the European Union (Beaumont & Maguire, 2013, p. 21).

In the Medián studies, researchers found that over the past decades frequency of sex decreased from about 8 times a month to 6 times a month, and every sixth person had no sexual relationships in the past 12 months. In the latest online survey in 2016, results showed that the frequency of sex varied from never/not yet (1.5%) to 6–7 times a week (4.7%), with the highest number (34.6%) indicating that they had sex 2–3 times a week, and the overall average being once a week (ELTE, 2016). The difference in frequency of sex can be due to the fact that an online self-administered questionnaire is more likely to elicit more positive attitudes about sex.

The Medián study in 2007 found a huge gender difference in the admitted frequency of sex – 24% of women but only 7% of men said that they had no "sex life" in the past 12 months. The traditional, conservative, and sexist script of sex contains a more active and dominant man and submissive and obedient woman who does not need, desire, or like sex, and only does it for her partner's sake (Kiefer & Sanchez, 2007). In consequence, women are usually fearful of confessing openly about their sexual life, as they internalize the sexist stereotype about a less sexual female ideal; therefore, they underestimate their frequency of having sex, as if these experiences had never even happened at all. Contrary to women, men may overestimate their sexual activity; they think that the

---

[6] www.euro.who.int/__data/assets/pdf_file/0003/303438/HSBC-No.7-Growing-up-unequal-Full-Report.pdf?ua=1

more the better, so when researchers ask them, they may confess more frequent sexual activity than is real.

Participant's age was the most relevant factor influencing the frequency of sex in 2007 (Median, 2007). The most active age group was the 18- to 29-year-olds – they had about 9 sexual acts[7] in a month, while for those younger than 18 and those older than 40, the frequency of sex was 5-6 times a month, and it decreased with age, so more than 50% of participants older than age 60 said they had no sex life at all.

All in all, sex is very pleasurable activity for most Hungarians. The majority of the participants of the Median study in 2007 said "it causes lots of pleasure" (49%) or "usually it causes pleasure" (41%), and the younger ones found it more pleasurable than the older ones (average scores: 91 and 70, respectively, on a 100-point scale). However, the elderly people who were sexually active found the sex very pleasurable too! There was a small but significant gender difference here too: men rated the sex more pleasurable than women (average scores 88 and 81, respectively in a 100-point scale) (Median, 2007).

Although sex is good, sexual activity does not occur in 23% of married and 15% of cohabiting participants (Median, 2007). It is understandable that half of the single (55%) and divorced (60%) people and the majority of the widows/widowers (86%) lacked a sex partner at the time of the Median study (2007). Using a sex worker's services is an option used only by men, and 12% of men confessed they did visit a prostitute at least once (Median, 2007).

In 2016 the number of sex partners varied from none (3.1%) to more than 50 (4.8%), with an average of 7. Sixty percent had less than 10 sex partners, 18% had 11–20 sex partners, and 22% had more than 21 sex partners until the time of the study (ELTE, 2016). The Median studies (1996, 2007) revealed that males reported more sex partners than females (average number of partners of males: 11, females: 5), and the difference is larger if only the less than one-year relationships and casual sex are taken into account. On average, male participants had 7 non-long-lasting sex partners, while females only had 2 in their life.

According to the Median study (2007), better-educated participants had more sex partners. Age was also a relevant factor related to the number of sex partners – not surprisingly the youngest and the oldest generations had the fewest sex partners in their lives, and people from the 30 to 39 age group had the most (3–4 and 11, respectively) (Median, 2007).

Demographic differences between sex partners are not uncommon in Hungary (Median, 2007). In 2007, male participants were more open to

---

[7] The study used a Hungarian phrase that covers all forms of sexuality not only intercourse. The closest English form is "live one's sex life."

differences in every aspect, they had more partners from a different social background (e.g., much better-educated partner [29% of males, 25% of females], much less-educated partner [27% of males, 10% of females], partners from a different ethnic or racial group [23% of males, 8% of females], partners who were 15 years older [13% of males, 11% of females] or 15 years younger than the participant [11% of males, 3% of females]). There is only one aspect where women are at the top – same-sex relationships. In 2007 in Hungary, 6% of women and 4% of men admitted that they had same-sex relationships at least once in their lifetime (Medián, 2007).

According to the Medián study in 2007, 80% of those who had a sexual relationship were satisfied with it (38% totally, 25% very, 17% moderately satisfied), and sexual satisfaction correlated with the novelty of the relationship and consequently the frequency of sex. Not surprisingly, those who had sex every day were the most satisfied with their sex lives (average 91 point on a 100-point scale) compared to those who only occasionally had sex with their partners (62 point in a 100-point scale) (Medián, 2007). Similarly, in 2016, while only 49% were satisfied with their frequency of sex, 68% were generally satisfied with their sexual life, and 75% indicated that they always or almost always had an orgasm during sex (ELTE, 2016).

Orgasm frequency was strongly related to sexual satisfaction. The Medián study (2007) found that those who thought sex very pleasurable experienced orgasm the most frequently (9.5 times in 10 sexual acts), and those who felt indifferent about sex had only 5.2 orgasms in 10 sexual acts. Very few participants had multiple orgasms (2%) and 2% admitted that they had never had an orgasm in their life. Although 20% of men and 65% of women confessed that they did not experience orgasm in every occasion of sex, 81% of the participants think that the simultaneous orgasm is one of the basic principles of good sex, and 51% of them try for multiple orgasms.

Relationship duration had a positive effect on sexual satisfaction at the beginning (while partners live together); after a couple of years, it had a negative relationship with sexual satisfaction, which is a well-known phenomenon. Parental sexual attitudes and open communication on sex also had positive relationships with actual sexual satisfaction – those who had sexually open-minded parents rated their sexual satisfaction higher than did those who had sexually restrictive parents (84 and 75 points, respectively). However, participants reported a low level of open communication about sexual topics in the family. Even the youngest generation rated their family communication as 39 points open in a 100-point scale and the oldest participants rated it at 13 points!

There is a slow "liberalization" of sex in Hungary related to the activities people think of as acceptable. Non-penile-vaginal forms of sex became more accepted between 1996 and 2007 (Medián, 2007). "Handwork" was the most accepted non-penile-vaginal sex, with about 90% of participants considering it acceptable from both male and female "givers" in 1996 and 2007 also. Other sexual activities became more accepted too: oral sex (1996: 65%, 2007: 74%), masturbation (1996: 51%, 2007:64%), sex toys (1996: 9%, 2007: 20%), anal intercourse (1996: 5%, 2007: 17%), role play (1996: n.a., 2007: 11%), multiple partners (1996: 3%, 2007: 8%), BDSM (1996: n.a., 2007: 3%). Younger participants were more open to every form of sex, but in 2007, 45% of people older than age 60 accepted oral sex, and 25% of them were open to role play, anal sex, or other forms, and only 10% kept themselves strictly to the traditional penile-vaginal intercourse.

Not only the acceptance but also the practice of anal sex has become more frequent since 1996. The more accepted a sex activity is, the more likely it is to be used in a real-life situation. The percentage of participants who said that they experienced anal sex in the past 12 months increased from 11% to 22 % from 1996 to 2007. Participants aged 18–29 were the most open to anal sex, with 33% of them reporting that they tried it at least once in the past 12 months. But even 7% of the oldest participants did at least once in the year. However, anal sex is not the most satisfying form of sex, at least not for women – 70% of men and 43% of women (from the subsample who practiced anal sex) experienced orgasm at least once during anal sex in the past 12 months (Medián, 2007).

Masturbation was less common in Hungary in 2007 (or Hungarian people didn't confess it), with 37% of participants having never practiced it (Medián, 2007). But in 2016 only 3.3% were totally against solitary sex (ELTE, 2016). The highest frequency of masturbation (23.8%) was 2–3 times a week. Only 12.8% indicated that they never watched porn during masturbation, but 40% always or almost always watched porn during solitary sex – in 2016 (ELTE, 2016).

According to the Medián study (2007), the frequency of masturbation-free life is higher among the people older than 60 (56%) or the youngest generation under age 18 (49%), among those who are the least educated (46%) or living in small villages (45%), among women (59%), among widows or widowers (62%), or among those who do not have a sexual partner (66%). Not surprisingly, participants who did not practice masturbation did not appreciate sex very much. Among those who rated sex as indifferent in their lives, 80% had never masturbated at all (Medián, 2007).

Frequency of adultery/cheating or openness about cheating has increased in the past few decades (Medián, 2007). In 1996, only 7% of participants admitted that they cheated on their actual partners, whereas in 2007 this number was 19%. Gender and relationship satisfaction were found to be relevant factors in cheating in 2007. Male participants were more likely to cheat on their partners than females (27% and 10%, respectively), and cheating was more likely among those who were dissatisfied with their relationships than those who were satisfied (32% and 15%, respectively). This relationship between satisfaction and cheating was new; it was not found in 1996.

It seems that sexual needs and preferences have become more important to the younger generation, and they were more likely to cheat on their partners in "substandard" relationships than previous generations. In addition to this, porn watching is also a relevant factor – those who watch porn are more likely to cheat on their partners than those who don't (28% and 15%, respectively). Religion, however, did not show any relationship with cheating in 2007. It seems that adultery/cheating is related more to participant needs and preferences than their values or beliefs; however, these last concepts were not studied at this time.

The Median study (2007) used a 100-point Likert-type scale to indicate how much people are in love with their actual sex partners. Not surprisingly, love and sexual satisfaction scales were highly correlated, so those who were most in love were the most satisfied sexually and had sex the most frequently. Women were slightly more in love and more satisfied sexually than men (F: 72, 80 and M: 68, 74, respectively).

Summarizing these results, we can say that Hungarians, like those in other nations, like sex and think of sex as a pleasurable, satisfying activity, and they have become more open and accepting in relation to every form of sex. However, traditional gender and age differences stayed intact in the past twenty years.

6

What Are the Dynamics of Exchange and Power?

Predictions of having a current partner, as well as relationship satisfaction and relationship commitment, are explored in terms of the following:

- Equal power
- Equal involvement
- Potential alternative partners
- Other exchange variables
- Gender role attitudes

WHAT ARE THE BASES OF POWER?

French and Raven (1959) identified five bases of power:

- **Coercion** – use of force
- **Reward** – relative dependence for rewards
- **Legitimacy** – socially defined right to exercise authority
- **Expert** – providing needed expertise
- **Referent** – identification with the influence agent or group

In intimate relationships, coercion can take the form of intimate partner violence, which is discussed in Chapter 7. Reward dependence is explained in terms of social exchange, which is discussed in this chapter. Legitimate power can occur when traditional gender role attitudes say that men should have more power. Expert power can occur when one partner relies on the other partner's expertise or experience, and referent power can occur when one partner identities with and wants to be in agreement with the partner. Different styles of exercising power are discussed in the SPOTLIGHT on Couple Power Dynamics in Mexico later in this chapter.

WHAT IS THE SOCIAL EXCHANGE PERSPECTIVE ON POWER AND COMMITMENT?

Blau (1964) viewed social interaction as a process of social exchange, in which one person gives rewards to another, and the other is obligated to reciprocate by giving something appropriate back. We are taught a norm that we are supposed to reciprocate (such as Christmas gifts and birthday presents), but even more important is the need to reciprocate to obtain future rewards. What is exchanged includes not only tangible things like goods and assistance but also intangible things like advice and love. For example, mothers who unselfishly do things for their children want love in return.

When the exchange is balanced, it promotes an ongoing relationship. But when it is unequal, it can lead to a power imbalance and to eventual termination of the relationship. If person A gives more than person B, and B wants to continue receiving rewards from A but cannot give as much back, that can give A power over B. The key is B's dependence on A for rewards (Emerson, 1962). Blau (1964) lists four alternatives to compliance, which affect one person's relative dependency on another:

- Give rewards to make the exchange more equal (so you can negotiate terms)
- Find an alternative source of the rewards
- Take by force (if it is the kind of thing that can be taken by force)
- Do without the rewards

The same kinds of alternatives apply to both persons in the relationship, so that person A's power may be increased by devaluing what B has to offer, limiting B's alternatives, or making B feel that B cannot do without A's rewards. What is important is **relative dependency** leading to **relative power** of the two persons. If both are equally dependent or non-dependent, there is no power difference.

The same analysis applies to emotional involvement in the relationship. The person less involved may more easily walk away, so the more involved person may comply with the other's wishes to keep the other in the relationship. Waller (1938) called this the **principle of least interest.** But eventually the person with less power may get tired of being dominated, or the person with more power may get tired of being pressured to become more committed, leading one or the other to become dissatisfied and end the relationship.

When deciding whether or not to continue a relationship, a person not only considers the **current rewards and costs** but also two additional costs:

- **Investment costs** – the time and effort devoted to developing the current relationship, which one may be reluctant to give up, even in a relationship that is now costly or not rewarding. So one might invest more and put up with more in the hope that the relationship will improve, even when there is a power imbalance or abuse.

• **Opportunity costs** – the potential other relationships that were forgone while pursuing the current relationship, and the time and effort and risk that might be involved in finding and developing an alternative relationship to the desired level of rewards.

These analyses are also influenced by **comparison levels**, in which one compares the current rewards and costs to previous relationships, or to real or hypothetical relationships of others, or to potential alternative relationships.

In the Boston Couples Study, the person seen by couple members as less involved was seen by couple members as having more power (Peplau, 1979). This was also found in other research on opposite-sex couples by Sprecher and Felmlee (1997) and Sprecher, Schmeeckle, and Felmlee (2006).

And those in the Boston Couples Study who were unequally involved were twice as likely to break up during the initial two years of the original study (Hill et al., 1976) and were less likely to marry as reported on the fifteen-year follow-up (Hill & Peplau, 1998). In other research, equal involvement was associated with greater relationship satisfaction and stability in opposite-sex couples (Sprecher et al., 2006). Equal power was associated with greater satisfaction (Gray-Little & Burks, 1983) and less marital discord (Xu & Lai, 2004) in opposite-sex married couples.

In addition, perceptions of imbalance in work to maintain an opposite-sex romantic relationship were associated with lower satisfaction and commitment (Sprecher, Regan, & Orbuch, 2016). Unequal commitment to the relationship predicted breakups among opposite-sex unmarried relationships (Stanley et al., 2017). And more generally, degree of commitment predicted relationship stability (r=.47) in a meta-analysis of fifty-two studies across five countries and various relationship types (Le & Agnew, 2003).

HOW ARE RELATIVE POWER AND RELATIVE
INVOLVEMENT MEASURED?

In the present online study, the relative power and relative involvement are measured using the same items as in the Boston Couples Study (CP=Current Partner):

• Who do you think has more of a say about what you and CP do together – CP or you?

___CP has much more of a say
___CP has somewhat more of a say

___We both have the same amount of say
___I have somewhat more say
___I have much more say

• Who would you say is more involved in the relationship – CP or you?

___CP is much more involved
___CP is somewhat more involved
___We are both involved to the same degree
___I am somewhat more involved
___I am much more involved

Contrary to expectations, the negative correlation between relative power and relative involvement was trivial ($r < -.10$), perhaps reflecting the complexity of factors predicting power in various cultural contexts. However, both items are recoded from 5 response categories to 3 categories so that 3=EQUAL, 2=either CP or I SOMEWHAT MORE, AND 1= either CP or I MUCH MORE. Then the degree of Equal Power was correlated with the degree of Equal Involvement ($r = .24^{***}$).

Equal Power correlated with Relationship Satisfaction ($r = .26^{***}$) and with Relationship Commitment ($r = .14^{***}$). And Equal Involvement was correlated with Relationship Satisfaction ($r = .49^{***}$) and with Relationship Commitment ($r = .39^{***}$). In other words, those with equal power and those with equal involvement had greater relationship satisfaction and relationship commitment, while those with unequal power and those with unequal involvement had less relationship satisfaction and relationship commitment. These and other measures are combined in SEM Structural Models later in this chapter.

A similar question about **relative disclosure** is also from the Boston Couples Study:

• Who would you say has revealed more about himself or herself to the other – CP or you?

___CP has revealed much more
___CP has revealed somewhat more
___We have both revealed the same amount
___I have revealed somewhat more
___I have revealed much more

Relative Disclosure is positively correlated with Relative Involvement ($r = .33^{***}$), meaning that the person who is more involved in the relationship tended to disclose more than the other person. But it was trivially correlated with Relative Power, Relationship Satisfaction, and Relationship Commitment. However, when Relative Disclosure was recoded to indicate degree of Equal Disclosure, the recoded measure was correlated with Equal

Involvement (r=.30***), Equal Power (r=.22***), Relationship Satisfaction (r=.24***), and Relationship Commitment (.18***).

DO COUPLE MEMBERS AGREE ON RELATIVE INVOLVEMENT AND RELATIVE POWER?

In the Boston Couples Study, there was high agreement between dating partners on what month they met and what month they started dating. But more than half of the partners disagreed on who was more involved and who had more say. One reason for disagreement on power is the personal **importance of the decisions** that are considered in determining who has more say. For one couple interviewed after they had married, the woman said that she had more say because she was the one who made the decisions about how to decorate their apartment. The man believed that they had equal say since they had together made the more important decision of whether or not to have children. How to decorate the apartment was not an important decision to him.

A second reason for disagreement involves **styles of influence**. There is an old *I Love Lucy* episode in which Lucy leaves travel brochures around the apartment, until Ricky finally sees one and says "Let's take a vacation." Lucy responds with something like "Good Idea. I'm glad you thought of it." Men were traditionally supposed to have more power and have been used to making assertive statements such as "Let's do this." Women have traditionally exerted influence by making suggestions, such as "Why don't we do this?" and letting the man "make the final decision" when he assertively says, "Yes, let's do this." Weigel, Bennett, and Ballard-Reisch (2006) found that wives used more indirect influence strategies, while husbands used more direct influence strategies, and use of these strategies was associated with their spouse's commitment.

A third reason for disagreement involves **delegation of power**. Imagine one person says "Let's go to a movie. You decide which one," and the partner selects the movie. Who exerted more power depends on which decision was more important, going to a movie or choosing the movie, but each could think they had more say. Another example would be a spouse who says "What color would you like our new car to be" as if that were the important decision rather than the decision to buy a new car. Structuring a decision to give another person a small amount of choice can lead the other to think that they have more say than they really do.

In the present study, responses from both partners were available from the married couples in Pakistan, so it was possible to compare their responses. On the question of who was more involved, recoded so that 0=THE MAN MUCH MORE to 5=THE WOMAN MUCH MORE, only 48 percent of the partners agreed. On the question of who disclosed more, similarly recoded, only

43 percent of the partners agreed. These moderate levels of agreement were similar to those found in the Boston Couples Study, where correlations between couple members were r=.56 for involvement, r=.40 for power, and r=.30 for disclosure (Hill, Peplalu, & Rubin, 1981). On the shorter printed questionnaire in the present study, the Pakistani married couples were not asked who had more say, since it was assumed in Pakistan that the man should have more say.

HOW ARE POTENTIAL ALTERNATIVES MEASURED IN THIS STUDY?

Ease of finding an alternative partner is discussed in terms of relational mobility in Chapter 4. Yuki, Yamamoto, and Tsuji (2018) distinguished between measures at the cultural level ("It is easy for them to meet new people") and at the personal level ("It is easy for me to meet new people"). In the present study, ease of finding an alternative partner is measured using the following items:

- If you were not involved with CP, how easy do you think it would be for you to find someone else for a romantic or sexual relationship?
- If CP were not involved with you, how easy do you think it would be for CP to find someone else for a romantic or sexual relationship?

Contrary to expectations, the correlations of these measures with Relative Power, Equal Power, Relationship Satisfaction, and Relationship Commitment were trivial (r<.10). Perhaps these questions were too hypothetical and should have asked if there were specific others with whom you could form an intimate relationship.

Availability of alternatives might also be reflected in the following question, which is discussed in Chapter 2:

- Throughout your life, how difficult has it been to find an appropriate partner for a committed relationship?

This question also had trivial correlations (r<.10) with Relative Power and Equal Power. Its negative correlation (r=−.17) with Relationship Commitment was accounted for by Anxious Attachment and other factors in SEM models discussed in Chapter 2.

HOW ARE OTHER EXCHANGE VARIABLES MEASURED?

- Overall, to what extent do you feel that you have gained benefits from your relationship with CP?
- Overall, to what extent do you feel that you have made sacrifices in your relationship with CP?

- To what extent do you feel that you have <u>invested</u> time, effort, or money into your relationship with CP?

Gaining Benefits, another term for **rewards**, is moderately correlated with Relationship Satisfaction ($r=.54^{***}$) and Relationship Commitment ($r=.47^{***}$). And Having **Invested** in the Relationship is somewhat correlated with Relationship Satisfaction ($r=.20^{***}$) and Relationship Commitment ($r=.38^{***}$). Sacrifices, another term for **costs**, is trivially negatively correlated with relationship satisfaction ($r<.10$) but slightly positively correlated with Relationship Commitment ($r=.13^{***}$). Those who are more committed are slightly more willing to make sacrifices for the partner.

IS POWER INFLUENCED BY GENDER ROLE ATTITUDES?

In the Boston Couples Study, power was also influenced by gender role attitudes. Those with more traditional sex role attitudes reported more male dominance, while those with more liberal gender role attitudes reported more egalitarian relationships (Peplau, 1979). And women with liberal gender role attitudes were more likely to plan on graduate school, and if so, to break up with their college boyfriend (Peplau, Hill, & Rubin, 1993).

Several additional types of **gender-role attitude scales** have been developed since the Boston Couples Study to measure hostile, benevolent, modern, and neosexist attitudes (Masser & Abrams, 1999; McHugh & Friese, 1997). In the present study, factor analyses indicated that only the following three items load on a single factor:

- Men should take the lead in decision making.
- It is natural for men and women to have different kinds of jobs.
- People's behavior should always be appropriate for their sex.

The first item is from the Boston Couples Study and the other two items were written specifically for this study. SEM Measurement Models reveal similar factor loadings across relationship types (CFI=968, RMSEA=.031) and cultural regions (CFI=.980, RMSEA=.023). These three items are averaged to create a Traditional Gender Role Attitudes Scale. Not included are egalitarian items that were expected to have negative factor loadings but do not load on this factor.

Contrary to expectations, the negative correlation of this scale with Equal Power is trivial ($r<.10$). It is also trivially correlated with Relationship Satisfaction and Relationship Commitment. In other words, those with these traditional gender role attitudes are as likely as those with liberal gender role attitudes to be satisfied with their intimate relationship and to be committed to it. Other research has found that consistency between ideal and actual power is associated with marital happiness, whether the actual power is equal or male dominated (Sarantakos, 2000).

HOW DO MEASURES OF POWER AND EXCHANGE COMBINE IN SEM MODELS?

Structural Equation Modeling is introduced in Chapter 1. SEM Structural Models combine measures of Equal Power, Equal Involvement, Equal Disclosure, Benefits, Sacrifices, and Invested to test indirect predictions of Relationship Commitment through Relationship Satisfaction, and direct predictions of Relationship Commitment independent of Relationship Satisfaction. These models make similar predictions across eight relationship types (CFI=.962, RMSEA=.027) and nine cultural regions (CFI=.965, RMSEA=.020).

These models reveal that Gained Benefits (γ=.42), Equal Involvement (γ=.30), and Equal Power (γ=.10) are Central Factors in predicting Relationship Satisfaction. They each predict beyond their common predictions and capture what they have in common with the other measures. In other words, those who gained benefits, those equally involved, and those with equal power are more satisfied with their relationships, while those with fewer benefits, those with unequal involvement, and those with unequal power, are less satisfied with their relationships.

In addition, Invested (γ=.16) has a direct effect on Relationship Commitment independent of Relationship Satisfaction. In other words, those who have invested time, effort, or money into their relationship are somewhat more committed to it, regardless of their relationship satisfaction.

SELF-REFLECTION

If you have a partner, are you equally involved in the relationship? How are decisions made, and does one of you have more say about certain decisions? How invested do you feel you are in your relationship?

IN SUMMARY, WHAT CENTRAL FACTORS ARE IDENTIFIED IN THIS CHAPTER?

For Relationship Satisfaction and Relationship Commitment, the Central Factors are Gained Benefits, Equal Involvement, Equal Power, Sacrifices, and Invested. SEM models reveal that these same Central Factors make similar predictions across eight relationship types and nine cultural regions.

The predictions of these Central Factors are similar, even though the levels of these factors may vary. These Central Factors will be combined with Central Factors from other chapters in a *Comprehensive Commitment Model* in Chapter 10. Variations in levels of factors will be discussed in Chapter 11.

SPOTLIGHT ON COUPLE POWER DYNAMICS IN MEXICO

JOSÉ ENRIQUE CANTO Y RODRIGUEZ

Although it is a commonplace to say that humans are social by nature, we can say that we still have a long way to go to understand how social interactions promote human development and well-being. Among the most important human relationships are couple relationships, since they have an important impact on the happiness and health of people.

According to Rivera Aragón and Díaz-Loving (2002), social influence and power are at the base of human relationships. Hence, it is necessary to study social influence and power in couples. In Mexico, there have been ethno-psychological studies of how couples use power to achieve their goals within the relationship. According to Rivera Aragón and Díaz-Loving (2002), this involves "who makes the decisions, who proposes ideas or solves problems, who receives the most agreement or who participates the most in discussions" (p. 3). A definition of power widely accepted in Mexico is that expressed by Díaz Guerrero and Díaz-Loving (as cited in Rivera & Díaz-Loving, 2002), who consider that power "is any type of behavior through which it is achieved that others do what we as individuals want done" (p. 24).

The study of power in the Mexican couple began with investigating the concepts regarding power. It was carried out through the use of natural semantic networks, a technique proposed by Figueroa, González, and Solís (1981) and used to obtain the psychological meaning of the concepts.

Rivera and Díaz-Loving (1999), and later Rivera (2000), found that men who have a partner use a greater number of words that define the concept of power, compared to women. In this way, men define power as force, money, command, dominion, responsibility, shared, security, authoritarianism, and love. On the other hand, women define power as love, command, strength, authority, money, control, and willingness, among the main words used.

In addition, the authors already mentioned have carried out some studies to know in which areas couples use the power to achieve their goals in the relationship, as well as if the couple differs in those areas. They found that the areas in which the man exerts more power in the couple are those that relate to (a) individual pastimes, (b) distribution of income, (c) discipline, (e) permissions given the children, and (f) purchase of houses. While, for women, their power is manifested in (a) education and parenting, (b) school the children attend, (c) hobbies as a couple, (d) tasks in the home, and (e) purchase of furniture. Subsequently, the studies focused on identifying the power styles of couples, as well as the strategies they use to exercise power within the relationship (Rivera, 2000; Rivera & Díaz-Loving, 1999; Rivera, Díaz-Loving, Sánchez, & Alvarado, 1996, among others).

It is important to point out that in Mexico, based on ethno-psychological studies, power has a negative connotation (Rivera Aragón & Díaz-Loving, 2002), since it is used in a destructive way as an imposition of authority, control, threat, and punishment. Couple members develop styles to ask their partner to do what they want and to do this they adopt a specific style that shows how power manifests in the relationship.

When one observes how power is handled in the couple's relationship, Rivera and Díaz-Loving (2002) affirm that in Mexican culture, "affiliative obedience plays a preponderant role in the interpretation of power" (p. 134). Affiliative obedience occurs when a member of the couple gives in "for love" to the requests of the partner. So the affiliative obedience is practically a hybrid in which power and love are mixed.

According to the results of different studies (Rivera, 2000; Rivera & Díaz-Loving, 1999), eight styles of power were found:

- Authoritarian – Rough, violent, brusque, explosive, strict
- Affectionate – Tender, cordial, expressive, understanding
- Democratic – Safe, direct, suggestive, communicative, equitable
- Calm-conciliatory – Friendly, approachable, flexible, patient, conciliatory
- Negotiating – Reciprocal, controlled, empathetic, tolerant, business-like
- Aggressive-avoiding – Superficial, confused, irresponsible, inaccessible
- Laissez-faire – Permissive, liberating, committed, open
- Submissive – Silent, distracted, messy, indirect

When the differences among power styles were analyzed taking into consideration the sex of the couple, it was found that women use the Authoritarian, Negotiating, and Aggressive-avoiding styles more than men. While men showed greater use of Affectionate, Calm-conciliatory, and Submissive styles compared to women. In addition, it was found that there were no differences between men and women in terms of the Democratic and Laissez-faire styles.

As could be observed, it is striking that the results go against what was expected, since the expectation was that the authoritarian style would be used more by men than women, and that the affectionate style would be used more by women than men. Thus, according to the findings, women are more violent, abrupt, explosive, and strict than men when they exercise power; men, on the other hand, are more affectionate, tender, cordial, expressive, and understanding.

To conclude, it is necessary to say that more research is needed on this important topic to understand the differences in the exercise of power in couples, identify which mechanisms are useful for their learning, as well as the effect that these styles of power have in the development and maintenance of the couple relationship. Likewise, it is necessary to expand the sample in a way that is more representative of the Mexican society of the twenty-first century.

7

How Do Couples Cope with Conflict?

Predictions of having a current partner (CP), as well as relationship satisfaction and relationship commitment, are explored in terms of the following:

- Sources of conflict
- Ways of coping with conflict
- Intimate partner violence
- Jealousy

In the Boston Couples Study, couples with more problems were more likely to break up (Hill, Rubin, & Peplau, 1976) and never marry (Hill & Peplau, 1998). But just as important as the amount of conflict in a relationship is the way that conflict is dealt with. Prior research on how couples cope with conflict will be reviewed later in this chapter when introducing questions used to measure conflict resolution styles.

WHAT ARE THE SOURCES OF CONFLICT?

In the present study, **conflict** is measured by asking, "To what extent has each of the following been a source of conflict with CP?" Nine of the topics, marked with an asterisk (*), are similar to ones from Rivera Aragón, Díaz- Loving, and Cruz del Castillo (2005). The others are written especially for this study and include topics recently cited as top issues in marital conflict (Whitton et al., 2018).

The possible responses are from 0=NOT AT ALL to 8=EXTREMELY. The overall means and standard deviations are listed Table 7.1 in order from highest to lowest.

The standard deviations indicate a fair amount of variation in ratings. Factor analyses revealed four factors reflecting areas of conflict:

- **Highest Sources**: time management, poor communication, our personalities, leisure activities

TABLE 7.1 *Mean sources of conflict*

	Mean	(s.d.)
• Time management	3.36	(2.51)
• Poor communication	3.31	(2.34)
• Our personalities*	2.43	(2.38)
• Leisure activities*	2.42	(2.41)
• Relatives	2.38	(2.53)
• Job responsibilities	2.29	(2.46)
• Sexual activities or desires*	2.27	(2.43)
• Money*	2.08	(2.39)
• Future plans	2.08	(2.39)
• Public displays of affection	1.98	(2.35)
• Our own attitudes and values	1.94	(2.30)
• Expectations of others	1.89	(2.29)
• Household chores	1.86	(2.30)
• Irresponsibility*	1.78	(2.33)
• Our interests and hobbies*	1.56	(2.04)
• Exclusivity (monogamy)	1.51	(2.45)
• Others' disapproval of us	1.49	(2.17)
• Addiction to alcohol or drugs*	1.06	(2.08)
• Childrearing*	1.04	(2.00)
• Religious beliefs*	0.99	(1.87)

- **Living Together:** money, household chores, relatives, sexual activities or desires
- **Expectations:** expectations of others, others' disapproval of us, our own attitudes and values, public displays of affection
- **Uncertainties:** irresponsibility, addiction to alcohol or drugs, exclusivity (monogamy), future plans

The Uncertainties factor includes topics that are related to marital complaints that are associated with mental health issues (Kitson & Sussman, 1982).

Structural Equation Modeling (SEM) is introduced in Chapter 1. SEM Measurement Models indicate that the factor leadings are similar across eight relationship types and nine cultural regions for each of these four factors (Table 7.2).

The items in each factor are averaged to form scales for further analyses. While the items in the Highest Sources of Conflict Scale all appear to be different, the factor loadings indicate that those items are correlated. In other words, intimate relationships that have one of the Highest Sources of conflict are very likely to have the other Highest Sources of conflict as well. The factor loadings indicate similar patterns for the other three sets of conflicts.

TABLE 7.2 *SEM measures for conflict factors*

	Relationship Types		Cultural Regions	
	CFI	RMSEA	CFI	RMSEA
• Highest sources	.963	.031	.953	.027
• Living together	.979	.020	.981	.015
• Expectations	.967	.028	.959	.024
• Uncertainties	.958	.031	.958	.023

Relationship Satisfaction is negatively correlated with the Uncertainties Conflict Scale (r=−.36***), Expectations Conflict Scale (r=−.34***), Highest Sources of Conflict Scale (r=−.34***), and Living Together Conflict Scale (r=−.14***). In other words, all four areas of conflict are associated with lower relationship satisfaction. Relationship Commitment is also negatively correlated with the Uncertainties Conflict Scale (r=−.19***), Expectations Conflict Scale (r=−.17***), and Highest Sources of Conflict Scale (r=−.11***). In other words, uncertainties, conflicting expectations, and highest sources of conflict have negative associations with commitment.

However, Relationship Commitment is slightly positively correlated with the Living Together Conflict Scale (r=.10***). Such conflicts are more common among people who were actually living together (r=.34***), and those living together are generally more committed to the relationship (r=.37***). Among those not living together, the correlation between the Living Together Conflict Scale and Relationship Commitment is trivial (r<.10), whereas it is negative among those who say they are living together "some of the time" (r=−.13*) or "most or all of the time" (r=−.22**). Due to its being confounded with actually living together, the Living Together Conflict Scale is not included among the conflict scales and ways of dealing with conflict in SEM Structural Models later in this chapter.

HOW DO INTIMATE PARTNERS DEAL WITH CONFLICT?

Blake and Mouton (1985) identified four types of negotiation styles used in business that have been applied to couples (e.g., Hallock, 1988; Mannarini et al., 2017). In the present study, the following items are used to measure these styles, under the question "To what extent do you agree with each of the following statements?"

- **Avoidance:** I try not to say things on which CP and I might differ.
- **Collaboration:** I try to find a mutual solution with CP for any problem.
- **Accommodation:** I adjust easily to CP's ways of doing things.
- **Competition:** I try to impose on CP my own ways of doing things.

Gottman (1999) found that couple members who reacted to negative comments with negative comments were distressed. But couple members who responded to a negative with a positive were not distressed. For example, when a partner overreacts to something, instead of reciprocating a negative comment that escalates the conflict, it is better to realize that the person is overreacting due to stress, and say something supportive like, "you must really be stressed about something." These responses are measured using the following items written especially for this study to reflect Gottman's findings:

- **Negative**: When CP criticizes me, I always say something negative back.
- **Negative:** When I criticize CP, CP always says something negative back.
- **Positive**: When CP reacts strongly to something, I try to find out what is stressing CP.
- **Positive:** When I react strongly to something, CP tries to find out what is stressing me.

Factor analyses of the negotiation items, and the responses to negative comments, revealed the following two factors for intimate partners dealing with conflict:

Negative Responses
- I try to impose on CP my own ways of doing things. (competition)
- When CP criticizes me, I always say something negative back. (Gottman)
- When I criticize CP, CP always says something negative back. (Gottman)

Positive Responses
- I try to find a mutual solution with CP for any problem. (collaboration)
- When CP reacts strongly to something, I try to find out what is stressing CP. (Gottman)
- When I react strongly to something, CP tries to find out what is stressing me. (Gottman)

Woodin (2011) also categorized conflict behaviors into positive and negative in a review of sixty-four studies.

The Negative Responses factor has similar loadings across relationship types (CFI=.999, RMSEA=.008) and across cultural regions (CFI=.998, RMSEA=.006). The Positive Responses factor also has similar loadings across relationship types (CFI=.995, RMSEA=.014) and across cultural regions (CFI=.995, RMSEA=.011). So each set of items is averaged to create a scale.

The Negative Response Scale is slightly negatively correlated with Relationship Satisfaction (r=−.12**) but trivially correlated with Relationship Commitment (r<.01). The Positive Responses Scale is moderately correlated with Relationship Satisfaction (r=.47***) and Relationship

Commitment (r=.41***). In other words, negative responses decrease satisfaction, while positive responses increase both satisfaction and commitment.

In addition, Rusbult, Zembrodt, and Gunn (1982) identified four responses to dissatisfaction in romantic relationships. They are measured by the following items in this study, which do not load consistently with the previous items and hence are analyzed separately:

- **Voice:** I would discuss what was wrong and try to fix things up.
- **Neglect:** I would get angry and wouldn't talk at all.
- **Loyalty:** I would wait, hoping that things would get better.
- **Exit:** I would end the relationship.

Voice is positively related to Relationship Satisfaction (r=.46***) and Relationship Commitment (r=.44***). Exit is negatively related to Relationship Satisfaction (r=−.33***) and Relationship Commitment (r=−.39***). Neglect (−.19***) and Loyalty (r=−.16***) are negatively correlated with Relationship Satisfaction, but trivially related to Relationship Commitment (r<.10). In other words, discussing what is wrong is associated with greater relationship satisfaction, while not talking, waiting, and willingness to end the relationship are associated with less relationship satisfaction. Discussing what is wrong is associated with greater relationship commitment, while willingness to leave the relationship is associated with less relationship commitment.

Failure to deal with conflict adequately, along with irritations and disappointment, can create marital tension, which over time can lead to divorce (Birditt et al., 2017).

HOW DO SOURCES AND WAYS OF DEALING WITH CONFLICT COMBINE IN SEM MODELS?

SEM Structural Models combine the sources of conflict scales, the Negative Response Scale, the Positive Response Scale, and the four Rusbult et al. responses to test indirect predictions of Relationship Commitment through Relationship Satisfaction, and direct predictions of Relationship Commitment independent of Relationship Satisfaction. These models make similar predictions across eight relationship types (CFI=.978, RMSEA=.023) and nine cultural regions (CFI=.983, RMSEA=.016).

These models reveal that the Highest Sources of Conflict Scale (γ=−.11), Uncertainties Conflict Scale (γ=−.12), Expectations Conflict Scale (γ=−.10), and Exit (γ=−.16) are negative Central Factors, while the Positive Responses Scale (γ=.28) and Voice (γ=.22) are positive Central Factors in predicting Relationship Satisfaction. Voice (γ=.10) also has a positive direct prediction of Relationship Commitment, while Exit (γ=−.16) has a negative direct prediction of Relationship Commitment, independent of Relationship Satisfaction.

Examples of how couples deal with conflict are provided in the SPOTLIGHT on Conflict Resolution in Spain and Colombia later in this chapter.

SELF-REFLECTION

If you have a partner, what causes conflict between you? How do you react when your partner says something negative? Do you say something negative back, or do you try to find out what is stressing your partner?

HOW IS INTIMATE PARTNER VIOLENCE MEASURED?

Strauss (1979, 2012) measured three types of responses to conflict: reasoning, verbal aggression, and violence. Reasoning includes discussion, which is part of the Positive Responses Scale and Voice measures discussed earlier. Verbal aggression and physical violence are considered to be forms of **intimate partner violence** (also called domestic violence), along with sexual violence. Further distinctions and examples are discussed in the SPOTLIGHT on Intimate Partner Violence later in this chapter.

Panuzio and DiLillo (2010) found that physical, psychological, and sexual violence were all associated with less marital satisfaction among newlyweds over a three-year period. In another longitudinal study, Lawrence and Bradbury (2007) found that changes in physical aggression predicted changes in marital satisfaction more than dissatisfaction predicted aggression.

To measure intimate partner violence in the present study, the questions asked with possible responses from 0=NEVER to 8=FREQUENTLY appear in Table 7.3.

Note that in each set, the first two items refer to **physical violence**, while the last three items refer to **verbal violence**. The overall means indicate that criticism was the most frequent kind of violence, while physical violence was much less common. The standard deviations indicate a fair degree of individual variation. **Sexual violence** includes engaging in unwanted sex, which is discussed in Chapter 5.

In each set, the three verbal items load on a single factor of Verbal Violence. This is similar across eight relationship types (CFI=.995, RMSEA=.020) and nine cultural regions (CFI=.991, RMSEA=.020) for Current Partner, and across eight relationship types (CFI=.989, RMSEA=.-28) and nine cultural regions (CFI=.997, RMSEA=.011) for self. Each set of items is averaged to form a scale. The two physical violence items are analyzed separately.

TABLE 7.3 *Mean violence behaviors*

	Mean	(s.d.)
How often has CP done each of the following to you?		
• Hit	0.46	(1.32)
• Shoved	0.57	(1.40)
• Shouted	1.97	(2.25)
• Criticized	2.79	(2.32)
• Used humiliating words	1.31	(2.05)
How often have you done each of the following to CP?		
• Hit	0.52	(1.34)
• Shoved	0.56	(1.34)
• Shouted	2.07	(2.32)
• Criticized	2.59	(2.27)
• Used humiliating words	1.15	(1.88)

Relationship Satisfaction is negatively correlated with the Partner's Verbal Violence Scale (r=−.17***), Own Verbal Violence Scale (r=−.11***), Partner Hit (r=−.13***), and Partner Shoved (r=−.16***), but trivially with Self Hit or Shoved the partner (r<.10). Only the Own Verbal Violence Scale was correlated nontrivially with Relationship Commitment, and the correlation was positive (r=.11). In other words, participants who were more committed to their relationship used slightly more verbal violence than those who were less committed, presumably in an effort to control their partners. A similar pattern occurred with own expression of jealousy.

HOW IS JEALOUSY MEASURED?

Previous research has found that **jealousy** can be associated with greater relationship satisfaction or with less relationship satisfaction (Buunk, Dijkstra, & Massar, 2018). To measure jealousy in the present study, items in Table 7.4 were asked along with the previous questions about how often CP or you have done these things.

The means indicate quite a bit of jealousy, and the standard deviations indicate a fair amount of individual variation. Partner's Expressed Jealousy had trivial correlations with Relationship Satisfaction and Relationship Commitment (r<.10). Own Expressed Jealousy was not correlated with Relationship Satisfaction (r=.02), but it was positively correlated with Relationship Commitment (r=.16***). In other words, own expression of jealousy is an indicator that one is committed to the relationship and is concerned about losing the partner. This positive correlation for expressing jealousy is similar to the previous finding that those who are more committed

TABLE 7.4 *How often expressed jealousy*

	Mean	(s.d.)
• CP: How often expressed jealousy	3.83	(2.53)
• You: How often expressed jealousy	3.55	(2.57)

TABLE 7.5 *Times broken up and come back*

	Mean	s.d.
• CP: Broken up with you for a period of time then come back to you – How many times?	0.70	(1.57)
• You: Broken up with CP for a period of time then come back to CP – How many times?	0.69	(1.55)

are more likely to use verbal violence. The questions in Table 7.5 are also asked along with the previous questions about how often CP or you have done these things.

Although this occurs rarely, Partner Breaking Up and Coming Back is negatively correlated with Relationship Satisfaction (r=−.23***) and Relationship Commitment (r=−.11***). Self Breaking Up and Coming Back is also negatively correlated with Relationship Satisfaction (r=−.20***) but trivially correlated with Relationship Commitment (r<.10). Coming back indicates some commitment to the relationship.

WHAT ARE THE COMBINED PREDICTIONS OF VIOLENCE, JEALOUSY, AND TEMPORARY BREAKUPS?

SEM Structural Models combine partner's and own verbal violence, partner hitting and shoving, jealousy, and temporary breakups to test indirect predictions of Relationship Commitment through Relationship Satisfaction, and direct predictions of Relationship Commitment independent of Relationship Satisfaction. These models are similar across eight relationship types (CFI=.987, RMSEA=.021) and nine cultural regions (CFI=.991, RMSEA=.013).

These models reveal that Partner's Verbal Violence (γ=−.12) and Partner Breaking Up and Coming Back (γ=−.16) are negative Central Factors in predicting Relationship Satisfaction. The other measures add trivial explained variance when these are taken into account. In addition, Own Expression of Jealousy is slightly linked to Relationship Commitment independent of Relationship Satisfaction (γ=.10). In other words, partner's verbal violence and partner breaking up and coming back have negative associations with relationship satisfaction. And persons who are more committed are more likely to express jealousy regardless of their level of relationship satisfaction.

IN SUMMARY, WHAT CENTRAL FACTORS HAVE BEEN IDENTIFIED IN THIS CHAPTER?

For Relationship Satisfaction and Relationship Commitment, the negative Central Factors are the Highest Sources of Conflict Scale, Uncertainties Conflict Scale, Expectations Conflict Scale, Exit, Partner's Verbal Violence, and Partner Breaking Up and Coming Back. The positive Central Factors are Positive Responses, Voice, and Own Expression of Jealousy. SEM models reveal that these Central Factors make similar predictions across eight relationship types and nine cultural regions.

The predictions of these Central Factors are similar, even though the levels of these factors may vary. These Central Factors will be combined with Central Factors from other chapters in a *Comprehensive Commitment Model* in Chapter 10. Variations in levels of factors will be discussed in Chapter 11.

SPOTLIGHT ON CONFLICT RESOLUTION IN SPAIN AND COLOMBIA

ANDRÉS A. FERNÁNDEZ-FUERTES,
NOELIA FERNÁNDEZ-ROUCO, ANNI M. GARZÓN,
RODRIGO J. CARCEDO, AND
JOSÉ L. MARTÍNEZ

The presence of conflicts is inherent in any interpersonal relationship, but even if they are not necessarily destructive, they often have harmful effects, especially in intimate relationships (Valor-Segura, Expósito, Moya, & Kluwer, 2014). The fact remains that relationships are a relevant aspect for the happiness and satisfaction of both adults and young people (Schmidt, Luquet, & Gehlert, 2016; Viejo, Ortega-Ruiz, & Sánchez, 2015). However, conflicts affect the perception of the quality of these relationships, and the ways in which they are resolved influence continuing or ending them (Laursen & Hafen, 2010).

In Spain, research on the presence of conflicts in relationships, their resolution, and possible consequences has traditionally been linked to studies of the existence of aggression and violence within said relationships. Little research has focused on the analysis of the process of resolving conflicts and difficulties. Some studies with adult subjects reveal that a characteristic that is able to mediate between satisfaction with the relationship and the likelihood of ending it after a purportedly mild conflict, such as one resulting from lies, is commitment. Thus, a lower level of satisfaction with the relationship is related to less commitment and therefore to a higher possibility of ending the relationship. This only appears applicable when the conflict is considered mild, however, as results differ when the conflict is considered serious (e.g., resulting from infidelity). In this sense, it seems that the severity of the conflict and commitment and satisfaction levels are especially relevant to continuity or lack thereof in the relationship (Garrido-Macías, Valor-Segura, & Expósito, 2017). These conclusions are likely connected with the important presence of the romantic love model among Spanish youth and adults (Ferrer, Bosch, Navarro, Ramis, & García, 2008).

At the same time, work with couples who have low levels of satisfaction with their purportedly conflictive relationship often shows inadequate strategies for solving conflicts, strategies that are considered fundamental for the success of social interaction (e.g., communication, assertiveness, empathy and negotiation). On the contrary, both men and women perceive that they are the ones who always or almost always end up giving in when it comes to resolving conflicts with their partner (Hurtado, Ciscar, & Rubio, 2004).

Research with young people, on the other hand, has been more closely focused on situations of coercion between peers and less on the analysis of the relationship characteristics. However, a replication study with young people as subjects has recently been carried out in Spain (Cheung et al., 2016), which in addition contributes to mitigating the current crisis of replication of results in psychology. This work was carried out to replicate the work published by Finkel et al. (2002). It focuses on the priming effect of commitment on conflict resolution strategies used by young couples. The study was developed in twenty-three countries, including Spain. While in the original study the priming effect on commitment influenced the ways in which the conflict was resolved, this effect was not found in the replication study. Rather it was the couple's true level of commitment that was relevant. People who showed a higher level of commitment to their partner were less likely to use negative conflict resolution strategies such as "Exit" or "Neglect"; in the Spanish version of this study, the same results were found. Positive conflict resolution strategies (i.e., Voice and Loyalty) were also more commonly used than negative ones (i.e., Exit and Neglect). Gender differences were also found: while women were more likely to use the "Exit" strategy, men were more commonly used "Loyalty."

When specifically referring to adolescent couples, those who have good communication show a tendency toward high levels of satisfaction with the relationship. In addition, expectations regarding relationship continuity are usually positive as well (Sánchez, Ortega, Ortega, & Viejo, 2008). On the contrary, the existence of jealousy in the context of this study seems to be an important predictor of aggressive behaviors (i.e., verbal-emotional and physical) among both the male and female in the couple (Fernández-Fuertes & Fuertes, 2010).

Research regarding strategies to resolve conflict and to improve relationship satisfaction and commitment among adolescents and young people nevertheless has been focused on situations of coercion and violence. In this sense, it seems that those who have a negative-based commitment (i.e., difficulties getting out of a relationship) and feel higher pressure to continue with the relationship are more likely to be victims of coercion and physical aggression. A positive-based commitment (e.g., well-being in the relationship), on the other hand, implies a lesser likelihood of being a victim of coercion in the relationship (Hernández & González, 2009). These data, indicating that negative-based commitment increases the risk of coercion and violence, highlight the importance that level of commitment has in understanding and predicting relationship dynamics. In addition, it seems that emotional blackmail (e.g., threatening to leave the relationship or to fall out of love) is, among other coercive strategies, the most frequently used (Hernández & González, 2009).

Speaking specifically of relation conflict resolving strategies, it seems that adolescents who have been classified as suffering from either high or low victimization and perpetration differ significantly in the destructive strategies that they employ. Thus, those with high victimization and also those who present higher levels of perpetration used the strategies of implication (i.e., referred to the use of personal attacks and loss of control) and withdrawal from the conflict (i.e., refusing to discuss a problematic issue, disconnecting from the relationship) more often than those who showed low levels of victimization and perpetration. However, no differences have been found between those who are victims and perpetrators in the use of positive conflict resolution strategies (Bonache, Ramírez-Santana, & González-Méndez, 2016).

In Colombia, research on what occurs in relationships is still in an initial stage. Although there have been important investigations on the family structure and its transformations (e.g., Gutiérrez de Pineda, 1976; Palacio, 2009), or on marital separations (e.g., Zamudio & Rubiano, 1991), little systematic research has been done on relationships between couples, the resolution of conflicts, satisfaction, and associated factors (Acevedo, Restrepo de Giraldo, & Tovar, 2007). In general, it has been observed that the studies in this field demonstrate the following tendencies: study of the frequency and modalities of partner violence, study of the factors that generate crisis in couples, and study of communication and coping strategies used by the couple prior to conflicts.

It has been found in Colombia that intimate partner violence occurs mostly toward women and in physical modalities (e.g., slapping, kicking, beating, among others), psychological modalities (e.g., restriction, shouting, humiliation, among others), and sexual modalities; often two or more modalities are used together (Canaval, González, Humphreys, De Leóne, & González, 2009; Jaramillo-Vélez, Ospina-Muñoz, Cabarcas-Iglesias, & Humphreys, 2005; Klevens, 2001; Londoño et al., 2014). In addition, a statistically significant association has been found between violence and lower levels of schooling and income, a greater number of children, a longer-lasting relationship with the current partner, the absence of other relatives in the home, a history of mistreatment within the birth family, couples with greater frequency of conflict, and a partner who issues restrictions, the last two of which presented the strongest associations (Klevens, 2001).

That being said, crises in Colombian relationships usually occur when unemployment and economic problems are factors because they generate changes in family dynamics, fueling a fear of instability, loneliness, and frustration (Agudelo et al., 2005; Ariza & Guevara, 2002; Londoño, 2005). In turn, in those relationships in which children are present, the children can become a source of motivation because the couple focuses their relationship around their responsibilities to their children (Londoño, 2005). However, children can also generate a crisis; when children display maladaptive behaviors, parents are afraid that they haven't educated their children well, or that there is a lack of respect between themselves and their children (Agudelo et al., 2005; Casadiego, Martínez, Riatiga, & Vergara, 2015).

In the same vein, when analyzing the relationships of couples who are conflictive and unstable, a lack of assertiveness, communication, and mutual understanding was found to be common. These couples use a passive-aggressiveness strategy as a main coping mechanism characterized by difficulty with clearly and directly expressing their opinions, thoughts, and feelings, if expressing them at all. Indirectly, coercion is another strategy used via threats and punishments, in this way coercing the other person to give in to their wishes (Casadiego et al., 2015; Díaz & Porras, 2011).

On the other hand, a positive association has been found between the relationships of stable and satisfied couples who have lived together for more than ten years, who come from homes in which the parents are still together, and who report their relationship as being a positive one. The study of these couples shows that a stable and satisfactory coexistence is possible when each member of the couple recognizes that being together entails obstacles and challenges but, at the same time, they seek to build a loving bond based on respect, tolerance, mutual admiration, trust, assertive communication, negotiation, and management of negative emotions. Gender differences in satisfaction were discovered among these couples in that men showed greater satisfaction with conjugal living, while women showed greater satisfaction with their partners' emotional reactions (Acevedo et al., 2007; Londoño, 2014; Vélez, 2017).

A moderate association has been found among university student couples that links emotional dependence to employing aggressive reaction as a coping mechanism. Also, couples who use problem solving and positive reevaluation as strategies for facing conflict were less likely to exhibit emotional dependence (Niño & Abaunza, 2015). Isaza (2011) has identified the most common causes of conflicts among young couples to be infidelity, lack of communication, and loss of freedom; in the face of conflict, the most frequent strategies to solve these issues are communicating well and seeking help from a friend or professional.

Young couples who have been trained in assertive communication techniques and how to actively search for ways to solve conflicts also improved their self-esteem, their emotional expression and their ability to adapt and be flexible in the face of problems (Díaz, Jaramillo, Silva, & Cerón, 2015). Accordingly, Mogollón and Villamizar (2013) have demonstrated that young couples consider good communication to be a factor that, in addition to helping to resolve conflicts, improves the couple's relationship by preventing cohabitation from worsening and projecting the relationship into the future. Likewise, these authors affirm that young couples consider their relationships to be stable when they have intimacy, passion, and commitment, intimacy being the most relevant component, followed by commitment and passion. Similarly, research with young couples concurs that men show higher levels of satisfaction with the relationship than women.

In conclusion, assertive communication has been identified among the Colombian couples to be a strategy that allows for conflict resolution, maintaining and improving long-term relationships, generating satisfaction, and preventing the use and escalation of violence (Agudelo et al., 2005; De la Puerta & Fossa, 2013; Londoño, 2005; Vélez, 2017; Yáñez, Ferrel, Ortiz, & Yáñez, 2017). In addition to this strategy, it has been found that couples can employ restructuring (i.e., redefining stressful issues to make them more manageable) and passive evaluation (i.e., accepting problematic issues by minimizing their reactivity); getting social and family support; and developing protective factors to ward against crises such as cohesion, adaptability, and engaging in leisure and other activities together (Ariza & Guevara, 2002).

IS THE SITUATION BETWEEN SPAIN AND COLOMBIA COMPARABLE?

The analysis regarding conflict resolution strategies in relationships, as well as the relationship between satisfaction and commitment, reveals the difficulty in comparing the situation within different cultural contexts. In this case, Spain and Colombia serve as examples of these cultural contexts in that there is considerable variance in both the theoretical models used, as there is in other aspects such as type of sample, or the variables and instruments used. Taking this into account, we find that the focus in both countries has frequently been on the analysis of violent or coercive situations.

An element that seems to make constructive resolution of conflicts rather difficult, at least as it pertains to youth, is the existence of aspects linked to emotional dependence and jealousy, even reaching the point of physical violence. This could be due to a lack of skills that, in many cases, would enable one to deal with relationship difficulties and problems in a positive way (Fernández-Fuertes & Fuertes, 2010; Niño & Abaunza, 2015). This ultimately speaks to the importance of promoting preventive actions, especially those of a psychoeducational nature, early on. This allows for improvements in the couple's well-being, cultivating such aspects as the ethics of mutual care or voluntary consent (Martínez-Álvarez et al., 2012).

In both countries, research has focused on exploring the kind of conflict resolution strategies that have been linked to other relational aspects. With respect to the adult population, however, in Spain a connection has been found between the use of positive conflict resolution strategies with respect to commitment and satisfaction and the relationship (Cheung et al., 2016; Martínez-Íñigo, 2005). In Colombia, a connection has been found between these kinds of strategies and low emotional dependence (Niño & Abaunza, 2015).

In both countries, studies identifying the use of positive resolution strategies such as assertive communication, negotiation, and the use of empathy (Acevedo et al., 2007; Hurtado et al., 2004; Londoño, 2014; Sánchez et al., 2008) as well as negative resolution strategies such as the use of coercion and violence (Fernández-Fuertes & Fuertes, 2010; Hernández & González, 2009; Klevens, 2001) have been carried out. However, other strategies have also been observed in Colombia, such as the search for social (e.g., friends and professionals) and family (Ariza & Guevara, 2002; Isaza, 2011) support.

In the same vein, with respect to the couple's relationship stability, it seems that commitment is shown to be a central aspect in both contexts, while intimate communication, due to its relationship with prevention, contributes significantly to satisfaction in the relationship and improved conflict resolution (Garrido-Macías et al., 2017; Mogollón & Villamizar, 2013; Sánchez et al., 2008). In this case, the work in Colombia was carried out via a young adult population; in Spain, research has been done with both adult and adolescent populations.

There does seem to be a difference, on the other hand, in the amount of importance given to the analysis of the context in which the couple is involved: while in Spain, research focuses on the analysis of the satisfaction of each member of the couple and on their interactions (e.g., Martínez-Íñigo, 2005; Sánchez et al., 2008), in Colombia, children tend to be involved in their relationship role (Agudelo et al., 2005; Casadiego et al., 2015; Díaz & Porras, 2011). The roles of the economy and unemployment are also taken into account in regard to crises and resilience in couples (Agudelo et al., 2005; Ariza & Guevara, 2002; Londoño, 2005). This difference generates additional difficulties in comparing the conflict resolution among the couples from both countries, because studies carried out in Spain focus on the relationship in great depth, whereas very few studies in Colombia analyze the couple outside of the family context.

In addition, some gender differences were identified in both countries: in Spain differences were identified in conflict resolution strategies (Cheung et al., 2016) and in Colombia they were identified in regard to the couple's level and type of satisfaction (Acevedo et al., 2007; Londoño, 2014; Vélez, 2017). In this way, although these studies are not directly comparable because they evaluate different variables, the need for further research that examines gender differences in relationships is referenced in both countries. Likewise, studies in both countries indicate that the majority of past research has been focused on heterosexual couples; therefore, more research needs to be done about ways to resolve conflicts among couples of other sexual orientations.

In short, the study of conflict resolution strategies in relationships, as well as the variables with which they relate, such as commitment or satisfaction in the relationship, is hardly comparable in both cultures, and the characteristics of the samples, the theoretical approaches, and the methodological procedures used have been different. This reinforces the need to do cross-cultural studies that allow comparisons to be made.

SPOTLIGHT ON INTIMATE PARTNER VIOLENCE

SILVIA MARI

Statistics report that the 35.6 percent of women and 28.5 percent of men in a lifetime will experience physical violence, sexual abuse, and/or stalking by an intimate partner (Black et al., 2011). Intimate partner violence (IPV), also known in literature as domestic violence, is a worldwide issue, diffuse in all cultures and societies (Ellsberg et al., 2014), with significant negative outcomes not only for the victims' well-being but also for the family and communities more broadly (e.g., Bonomi et al., 2006; Coker, Smith, Bethea, King, & McKewon, 2000).

IPV is a multidimensional phenomenon and understanding its multi-faceted nature, its various causes, correlates, and outcomes may help the promotion of more efficacious targeted interventions (Ali, Dhingra, & McGarry 2016). Additionally, this knowledge may be useful in developing more accurate IPV risk assessments or when it is necessary to make decisions about the family life, for instance, in the case of post-divorce parenting decisions during the divorce period (Beck, Anderson, O'Hara, & Benjamin, 2013).

The World Health Organization (WHO, 2010) defined IPV as the "behavior within an intimate relationship that causes physical, sexual or psychological harm, including acts of physical aggression, sexual coercion, psychological abuse and controlling behaviors" (p. 11). IPV is a type of violence that can be committed by both men and women in an intimate relationship independently of their marital status, or their heterosexual or homosexual orientation (Archer, 2000; Capaldi & Owen, 2001).

When considering the *forms* of abuse, WHO (2002) also described categories useful to tackle IPV from a public policy viewpoint. *Physical violence* refers to the use of physical force to inflict harm, hurt, or physical suffering to the partner, such as, for instance, beating, kicking, or using a knife (García-Moreno, Jansen, Ellsberg, Heise, & Watts, 2005). *Sexual violence* within IPV indicates the sexual abuse committed toward the partner by forcing them to have unwanted sexual intercourse by obliging them to carry out a sexual practice that is considered degrading or humiliating (García-Moreno et al., 2005). The definition has considered also the harm committed toward the partner during sexual intercourse or sex without protection (WHO, 2014).

The third type of abuse in IPV refers to *psychological violence*, which consists of a number of behaviors that humiliate or control the partner in public or private situations. Just to provide some examples, psychological violence includes verbal aggression, repetitively criticizing, monitoring and limiting movements, controlling contacts with the family and the friends, and limiting financial independence (Follingstad & DeHart, 2000; WHO, 2002). Such forms of abuse may occur individually or in combination (Devries et al., 2013). Showalter (2016) specified that this form of domestic violence is actually quite underreported by victims because they may not perceive them as abusive tactics and additionally it is not clearly visible from outside by bystanders.

Ali and colleagues (2016) in their review of the literature classified the diverse typologies of IPV based on the *type* of perpetrated violence. According to the authors, the Johnson's typology (Johnson, 1995, 2008; Kelly & Johnson, 2008) may be considered the most influential and the most comprehensive in describing IPV in a series of contexts and situations (Anderson, 2009). Ali et al. (2016) clarified that Johnson's typology is able to integrate two perspectives in the study of IPV: the feminist perspective and the family research perspective. The former considers IPV as a tactic perpetrated by men in a heterosexual relationship to exhibit control over their partners. The feminist perspective indeed focuses the attention toward how structural societal arrangements created an atmosphere of oppression that promoted violence against women, both in relational and cultural contexts (e.g., Adams, 1988). Thus, IPV is a way of maintaining male dominance, and the patriarchal ideology contributes to legitimize it. On the other hand, the family perspective considers IPV as a consequence of conflict in couples, both heterosexual and homosexual.

Initially, Johnson (1995) distinguished between patriarchal terrorism (more in line with the feminist perspective) and common couple violence. Then, the IPV conceptualization evolved and now the Johnson's typology includes five types of IPV: coercive controlling violence, violent resistance, situational couple violence, mutual violent control violence, separation-instigated violence.

Coercive controlling violence (CCV) is the most severe form of IPV and indicates a behavioral pattern of emotional abuse, control, and coercion exerted toward the intimate partner (Kelly & Johnson, 2008). The perpetrator generally tends to monitor the partner, to control any activity and relationship, and to impose rules for the couple that result in punitive actions when not met (Beck et al., 2013). Ali and colleagues (2016, p. 18) indicate that the types of violence may "include intimidation, emotional abuse, isolation, minimizing, denying, and blaming, use of children, asserting male privilege, economic abuse, and coercion and threats" (see also Pence & Paymar, 1993) and tend to escalate over time (Johnson & Leone, 2005).

Showalter (2016) in her review found that IPV is strictly linked to women's employment instability due to workplace disruptions and sabotage perpetrated by their partners.

Literature has described that in heterosexual relationships, women are more frequently victims of abusive men partners: the National Crime Victimization Survey has reported that, among the denounced abuses, women are victims in 84 percent of the cases among married couples and 86 percent of abusive dating (Catalano, 2007). However, more recent research has also shown that women in both heterosexual and homosexual relationship may recur to CVV (Beck et al., 2013).

Hamberger, Larsen, and Lehrner (2017), in a review of the literature concerning coercive control, have noticed that coercive control in IPV has been inconsistently conceptualized and measured. The authors highlight that a common core in the conceptualizations refers to an imbalance of power that makes the mate submissive to the partner. Additionally, three main characteristics may be identified: (a) the intentionality and motivation of the abuser to get control over the partner; (b) the perceived negativity of the behavior by the victimized partner; (c) the capacity of the perpetrator to make a credible threat, which implies also the capitulation of the victim to this threat. Hamberger et al. (2017, p. 10) pointed out that "the accurate assessment of coercive control should include an evaluation of threatened consequences of failure to comply with demands (i.e., coercion), and the achievement of the demanded behaviors (i.e., control)." There is still a need to explore victims' perceptions about different types of IPV (Wangmann, 2011).

In the Johnson's typology, *violent resistance* is the "type of violence used by the victim of violence to resist violence from a coercive controlling partner" (Ali et al., 2016, p. 18), independent of the gender of the victim. However, alternative terms have been used in literature, such as *female resistance* (in the feminist perspective), *resistive/reactive violence*, and *self-defense* (Beck et al., 2013; Kelly & Johnson, 2008). Ali and colleagues noted that this type of violence in some circumstances is ineffective and may cause the situation to deteriorate, as in the case of the murder of the perpetrating partner (Ferraro, 2006).

With the term *situational couple violence* (SCV), Kelly and Johnson (2008) refer to occasional conflict situations in which there is an escalation of disagreement that may lead to physical violence perpetrated by one or both partners. In this type of violence, that is the most common in the population, the main intent of the violent partner is not the control of the other as in CCV and tends to involve verbal abuse (e.g., shouting, name calling, accusation of infidelity). Generally, SCV emerges because of the inability of the mates to manage the conflictual situation or the anger (Johnson, 2008).

The label *mutual violent control violence* indicates situations in which both partners are "intimate terrorists"; that is, they tend to be violent and controlling of the mate. However, this type of IPV is considered to be quite rare (Beck et al., 2013).

The last type of IPV described by Kelly and Johnson (2008) is labeled *separation-instigated violence* and refers to the violence within the couple that is elicited by the trauma of the separation or divorce. It may occur in both men and women, but generally the episodes, which include humiliation and insult, such as throwing partner's objects away, intimidating the other about a new partner, tend to be limited to the separation period.

The social and economic consequences of IPV are extremely relevant. For instance, the financial cost of IPV in the United States was estimated at more than $8.3 billion annually (National Center for Injury Prevention & Control, 2003). IPV perpetrated by men toward women results in more severe negative health consequences than that of women toward men (Archer, 2000). Additionally, the incidence of physical and mental health issues in women who experienced IPV is greater compared to women who did not, for instance, by manifesting symptoms of post-traumatic stress disorder (PTSD), time off from work (Johnson & Leone, 2005), as well as the likelihood of developing chronic diseases (Black et al., 2011). Moreover, the effect of IPV victimization on mental health in women has been found in several long-itudinal studies (e.g., Lawrence, Orengo, Langer, & Brock, 2012); evidence also exists of an increased risk for mental health symptoms in male victims of IPV (Hines & Malley-Morrison, 2001).

8

How Do External Factors Matter in Intimate Relationships?

Predictions of having a current partner, as well as relationship satisfaction and relationship commitment, are explored in terms of the following:

- Approval of partner by parents and others
- Impacts of life domains
- Coping with stress
- Racial-ethnic identities
- Religious identities
- Timing of external events

HOW DO PARENTS INFLUENCE MATE SELECTION?

Historically, parents often arranged marriages (Hunt, 1959). People married at a young age, and it was believed that marriage was too important to be left to the whims of adolescents. Marriages were often used to consolidate land holdings and political alliances, ensure the passing on of cultural traditions and religious beliefs, and preserve or move upward in social status. Marriages based on love became more widespread about the time of the Industrial Revolution, when land holding became less critical as many moved from farms to cities. It was especially common in the United States, where young immigrants were often freer from the influence of parents back in the old country.

To explain the phenomenon of marrying for love, notions of romantic love were spread in fairy tales and movies (such as "Cinderella"), that "True love lasts forever" and "True love overcomes all obstacles." The Boston Couples Study and other research found that men were more likely to endorse such romantic beliefs, while women were found to be more practical about love (Hill & Peplau, 2002). Traditionally, women were dependent on their husband for income and social status, so women had to be practical in deciding whom to marry. Even today when women may have their own income and social status, they are concerned about marrying a man who is at least their equal in income and occupational prestige. When the woman has more income or occupational prestige, the man may feel threatened in regard to the balance of power, and she may feel that he is not "pulling his weight."

Arranged marriages are still practiced in some cultural contexts today, due to cultural emphasis on interdependence and kin relationships (Imamoglu & Seluk, 2018). However, attitudes and practices have been changing. See the SPOTLIGHT on Parent-Choice vs. Own-Choice Marriages in Pakistan, and the SPOTLIGHT on Traditional Norms and Social Changes in China, later in this chapter. Effects of economic factors and other social changes are discussed in the SPOTLIGHT on Changes in Family Life in Greece.

But even when people choose their own spouses, parents exert influence in many ways. They may emphasize marrying someone within one's own race, culture, religion, social class, education, and other characteristics. They may express approval or disapproval when a potential spouse is brought home. Even before then, they may try to live in a neighborhood and have their children attend schools where they are likely to meet, play with, date, and eventually marry the "right" kind of people. Apostolou (2013) identified other tactics used by parents to manipulate mate choices.

When you marry someone, you are marrying into their network of family and friends. Previous research (Parks, 2006) has found that those in relationships feel closer when they believe that network members support their relationship. And interactions with network members affect dating partners becoming more or less committed to wed over time (Surra & Hughes, 1997).

HOW ARE THE INFLUENCES OF PARENTS AND OTHERS MEASURED?

The importance of other people in meeting partners and the importance of socioeconomic factors in mate selection are discussed in Chapter 3. External factors are also included in sources of conflict discussed in Chapter 7.

To assess parents' and others' **knowing the current partner** (CP), the following questions are asked:

- How well do (or did) your parents know CP?
- How well do (or did) your closest friends know CP?
- How well do (or did) your co-workers or classmates know CP?

These three items do not load on a single factor so they were analyzed separately. Parents and friends may vary knowing the current partner, depending on whether their parents or friends introduced them, and whether the relationship is serious enough to introduce the partner to parents or friends. Depending on living arrangements, parents might not meet the partner until marriage is being considered.

Relationship Satisfaction is positively correlated with each of these three measures: Parents Know CP (r=.33***), Closest Friends know CP (r=.33***), and Co-workers or Classmates K; now CP (r=.20***). Similarly, Relationship Commitment is positively correlated with each of them: parents know CP (r=.44***), closest friends know CP (r=.35***), co-workers or classmates know CP (r=.23***). These measures are combined with other measures in SEM Structural Models later in this chapter.

Previous research has found that parental approval affects marital quality (Booth & Johnson, 1988). Approval by others could also matter. In the Boston Couples Study, one woman who was interviewed said that she broke up with her boyfriend after her best friend died in an auto accident, because her best friend disapproved of the boyfriend. She apparently felt compelled to fulfill her best friend's wishes.

To assess parents' and others' **approval of the current partner** in the present study, the following questions are asked:

- How much do you think your parents do (or would) approve of CP as a committed partner?
- How much do you think your closest friends do (or would) approve of CP as a committed partner?
- How much do you think your co-workers or classmates do (or would) approve of CP as a committed partner?

These three items do load on a single factor that is similar across eight relationship types (CFI=.994, RMSEA=.015) and nine cultural regions (CFI=.995, RMSEA=.018). They are averaged to create an Approval of Partner Scale, which is moderately correlated with Relationship Satisfaction (r=.55***) and with Relationship Commitment (r=.51***).

HOW DO LIFE DOMAINS IMPACT INTIMATE RELATIONSHIPS?

Previous research has found that spouses of workaholics reported more marital estrangement than spouses of non-workaholics (Robinson, Carroll, & Flowers, 2001). However, a longitudinal study found that marital satisfaction predicted job satisfaction more than the reverse (Rogers & May, 2003). Leisure activities together versus alone can have positive or negative effects on marital satisfaction depending on the leisure preferences of the two spouses (Crawford et al., 2002).

To measure **impacts of life domains** on the relationship and vice versa, in the present study, the questions in Table 8.1 are asked with possible responses from 0=NOT AT ALL to 8=EXTREMELY.

Note that the standard deviations indicate a fair amount of variation in the responses. The first three items load on a single factor of Impacts of Life

TABLE 8.1 *Impacts of life domains*

	Mean	(s.d.)
To what extent does each of the following have a negative impact on your relationship with CP?		
• Your job or career	2.29	(2.47)
• Your friendships	1.84	(2.23)
• Your activities by yourself	2.23	(2.42)
To what extent does your relationship with CP have a negative impact on each of the following?		
• Your job or career	1.70	(2.24)
• Your friendships	1.88	(2.23)
• Your activities by yourself	2.08	(2.42)

Domains on the Relationship, which is similar across relationship types (CFI=.999, RMSEA=.007) and cultural regions (CFI=.996, RMSEA=.009). The second three items load on another single factor of Impacts of the Relationship on Life Domains, which is similar across relationship types (CFI=.995, RMSEA=.019) and cultural regions (CFI=.997, RMSEA=.066). Each set of items is averaged to form a scale.

The Impacts of Life Domains on the Relationship Scale is negatively correlated with Relationship Satisfaction (r=−.27***) and Relationship Commitment (r=−.17***). Similarly, the Impacts of the Relationship on Life Domains Scale is negatively correlated with Relationship Satisfaction (r=−.28***) and Relationship Commitment (r=−.14***).

HOW DOES COPING WITH STRESS IMPACT INTIMATE RELATIONSHIPS?

Previous research has found that social support in marriage can buffer stress caused by external factors (Bradbury, Fincham, & Beach, 2000). And a review of research on dyadic coping (how married couples help each other cope with stress) found that it affects both relationship functioning and personal health (Staff, Didymus, & Backhouse, 2017).

To measure **coping with stress** in the present study, the following questions are asked, with responses from 0=NOT AT ALL to 8=EXTREMELY, which load on a single factor:

• To what extent do you feel that you have control over events in your life?
• To what extent do you feel that you are able to cope with the stress in your life?
• To what extent do you feel that you have social support from others?

These items are averaged to create a Coping with Stress Scale, which is similar across eight relationship types (CFI=.998, RMSEA=.007) and nine cultural regions (CFI=.996, RMSEA=.010). This scale is positively correlated with Relationship Satisfaction (r=.26***) and Relationship Commitment (r=.12***). In other words, while negative impacts involving life domains are associated with less relationship satisfaction and relationship commitment, successful coping with stress is associated with greater relationship satisfaction and relationship commitment.

HOW DO THE PREVIOUS MEASURES COMBINE IN SEM MODELS?

Structural Equation Modeling (SEM) is introduced in Chapter 1. SEM Structural Models combine knowing the partner, approval of the partner, impacts of life domains on the relationship, impacts of the relationship on life domains, and coping with stress to test indirect predictions of Relationship Commitment through Relationship Satisfaction, and direct predictions of Relationship Commitment independent of Relationship Satisfaction. These models are similar across eight relationship types (CFI=.970, RMSEA=.027) and nine cultural regions (CFI=.979, RMSEA=.017).

The standardized regression coefficients in these models reveal that parents' knowing the partner (γ=.11); parents', friends', and co-workers' approval of the partner (γ=.40); and coping with stress (γ=.13) are positive Central Factors, while impacts of life domains on the relationship (γ=-.11) is a negative Central Factor, in predicting Relationship Satisfaction. In addition, parent's knowing the partner (γ=.15) has a direct effect predicting relationship commitment independent of relationship satisfaction. In other words, parents' not knowing the partner reflects less commitment to the partner.

HOW ARE RACIAL-ETHNIC IDENTITIES MEASURED?

In research on families, "racial" categories are often used to define ethnic groups, even though those within those categories further distinguish themselves by their country of origin or that of their ancestors (e.g., McAdoo, 1999). For example, Latinos distinguish themselves as Mexican and Guatemalan, while Caucasians distinguish themselves as German and Italian. When Americans speak about their race or ethnicity, they often report fractions, being half or a quarter or an eighth of one category and another fraction of one or more other categories. To measure this, all participants are asked the question in Table 8.2 from the Multiple Identities Questionnaire (Hill, 2001a), with possible responses from 0=NOT AT ALL to 8=COMPLETELY, so that 1=1/8, 2=2/8, 4=4/8, etc.

TABLE 8.2 *Racial-ethnic identities of participants*

To what extent do you consider yourself to be a member of each of the following "racial" categories?	
• Asian	(N=1364 partly, 1388 fully)
• Black or African	(N=1141 partly, 230 fully)
• Hispanic or Latino	(N=1921 partly, 794 fully)
• Native American or other Indigenous	(N=1408 partly, 70 fully)
• Pacific Islander	(N= 754 partly, 74 fully)
• White or Caucasian	(N=2536 partly, 2885 fully)
• Other_____	(N=319 partly, 152 fully)

The numbers for racial-ethnic identities show the numbers of participants who answered 1–7 for partly or 8 for fully, although the full range of
values is used in correlations with each category. But 40 percent use more
than one category, and when they do it often adds up to more than 8/
8=100 percent, as found in other research using the Multiple Identities
Questionnaire (Hill, 2001a). For example, a woman might consider herself
8/8 Latina since she was raised as a Latina, yet she is also 2/8 Native
American since one grandmother was Native American. It is common to
have one or more family members of a different racial-ethnic identity than
the way you are raised. Hence many respondents are counted in more than
one category.

HOW DO RACIAL-ETHNIC IDENTITIES MATTER?

Previous research found that Blacks reported lower marital quality than
Whites, with spousal support and financial satisfaction important factors
(Broman, 1993). But other research revealed that differences in marital happiness between Blacks and Whites have decreased from the 1970s to the 1990s
(Corra et al., 2009). Mexican Americans and Whites had similar levels of
marital quality (Bulanda & Brown, 2007). In the present study a wider range of
racial-ethnic identities is compared.

The correlations between each racial-ethnic identity and Having
a Current Partner reveal that there is a only a negative correlation for Asian
Identity (r=−.22***) and a positive correlation for White or Caucasian
Identity (r=.15***). This finding for Asian Identity is consistent with the
finding reported in Chapter 1 that participants in the East Asia and
Southeast Asia cultural regions are less likely to have a current partner.
Other research using the Multiple Identities Questionnaire has found that
Asian American college students were less likely than other racial-ethnic
groups to report having had sexual intercourse before marriage (Hill, 2016).

TABLE 8.3 *Religious identities of participants*

To what extent do you consider yourself to be a member of each of the following religious categories?

• Protestant Christian	(N=1633 partly, 726 fully)
• Roman Catholic	(N=2372 partly, 1031 fully)
• Eastern Orthodox Christian	(N=858 partly, 345 fully)
• Jewish	(N=548 partly, 97 fully)
• Buddhist	(N=1524 partly, 111 fully)
• Taoist	(N=465 partly, 13 fully)
• Hindu	(N=370 partly, 49 fully)
• Muslim	(N=307, 381 fully)
• Sikh	(N=154 partly, 15 fully)
• Indigenous	(N=620 partly, 39 fully)
• Other–which?	(N=309 partly, 234 fully)
• No religious group	(N=2027 partly, 1523 fully)

These findings are likely the result of greater emphasis on obedience by Asian parents (Argyle et al., 1986), who are expected to control their offspring so that they do not engage in intimate relationships that lead to premarital sex, which would reflect poorly on their parenting. See the SPOTLIGHT on Filial Piety in Chapter 1.

The correlations between each racial-ethnic identity and Relationship Satisfaction are trivial (r<.10). So are the correlations between each racial-ethnic identity and Relationship Commitment. These findings are consistent with the findings of SEM Structural Models throughout this book that the predictors of Relationship Satisfaction and Relationship Commitment are generally similar across nine cultural regions.

HOW ARE RELIGIOUS IDENTITIES MEASURED?

Religions are an important part of cultures (Cohen, 2011), and they often have restrictions on sexual activities (Li & Cohen, 2014). To measure **religious identities,** the question from the Multiple Identities Questionnaire (Hill, 2010) shown in Table 8.3 is asked, with possible responses from 0=NOT AT ALL to 8=COMPLETELY for each category.

The numbers for Religious Identities show the numbers of participants who answered 1–7 for partly or 8 for fully, although the full range of values is used in correlations with each religious category. But 39 percent use more than one category, and when they do it often adds up to more than 8/8=100 percent, as found in other research using the Multiple Identities Questionnaire (Hill, 2010).

Among those rating partly for "No religious group," 96 percent identify at least partly with one or more religions. Even among those rating fully for "No religious group," 77 percent identify at least partly with one or more religions. In other words, they at least partly identify with a religious belief or background that they may have been raised in even if they do not fully identify with a religious group or organization now. Other research using the Multiple Identities Questionnaire has found that it is common for college students to have weaker religious identities than their parents (Hill, 2015).

HOW DO RELIGIOUS IDENTITIES MATTER?

The overall correlations between each religious category and Having a Current Partner are trivial (r<.10). So are the correlations between Relationship Satisfaction and Religious Commitment (r<.10). Hence, they are not included in SEM models predicting relationship satisfaction and relationship commitment.

However, among those with a current partner, there are correlations between specific religious categories and having **premarital sex**, and as well as correlations with having **same-sex partners**. For unmarried women, having sexual activities is slightly negatively correlated with Roman Catholic (r=−.16**) and Eastern Orthodox Christian (r=−.12**), but positively correlated with No Religious Group (r=.22**). For unmarried men, having sexual activities is slightly negatively correlated with Eastern Orthodox Christian (r=−.13**) and Muslim (r=−.15**), but slightly positively correlated with No Religious Group (r=.13***).

Among all women with a Current Partner, having a Same-Sex Partner is negatively correlated with Protestant (=−.17**) and Muslim (r=−.10**), but positively correlated with No Religious Group (r=.17**). Among men, having a Same-Sex Partner is slightly negatively correlated with Jewish (r=−.17**), Hindu (r=−.11**), and Muslim (r=−.12**), but positively correlated with No Religious Group (r=.16**).

The most striking findings are that premarital sex and same-sex relationships are slightly more common among those rating "No Religious Group." Religions have often placed restrictions on sexual behaviors, especially monotheistic religions (Christian, Jewish, and Muslim), to emphasize reproduction in families (Benagiano, Carrara, & Filippi, 2012). But attitudes of believers do not always agree with the restrictions of their religion, and religious behavior is a strong predictor of sexual behavior (Lefkowitz et al., 2004; Rostosky et al., 2004). See the SPOTLIGHT on Family Tradition and Catholic Religion in Poland later in this chapter.

SELF-REFLECTION

In what ways have your parents tried to influence you to marry or not marry a particular kind of person? Have they made comments about marrying someone similar to you in race, ethnicity, social class, religion, or education? Have they approved or disapproved your dating particular persons?

HOW DOES THE TIMING OF EXTERNAL EVENTS IMPACT INTIMATE RELATIONSHIPS?

In the Boston Couples Study, breakups of college dating relationships were more likely to occur at the beginning and end of semesters: September-October, December-January, and May-June (Hill, Rubin, & Peplau, 1976). These are times when decisions have to be made about whether or not to coordinate classes, work schedules, and living arrangements. These decisions raise issues about the relationship – is the relationship worth it? These are also times when it is easier to meet potential new partners due to new classes, work schedules, and living arrangements. And finally, the separations caused by these changes may make it easier to call off a relationship. It is easier in May to say, "while we are apart we should date others," instead of saying in April that "I don't want to date you anymore." This is especially important since the desire to break up was rarely mutual. In 93 percent of the breakups, one person wanted to the relationship to end more than the other.

Breakups among non-students might not occur during the same months of the year, but external events might have similar effects. When a person changes jobs or living arrangements or a parent dies, one may reassess one's relationships and decide whether or not to break up or make a firmer commitment such as marriage.

In the present study, participants are asked the following questions:

- Have you ever had a romantic or sexual relationship that ended? NO YES
- If YES, when did your most recent previous relationship end? MONTH YEAR

Among students, 60.1% say YES to the first question, while among non-students 77.2% say YES. Among students the most frequent months are August (11.7%) and September (10.5%). Among non-students the most frequent months of breakups are May (10.9%), June (10.5%), and September (9.9%). In other words, it is common to have had a previous relationship that ended, and summer breakups are more common for both students and non-students.

IN SUMMARY, WHAT CENTRAL FACTORS HAVE BEEN IDENTIFIED IN THIS CHAPTER?

For Relationship Satisfaction and Relationship Commitment, parents' knowing the partner, parents' and others' approval of the partner, and coping with stress are positive Central Factors, whereas the Impacts of Life Domains on the Relationship Scale is a negative Central Factor. SEM models reveal that these same Central Factors make similar predictions across eight relationship types and nine cultural regions.

The predictions of these Central Factors are similar, even though the levels of these factors may vary. These Central Factors will be combined with Central Factors from other chapters in a *Comprehensive Commitment Model* in Chapter 10. Variations in levels of factors will be discussed in Chapter 11.

SPOTLIGHT ON PARENT-CHOICE VS. OWN-CHOICE
MARRIAGES IN PAKISTAN

CHARLES T. HILL, RUKHSANA KAUSAR, AND SHEHNAZ BANO

In what ways are parent-choice marriages and own-choice marriages similar or different? Previous research has found love-match marriages to be more intimate (Blood, 1967), have higher satisfaction (Xiaohe & Whyte, 1990), and have better marital quality as measured by satisfaction, communication, togetherness, problems, and disagreements (Allendorf & Ghimire, 2013). However, other studies have found arranged marriages to have higher satisfaction (Yelsma & Athappilly, 1988; Raina & Maity, 2018), or found no difference (Regan, Lakhanpal, & Anguiano, 2012). Fox (1975) found homogamy in own-choice marriages as well as in arranged marriages.

A key factor in both kinds of marriages is parental approval. Arif and Fatima (2015) found that arranged marriages and own-choice marriages with parental approval had similar levels of marital satisfaction, which were higher than in own-choice marriages without parental approval.

The cross-cultural study that is the focus of this book found that approval by parents and others predicts relationship satisfaction and relationship commitment across eight relationship types and nine cultural regions, as reported earlier in this chapter. As noted in Chapter 1, a printed version of the online questionnaire in Urdu was distributed to both members of 125 married couples in Pakistan. Sixty-five couples described their marriage as parent choice while sixty described it as own choice. There were no average differences between the two types of marriage in parental approval of the marriage or how important they considered parental advice.

On the average, own-choice spouses were younger ($p<.05$), and had a smaller age gap ($p<.05$), than parent-choice spouses: own-choice women 30.2 and men 33.5, parent-choice women 34.1 and men 38.7. Own-choice couples had been married fewer years: 6.2 vs. 10.8 ($p<.001$). And own-choice couples were less likely to live with parents: 43.3% vs. 73.8% ($p<.05$).

Only three differences were found on 21 mate selection criteria, on scales of 0=NOT AT ALL to 8=EXTREMELY important. Own-choice women rated greater importance for physical attractiveness (6.62 vs. 6.12, $p<.05$), while own-choice men rated greater importance for religious beliefs (6.52 vs. 6.03, p <.05) and willingness to have children higher (7.02 vs. 6.42, $p<.05$).

Own-choice husbands and wives reported being emotionally closer (6.63 vs. 5.15, $p<.001$ for men and 6.50 vs. 5.41, $p<.001$ for women). They had higher Four Component Love Scale scores (6.49 vs. 5.09, $p<.001$ for men and 6.61 vs. 5.36, $p<.001$ for women). And they reported expressing more affection (6.38 vs. 4.89, $p<.001$ for men and 6.52 vs. 4.60, $p<.001$ for women).

Own-choice wives and husbands reported disclosing more (6.09 vs. 5.11, $p<.001$ for women and 6.39 vs. 5.26, $p<.001$ for men). They also trusted their partner more not to lie (6.30 vs. 5.12, $p<.001$ for women and 6.37 vs. 4.83, $p<.001$ for men).

Own-choice husbands and wives reported fewer problems (2.64 vs. 3.48, $p<.001$ for men and 2.54 vs. 3.37 for women, $p<.001$). And they were more likely to report trying to find a mutual solution as a way of dealing with conflict (6.35 vs. 5.43, $p<.001$ for men and 6.58 vs. 5.45, $p<.001$ for women).

Own-choice wives and husbands reported greater sexual satisfaction (6.65 vs. 5.31, $p<.001$ for women and 6.70 vs. 5.37 for men, $p<.001$). They also reported greater relationship satisfaction (6.67 vs. 5.25, $p<.001$ for women and 6.38 vs. 5.36, $p<.001$ for men). And they reported greater relationship commitment (6.55 vs. 5.54, $p<.001$ for women and 6.78 vs. 5.46, $p<.001$ for men).

Own-choice husbands and wives were better able to cope with stress (6.60 vs. 5.55, $p<.001$ for men and 6.24 vs. 5.32, $p<.001$ for women). They were happier (6.63 vs. 5.41, $p<.001$ for men and 6.32 vs. 5.14, $p<.001$ for women). And they were more satisfied with their lives (6.70 vs. 5.65, $p<.001$ for men and 6.52 vs. 5.51, $p<.001$ for women).

Overall, own-choice couples were more intimate in many ways, and more satisfied with their relationships and their lives. This is consistent with the prediction of Relational Mobility Theory discussed in Chapter 1 of this book. When there is more choice of partners, there is greater expression of affection and commitment to keep a partner in the relationship.

Yet participants in parent-choice marriages were not dissatisfied. On every measure (except problems), their average ratings were significantly above the scale midpoint of 4.0 on scales from 0 to 8. They were just not as intimate and satisfied as own-choice couples.

SPOTLIGHT ON TRADITIONAL NORMS AND SOCIAL CHANGES IN CHINA

XIAOMIN LI

Culture is among the salient catalysts for the development, maintenance, and dissolution of intimate couple relationships (Markus & Kitayama, 2003). Specific to couple relationships in modern China, there appear to be coexisting influences of traditional cultural norms and recent social changes on modern Chinese couples. As such, Chinese couples' relationships reflect characteristics that are similar to but still different from those in Western couples' relationships.

Concerning mate selection, the majority of marriages in traditional Chinese society were assigned by parents or families for purposes including keeping the family lineage alive (Pimentel, 2000). To this end, family background, economic worth, and social status tended to be superior to love for mate selection. However, since the passing of the marriage law in 1950s that shifted the right of mate selection from parents or families to individuals themselves, love and companionship are now among the major driving forces to enter into marriage (Davis, 2014). However, despite the increasing freedom for mate selection, parents and families could still exert influence on mate selection among Chinese youth. In fact, there are still a large proportion of individuals in modern China who met their intimate partners via parents or/ and relatives (Xu, Xie, Liu, Xia, & Liu, 2007).

With respect to couple interactive processes, of note is that traditional Chinese culture is described as collectivistic and hierarchical, which increases the possibility for Chinese partners to engage in high-context communication that is indirect, implicit, and potentially ambiguous (e.g., Kapoor, Hughes, Baldwin, & Blue, 2003). In addition, interpersonal harmony, which is regarded as one of the central values in traditional Chinese culture, would also make Chinese partners repress personal opinions and feelings in attempting to minimize conflicts (Lee, Nakamura, Chung, Chun, Fu, Liang, & Liu, 2013).

However, the unprecedented social, legal, and economic reforms that have happened in Chinese society during recent decades have also reshaped couples' interactive processes among Chinese couples. For example, as the 1978 "reform and openness" policy increases Chinese individuals' exposure to Western culture values, assertiveness about personal feelings and opinions has been embraced by an increasing number of Chinese (Dong & Li, 2007). As a result, the way in which Chinese partners communicate with each other tend also be increasingly similar to that among Western couples.

In addition, attitudes toward premarital sex have changed over recent decades in China. To our knowledge, chastity is considered an important value in traditional Chinese culture and premarital sexual involvement is regarded as a social vice (Xu et al., 2007). However, with Western cultural values relevant to intimacy and compassion introduced to Chinese society, premarital sex has become more acceptable among Chinese youth: one study on sexual attitudes has demonstrated that a growing number of Chinese youth believe that "the concept (i.e., chastity is the most important) was too traditional, and should be abolished" (Zhen, Zhang, Li, Mao, & Wang, 2000).

Besides, wedding rituals have also been reshaped by social changes occurring in China. In the past, the main color for a wedding dress would be red, which means happiness and celebration. The Western wedding dress of white has also become popular in China since Chiang Kai-shek and his wife were married, and she wore a Western style wedding dress in the 1920s (for more details, see www.topchinatravel.com/china-guide/chinese-wedding-customs.htm).

Nevertheless, some traditional norms for wedding celebrations still persist in China. For example, it is quite common that the groom's parents present grand gifts to the bride's parents to formally announce the young couple's wedding, whereas it is the groom himself who usually buys the bride an engagement ring in Western societies (for more details, see www .topchinatravel.com/china-guide/chinese-wedding-customs.htm).

SPOTLIGHT ON CHANGES IN FAMILY LIFE IN GREECE

ARTEMIS Z. GIOTSA

Many researchers have studied the Greek family during the past two decades (Babalis, Tsoli, Nikolopoulos, & Maniatis, 2014; Georgas, Berry, van de Vivjer, Kagitçibasi, & Poortinga, 2006; Georgas, Van de Vivjer, & Berry, 2004; Giotsa, 2003; Giotsa & Mitrogiorgou, 2014a, 2014b, 2016; Giotsa & Touloumakos, 2014a, 2014b; Kataki, 2012; Mylonas, Gari, Giotsa, Pavlopoulos, & Panagiotopoulou, 2006). Their findings will be highlighted in terms of changing family types, statistical data on life in Greece, and family values in Greece.

CHANGING FAMILY TYPES

Social changes in Greece have led to changes in family types as a result of urbanization, industrialization, and in recent years the financial crisis. The traditional Greek family was patriarchal and extended. It consisted of at least three generations that lived together under the same roof (the parents; the children; and the grandparents, uncles, aunts, cousins). They had the same professional activity such as working in the small family factory. They focused on the whole family's benefit and they decided the future of the children. The father was the leader of the family; he made the final decisions and the other members of the family obeyed him. Also, the choice of the spouse constituted a family matter, and in many rural areas the marriage was arranged between the two families. However, in recent days in Greece, the individual makes the decision about the selection of the spouse.

As a result of the financial crisis, the economic and social difficulties have led to the empowerment of new family relationships. After the decrease of salaries and the increase of the taxes over the past seven years, the aging generation tends to be installed in the same house with their children's family in an effort to manage the economic difficulties that they face. The two generations unify their incomes and support each other in various duties and functions (e.g., housekeeping, child-rearing, and shopping; Giotsa & Mitrogiorgou, 2014b).

A new family type has replaced the extended family due to families' movement toward the big cities. This family type is called the *urban extended family* (Georgas, 1989, 1991). The members of the nuclear family live together and the members of the extended family such as the grandparents, uncles, and cousins live in the same building or in the same area. The members can help each other and take care of the older persons. In this family type, the members of the family have different professions and economic independence from the extended family.

Also, in contemporary Greece, we have the following family types:

The *double-nuclear family,* consisting of the divorced parents and their child/ children (Chatzichristou, 1992). The double-nuclear family results from the split of the nuclear family into two different nuclear families, the father's and the mother's. Both parents are responsible for raising and supporting their children.

Single parenting refers to a one-parent household, due to the death of the other parent, or intentional artificial insemination, or unplanned pregnancy. *The lame family* is one in which the financial crisis led to unemployment. Many Greek people are forced to find a profession in another country to financially support their family. They have intimate relationships with their children, spouse, and other relatives and travel frequently to their country of origin. This new family type is called the lame family, where the one of the two parents is absent for professional reasons and the other parent is responsible for raising the children (Mousourou, 1999).

In Greece, the extended family network (grandparents, siblings, other family members) supports the single parent families, the double nuclear families, and the lame families by offering help on many levels (sentimental, financial, social). In Greece the single parent family resulting from parental divorce is very often supported by the single parent's siblings, parents, extended family members, and friends (Babalis, Tsoli, Nikolopoulos, & Maniatis, 2014; Georgas, Berry, van de Vivjer, Kagitçibasi, & Poortinga, 2006; Georgas, Van de Vivjer, & Berry, 2004; Giotsa, 2003; Giotsa & Mitrogiorgou, 2014a, 2014b, 2016; Mylonas, Gari, Giotsa, Pavlopoulos, & Panagiotopoulou, 2006).

STATISTICAL DATA ON LIFE IN GREECE

According to the Greek Statistical Service, during the period 1991–2015, the percentage of marriages in Greece has decreased by 22%. In addition, the number of divorces has increased by 240% (Hellenic Statistical Authority, 2017). More specifically, one in three marriages ends in divorce. Also, there is a decrease of 10% in the number of births, in contrast to the other European countries where there is an augmentation in the fertility rate (Eurostat, 2017).

We must consider that long-term unemployment is extremely demoralizing and influences the relationships between the members of the family (Giotsa & Mitrogiorgou, 2016). Greece has the highest rate of unemployment among all 28 European countries (Eurostat, 2017), with an overall rate of 21.7%, where especially almost half of the young people younger than age 25 are unemployed (45.2%).

From a psychological point of view, during the years of economic crisis (2009–2017) in Greece, the rate of suicide attempts rose 29% and rates of depression have risen 25% (Karanikolos, Mladovsky, Cylus, Thomson, Basu, Stuckler, McKee, & Mackenbach, 2013). Although the number of Greeks seeking mental health support has increased 120% (Anagnostopoulos & Soumaki, 2013), the public subsidy has been decreased by 55%.

FAMILY VALUES IN GREECE

Also, many researchers in Greece have studied family values (Georgas, 1989, 1991; Georgas, Berry, van de Vivjer, Kagitçibasi, & Poortinga, 2006; Giotsa, 2003, 2007). Values are transmitted through the family from generation to generation (Georgas, 1989, 1991; Giotsa, 2003, 2007; Kataki, 2012). The emotional bonds between the family members and the support they provide to one another constitute a crucial factor in the transmission of family values (Georgas & Dragona, 1988; Hogg, 1992). According to Triandis (1992), Greek people trust family members and turn to relatives for emotional support during difficult times.

In Greece, many studies in the field of family values have focused on three principal factors: the hierarchical roles of father and mother, the responsibilities of parents toward the children, and the responsibilities of children toward the family and the relatives (Mylonas, Gari, Giotsa, Pavlopoulos, & Panagiotopoulou, 2006). The first factor *hierarchical roles of father and mother* contains values referring to the traditional gender roles such as father is the head of the family, punishes the children, controls the finances of the family; mother accepts father's decisions and mother's place is at home. The second factor *responsibilities of parents toward the children* contains values related to the behavior of parents in front of children, the resolution of problems in the family, etc. The third factor *responsibilities of children toward the family and the relatives* contains values such as children must take care of their old parents, obey they parents, and respect their grandparents.

Findings indicated that young people in Greece reject values related to the first factor of the hierarchical roles of father and mother and accept values related to the two other values related to the reciprocal responsibilities between the family members (Giotsa, 2003, 2007; Georgas, 1989, 1991; Georgas, Berry, van de Vivjer, Kagitçibasi, & Poortinga, 2006). Those findings and other findings referring to the close relationships between the family members and the warmth dimension in the Greek family (Rohner, 2017) play an important role during this period of crisis. The emotional bonds in the Greek family and the transmission of family values between generations help people deal with their difficulties such as unemployment (Giotsa, Anifanti, Lampaki, Mouzou, Xylagras, & Kastriotis, 2015). In spite of the social changes and the differences in family types, bonds between the members of the Greek family are still very strong.

The emotional bonds between the family members are irreplaceable. Many studies have been conducted worldwide in the field of family relationships and the emotional bonds between the family members (Georgas, 1989, 1991; Giotsa, 2003). Findings from cross-cultural research indicated that in spite of changes in roles, the emotional bonds in the Greek family remain strong (Georgas, Berry, van de Vivjer, Kagitçibasi, & Poortinga, 2006; Kagitcibasi, 2007) and children feel accepted by their parents (Giotsa & Touloumakos, 2014a, 2014b; Giotsa & Zergiotis, 2010; Rohner, 1986, 2004; Rohner & Khaleque, 2005; Rohner, Khaleque, & Kournoyer, 2012). The mother remains the person with the most emotional closeness to the children not only in the early childhood (Giotsa, 2012) and adolescence (Giotsa & Touloumakos, 2014a) but also in the life cycle of an individual (Georgas, Berry, van de Vijver, Kagitcibasi, & Poortinga, 2006).

SPOTLIGHT ON FAMILY TRADITION AND CATHOLIC RELIGION IN POLAND

KAROLINA KURYŚ-SZYNCEL AND BARBARA JANKOWIAK

Poland is a country characterized by a strong family tradition as reflected in its population structure according to marital status. According to data from the Central Statistical Office (GUS), among the almost 30 million Polish citizens 20 years of age and older, about 60% were legally married in 2011. More than 2% were in an informal relationship (cohabitation/common law marriage), almost 22% were unmarried, almost 5% were divorced, and less than 1% were separated (Stańczak, Stelmach, & Urbanowicz, 2016). In Poland currently about 50% of singles are aged 18–24 (Paprzycka & Izdebski, 2016).

Partners' relationship may be formalized in Poland solely by way of marriage, which pursuant to the provisions of the Constitution of the Republic of Poland and the Family and Guardianship Code means exclusively a relationship between a woman and a man (art. 18 of the Constitution of RP and art. 1 of the Family and Guardianship Code of February 25, 1964). There exists no legal possibility of formalizing same-sex relationships or the possibility of formalizing different-sex relationships in a way other than marriage.

Alternative forms of family life to marriage and nuclear family exist, such as reconstructed families, single parenthood, cohabitation relationships, "living apart together" (having an intimate relationship but living at different addresses), homosexual relationships, single life (Kwak, 2005; Slany, 2002). And current research comparing cohabitation relationships to marital relationships in Poland does not show any significant differences in intimate relationship quality (Jankowiak, 2010). Yet marriage continues to be the most desired form of partner life.

Today more and more often homosexual and bisexual persons stop hiding their sexual orientation and the relationships they form. And the recognition of homosexuals' rights has steadily grown. However, the views of Poles on same-sex relationships and sexual minorities are not free from myths and prejudices. The report on Poles' sexuality by Zbigniew Izdebski shows that two-thirds of respondents (65.3% of all persons aged 18–49) consider that sexual contacts between persons of the same sex are not normal; 24.6% of respondents were of a different opinion; and 5.2% did not have any opinion. In addition, 54.9% of respondents considered that persons sexually attracted to persons of the same sex should undergo "treatment." However, for same-sex relationships, 57% of persons approved the possibility of filing a common tax return; 48% approved adopting the partner's name, 50% approved taking over social rights such as pension, retirement benefits, industry authorizations; 50% approved inheritance on the principles of the closest family members; and 9% approved child adoption and raising children (Izdebski, 2012).

For several years now, more than 200,000 marriages have split up each year, 70% by the spouse's death, and 30% by divorce. About 65,000 divorces are registered each year. In 2013, about 66,000 occurred, the divorce coefficient amounting to 1.7% (73 out of 10,000 marriages were dissolved by court judgment) (Stańczak, Stelmach, & Urbanowicz, 2016). In comparison, in 2011 the EUROSTAT data show almost 1 million divorces registered in European Union countries, with the divorce coefficient amounting to 2.0%[1].

At present in Poland, no arranged marriages[2] are observed, and family influence on contracting marriage has been dwindling. As shown in the research by Iwona Przybył (2017) carried out in 2007–2014, the situation clearly differs between the beginning of the young people's relationship and the engagement and marriage phase. In the initial phase, the views of acquaintances and peers are of importance, their positive opinions motivate the strengthening of ties, while negative opinions cause the ties to loosen and frequently lead to splitting up. On the other hand, in the phase directly preceding the decision to form a lifelong relationship, the opinions of the closest family members, especially the parents, count the most.

Despite the preceding, many marriages are contracted against the opinion of the immediate social environment:

Over 15% of marriages were contracted against the will of both of the respondent's parents (11.1%) or one parent (4.6%), and over 14% of marriages were contracted despite the objection of both future parents-in-law (9.7%) or one of them (4.6%). 4.3 % of all respondents declared that the marriage was contracted without the support of any parents and parents-in-law of bride and groom)." (Przybył, 2017, 396–397)

---

[1] http://ec.europa.eu/eurostat/statistics-explained/index.php?title=Special%3ASearch&profile=default&search=Marriages+and+births+&fulltext=Search [2018, August 7]; http://ec.europa.eu/eurostat/statistics-explained/index.php/Marriage_and_birth_statistics_-_new_ways_of_living_together_in_the_EU [2018, August 7].

[2] In 2016 a paradocumentary film was produced by one of the Polish TV stations entitled: "Marriage at First Sight," where an experiment was arranged by an "expert" psychologist, anthropologist and sexologist. Out of a few hundred candidates, three couples were put together based on the identified similarities, and married without knowing each other (they saw each other for the first time on the day of marriage). Their life was then monitored with a camera. All three couples decided to divorce. The public did not approve of the program. Notwithstanding, the TV station planned another edition. The first episode of the second series was to be shown on September 11, 2017.

According to the respondents, parents and/or parents-in-law most frequently objected to the marriage because the candidate did not meet the expectations of the older generation with respect to character and personality (51.5% of cases on average), because the differences between future spouses in terms of age, wealth, or social background were too big (31%) and because a possessive parent expected the child to take care of them, instead of founding a family and moving out of the house (9%). As per the research carried out by I. Przybył, women respondents more frequently stated the possessiveness of their parents (Przybył, 2017).

At present the choice of a partner and the decision to marry are not made in consultation with parents. Very rarely are relationships formalized under direct financial pressure of the older generation. The situation changed during the past decade, as still in the 2007 in the research carried out by Henryk Domański and Dariusz Przybysz (2007, 19–20) the control by the family was observed, taking the form of advice, opinions, encouragement, or financial support. Currently financial issues play a minor role; young people want to make their own choice, do not ask for others' opinions, and point out the volitional nature of their decision (Przybył, 2017, 398–399). On the one hand, such change may be due to greater maturity of partners deciding to marry – in Poland the age of newlyweds has definitely increased. Currently, men most often marry "before they turn thirty," at the average age of 29, and the median age for women is about 27 (Stańczak, Stelmach, & Urbanowicz, 2016). On the other hand, people are aware of the possibility of formally dissolving marriage by way of divorce, which is no longer socially stigmatizing.

It is worth pointing out that tradition still prevails in Poland, and rites related to marriage are maintained (engagement, wedding ceremony). Young women mostly declare that a girl's dream is to get an engagement ring, wear a white wedding dress, and have a wedding ceremony in church (Przybył, 2017). Women initiate a long-term intimate relationship in earlier phases of their lives, i.e., during studies when they are still financially dependent on their parents, while men initiate such a relationship once they are financially independent (Przybył, 2017, 468). The majority of common law relationships are eventually legalized as marriages, because a marriage warrants more advantageous formal and legal benefits in Poland, securing the spouses and their offspring (e.g., inheritance). Marriage is also viewed as access to normality: "a marriage 'normalises' a woman, giving her more value and status" (Przybył, 2017, 387).

Poland is a country strongly bound to the Catholic religion. According to the research by the Central Statistical Office, 94.2% of inhabitants of Poland at the age of 16 and older identify themselves with religious institutions. At 92.8%, the Catholic Church faithful form

the most numerous community. The members of other churches correspond to 1.4% in total; 3.1% of the respondents do not subscribe to any
religion, and 2.2% refuse to answer this question. According to the self-
declaration of faith, the vast majority of adult Poles (80%) are believers,
more than 18% are indecisive, seeking or indifferent to religion, and
almost 3% are declared nonbelievers. Almost 70% participate in masses,
services, or religious meetings at least once a month, and half of them do
it at least once weekly. More than 65% pray at least once a week, of
which 40% nearly every day or more often (Ciecieląg & Boryszewski,
2017).

However, as shown in the data of the Centre for Public Opinion
Research (CEBOS), Poles have adopted a more and more selective approach
to the Catholic moral principles and consider them as not fitting into the
present reality. Such an approach is clearly reflected in the position taken by
Poles with respect to some moral issues regarding sexuality and family life.
About three-fourths of adult Poles consider using contraceptive means and
engaging in sexual intercourse before marriage as admissible (77% and 74%,
respectively). Almost two-thirds (63%) give their consent to divorce, and
more than one-fourth (27%) approve of abortion. In addition, 22% of the
respondents accept sexual intercourse between persons of the same sex, and
every eleventh respondent allows for sex with persons other than one's wife
or husband (9%).

Such data do not differ substantially in a sample limited exclusively to
persons defining themselves as Catholic. More than two-thirds of them
(77%) acquiesce to contraception, 73% allow for premarital sex, 62%
accept divorces, 26% are for the possibility of abortion, 20% think that
sexual intercourse between persons of the same sex is admissible, and 9%
do not condemn adultery. Positions taken with respect to the discussed
issues differ substantially depending on the level of religiosity of the
respondents; yet also in the group of people who consider themselves as
religious and regularly practicing, it is common to accept using contraceptive means, having sexual intercourse before marriage, or divorcing.
For example, among the respondents participating in religious practices
once a week, three-fourths (76%) declare their support for contraception,
a few less accept premarital sex (71%), and more than half allow for
divorces (57%) (Boguszewski, 2014).

The report on the Poles´ sexuality by Zbigniew Izdebski (2012) shows
that 20.6% of persons remaining in a regular relationship declare having
had sexual contacts outside the couple (25.6% for men, and 15.4% for
women). Adultery was declared less often by believers and regular practitioners of religion (15.8%), and by people deeply believing and regularly
practicing (11.3%). The symptoms of increasing secularization of morality
have been observed in Poland, and Poles feel less and less need for

religious justification of their own moral principles, often declaring moral views that are not in line with their professed religion. Nevertheless, the moral principles proposed by the Catholic Church, although considered by most Catholics as not adaptable to the current reality and necessitating completion, are frequently recognized also by persons who declare themselves as nonreligious or nonbelievers (Boguszewski, 2014).

To sum up, it is worth pointing out that pregnancy of teenage girls is a relatively common phenomenon in Poland. The data from the report on the sexuality of adult Poles show that the average age of sexual initiation in the research of 2005 was 18.42 years (18.82 for women, 18.08 for men) (Izdebski, 2012). Although the average age of women having their firstborn in Poland is 29.3 years, in 2013 GUS[3] registered about 10% of teenage live births (below 19 years of age). This issue is of great interest to young Polish researchers in the field of social sciences. As an effect of risk behavior of young people (Jankowiak, 2018), it is also an essential pedagogical problem. As shown in the research, only 33% of persons who initiated sexual life indicated the use of contraception (Izdebsk, 2006, 59).

Intimate relations of teenagers often result in unplanned pregnancy, which usually is regarded as a problem of the girl/mother, and not the boy/father (Jankowiak, 2018). The relationship of juvenile parents is rarely finalized in a marriage (consent of legal guardians is required), although, as the respondents declare, they wish to have a common household and take care of the child together, as a result of their own decision, and not under pressure of family or friends (Ratajczak, 2016; Skowrońska-Pućka, 2016). However, only 4 out of 21 juvenile fathers who turned adult during the research carried out by Łukasz Ratajczak (2016) decided to change their marital status and marry the mother of their child.

The low level of sexual awareness is still due to insufficient sexual education provided by Polish schools. Textbooks for Education for Family Life (EFL) depart from the assumptions and recommendations of the World Health Organization and do not fit into holistic sexual education (Paprzycka-Dec, Walendzik-Ostrowska, & Gulczyńska, 2016). The family in EFL textbooks is mainly understood in traditional categories. No information and indications concerning alternative family patterns exist (Waszyńska, 2016). Textbooks only include relationships of white, healthy heterosexuals of Catholic faith and conservative views (Paprzycka, Dec-Pietrowska, & Walendzik-Ostrowska, 2016). The world of men and women presented in textbooks mostly reflects stereotyped images of sex roles and obligations (Pietrowska-Dec, Walendzik-

---

[3] http://stat.gov.pl/obszary-tematyczne/roczniki-statystyczne/roczniki-statystyczne/rocznik-demograficzny-2013,3,7.html

Ostrowska, Gulczyńska, Jankowiak, & Waszyńska, 2016). In the description of contraceptive methods, natural methods are strongly favored (with a focus on advantages and strong points), and nonnatural contraceptive methods are devalued (with a focus on harmful effect, side effects, unreliability) (Paprzycka, Dec-Pietrowska, & Walendzik-Ostrowska, 2016).

9

How Do Intimate Relationships Relate to Well-Being?

Previous research has indicated that social relationships are important predictors of well-being, but that the quality of the relationships is more important than merely having the relationships (Saphire-Bernstein & Taylor, 2013).

In this chapter, associations with having a current partner, as well as with relationship satisfaction and relationship commitment, are explored in terms of the following:

- Happiness
- Depression
- Anxiety
- Life satisfaction
- Life as fulfilling and meaningful
- Self-esteem

HOW HAS WELL-BEING BEEN CONCEPTUALIZED IN THE PAST?

Happiness is viewed by psychologists as an emotional response, while **life satisfaction** is viewed as a cognitive evaluation (Diener, Oishi, & Lucas, 2002). Across a sample of 123 countries, Tay and Diener (2011) found that positive feelings were most associated with fulfilling social and esteem needs, while life evaluation was most associated with fulfilling basic needs such as food and shelter.

Seligman (2012) expanded the conceptualization of happiness and well-being to include not only positive emotions but a life that is flourishing. He argued that the following contribute to well-being:

- Positive emotions – happiness plus excitement, pride, awe, positive outcomes
- Engagement – involvement, passion, challenge, absorption, flow*
- Relationships – essential for positive emotions
- Meaning – finding meaning and purpose in life

- Accomplishments – pursuit of success and mastery

*Flow is described by Csikszentmihályi (1990) as involving deep concentration in an activity that is intrinsically rewarding, in which you lose track of time. It is also called being "in the zone" in which you are oblivious of everything around you.

Negative emotional responses include **depression** and **anxiety.** Seligman (1972) explained depression in terms of learned helplessness. This occurs from a feeling of lack of control in an aversive situation. Beck argued that depression involves negative thoughts about the world, the future, and the self. He developed the Beck Depression Inventory to measure these negative thoughts (Beck et al., 1961).

Anxiety is distinguished from fear in being a response to a perceived future threat instead of a perceived immediate threat (American Psychiatric Association (2013). A certain amount of anxiety is motivating, but too much is debilitating. And persistent anxiety can be a psychiatric condition.

Evaluation of one's own worth and abilities is called **self-esteem.** It involves both thoughts and feelings about the self. One of the most widely used measures is the Rosenberg Self-Esteem Scale (Rosenberg, 1965). Previous research has found that self-esteem has a positive effect on relationship quality in romantic relationships (Erol & Orth, 2016).

Other researchers have documented the importance of personal relationships for physical health (Holt-Lunstad, 2018; House, Landis, & Umberson, 1988;). In the present study "your health and fitness" is part of the Appearance Satisfaction factor discussed later in this chapter.

HOW IS HAPPINESS MEASURED AND CORRELATED?

In the present study, happiness is measured using the following single question that is often used in social surveys, such as the European Social Survey (Greve, 2010), except that the present study uses possible responses from 0=NOT AT ALL to 8=EXTREMELY.

- Taking all things together, how happy would you say you are?

Happiness is somewhat correlated with Having a Current Partner (r=.19***), and strongly correlated with Relationship Satisfaction (r=.60***) and Relationship Commitment (r=.40***). It is likely that having a satisfying and committed relationship promotes happiness, but it is also likely that happy people are more likely to be successful in establishing and maintaining satisfying and committed relationships (Stutzer & Frey, 2006). Happiness is combined with other measures of emotional well-being in SEM models later in this chapter.

HOW IS DEPRESSION MEASURED AND CORRELATED?

Previous research has found depression negatively related to commitment in both opposite-sex and same-sex couples (Kurdek, 1997). Depression is measured in this study using the following five items, which load on a single factor that is similar across relationship types (CFI=.981, RMSEA=.020) and cultural regions (CFI=.968, RMSEA=.025). The minus indicates that the item is scored in reverse.

- + I feel discouraged about the future
- + Enjoyable vs. Miserable
- + Full vs. Empty
- + Brings out the best in me vs. Doesn't give me a chance
- − Discouraging vs. Hopeful

The first item is from the Beck Depression Inventory (Beck et al., 1961). The other four are from Ways of Characterizing "Life in General" (Campbell, Converse, and Rodgers, 1976), which appear in this study under the question "How would you describe your present life?" Possible responses are from 0 to 8, which are averaged to create a Depression Scale.

This Depression Scale is negatively correlated with Having a Current Partner ($r=-.19^{***}$), Relationship Satisfaction ($r=-.38^{***}$), and Relationship Commitment ($r=-.21^{***}$). In other words, those without a current partner, and those who have low relationship satisfaction or low relationship commitment, are more depressed. Conversely, those who are more depressed have lower relationship satisfaction and lower relationship commitment. Longitudinal research has found that the causal direction goes both ways over time among newlyweds (Davila et al., 2003).

HOW IS ANXIETY MEASURED AND CORRELATED?

Anxiety is measured in this study using the following items, which load similarly on a single factor that is consistent across relationship types (CFI=.950, RMSEA=.029) and cultural regions (CFI=.966, RMSEA=.025):

- − I generally feel at ease
- − Worried vs. Confident
- − Nervous vs. Calm
- − Tense vs. Relaxed
- + Easy vs. Hard

These items also have possible responses from 0 to 8, which are averaged to form an Anxiety Scale. This scale is trivially correlated with Having a Current Partner ($r<.10$) but negatively correlated with Relationship Satisfaction ($r=-.25^{***}$) and Relationship Commitment ($r=-.11^{***}$). In other words, those with low relationship satisfaction or low relationship commitment have more anxiety. Conversely, those with high anxiety have lower relationship satisfaction and lower relationship commitment. A longitudinal study of newlyweds found that the negative relationship between anxiety and marital satisfaction remained stable over time (Caughlin, Huston, & Houts, 2000).

HOW DO EMOTIONAL RESPONSES COMBINE IN SEM MODELS?

Structural Equation Modeling (SEM) is introduced in Chapter 1. SEM Structural Models combine Happiness, Depression, and Anxiety to reveal associations with Having a Current Partner. These models are similar across gender (CFI=999, RMSEA=.017) and cultural regions (CFI=998, RMSEA=.007).

These models reveal that Happiness is a Central Factor (γ=.15). Depression and Anxiety add trivial explained variance when Happiness is taken into account. Reasons why those with a current partner might be happier are discussed in the SPOTLIGHT on Well-Being of Partnered vs. Single People later in this chapter. On the other hand, family members can be a source of stress, especially if a family member is disabled. See the SPOTLIGHT on Spouses with a Special Needs Child later in this chapter.

SEM Structural Models also combine Happiness, Depression, and Anxiety to reveal links with Relationship Satisfaction, and links with Relationship Commitment independent of Relationship Satisfaction. These models are similar across relationship types (CFI=.982, RMSEA=.025) and cultural regions (CFI=.986, RMSEA=.018).

These models reveal that Happiness is a Central Factor (γ=.54) in links to Relationship Satisfaction. And Depression and Anxiety add trivial explained variance when Happiness is taken into account. Previous research has found that positive emotions of well-being and negative emotions of depression loaded on a single dimension instead of separate dimensions (Siddaway, Wood, & Taylor, 2017).

There are no direct associations between emotional responses and Relationship Commitment independent of Relationship Satisfaction. In other words, Relationship Commitment is correlated with Happiness only because Relationship Commitment is associated with Relationship Satisfaction, which is associated with Happiness.

HOW IS LIFE SATISFACTION MEASURED AND CORRELATED?

Previous research has found that persons high in life satisfaction are more likely to marry (Mastekaasa, 1992). A study in China found that lower marital adjustment was correlated with lower life satisfaction as well as with psychiatric symptoms and reports of poor health (Shek, 1995). A review of twenty-three studies found that job satisfaction and overall life satisfaction are somewhat correlated (Rice, Near, & Hunt, 1980). And two studies found that body image dissatisfaction was related to marital dissatisfaction (Friedman et al., 1999; Meltzer & McNulty, 2010).

In the present study life satisfaction is measured using items from the twenty-five-year follow-up of the Boston Couples Study (Hill & Peplau, 2001), under the question, "Currently, how satisfied are you with each of the following aspects of your life?"

Factor analyses reveal four factors:

- **General life satisfaction**: your life as a whole, your educational level, your interests and hobbies, your relationships with other family members, your relationships with friends
- **Job satisfaction**: your employment status (full time or part time or unemployed), your job, your household income
- **Appearance satisfaction**: your appearance, your weight, your health and fitness
- **Partner satisfaction**: your commitment status (single, married, or other committed relationship), your relationship with your spouse or partner, your sex life

General Life Satisfaction has similar factor loadings across relationship types (CFI=.952, RMSEA=.0–28) and cultural regions (CFI=.952, RMSEA=.025). Job Satisfaction has similar loadings across relationship types (CFI=.999, RMSEA=.009) and cultural regions (CFI=.992, RMSEA=.021). And Appearance Satisfaction has similar loadings across relationship types (CFI=.997, RMSEA=.015) and cultural regions (CFI=.001, RMSEA=.023). Each of these sets of items is averaged to form a scale.

The Partner Satisfaction factor is confounded (overlaps) with Relationship Satisfaction and Relationship Commitment in this study, so it is omitted from further data analyses. Separate from these four factors are two items: satisfaction with your number of children, and satisfaction with your childcare arrangements.

Having a Current Partner is slightly correlated with the General Life Satisfaction Scale (r=.10***), Job Satisfaction Scale (r=.11***), Appearance Satisfaction Scale (r=.12***), Satisfaction with Number of Children (r=.16***), and Satisfaction with Childcare Arrangements (r=.16***).

Relationship Satisfaction is also correlated with the General Life Satisfaction Scale (r=.37***), Job Satisfaction Scale (r=.19***), Appearance Satisfaction Scale (r=.21***), Satisfaction with Number of Children (r=.10***), and Satisfaction with Childcare Arrangements (r=.11***).

And Relationship Commitment is correlated with the Life Satisfaction Scale (r=.18***) and Job Satisfaction scale (r=.14***), but only trivially (r<.10) with the Appearance Satisfaction Scale, Satisfaction with Number of Children, and Satisfaction with Childcare Arrangements.

It is likely that having a partner can contribute to life satisfaction, but it is also likely that those with greater life satisfaction can more easily achieve and maintain a satisfying and committed relationship. Since childcare arrangements are not relevant to all participants, it is omitted from SEM Structural Models later in this chapter.

The following questions evaluating **life as fulfilling and meaningful** are also asked:

• My job or career is (or was) very fulfilling to me.
• My leisure activities are very fulfilling to me.
• My personal relationships are very fulfilling to me.
• Overall, my life is meaningful to me.

These four items load on a factor that is consistent across relationship types (CFI=.966, RMSEA=.029) and cultural regions (CFI=.965, RMSEA=.027). They are averaged to create a scale of Life Fulfilling and Meaningful that is correlated with Having a Current Partner (r=.15***), and with Relationship Satisfaction (r=.32***) and Relationship Commitment (r=.18***). Life Satisfaction and Evaluating Life measures are combined with other evaluative well-being measures in SEM models later in this chapter.

HOW IS SELF-ESTEEM MEASURED AND CORRELATED?

Previous research on opposite-sex dating couples has found that lower self-esteem of individuals and their partners predicts lower relationship satisfaction and commitment (Robinson & Cameron, 2012). To measure self-esteem in the present study, the following three items from the Rosenberg (1965) Self-Esteem Scale are used, with the negative indicating that the item is scored in reverse:

• + On the whole, I am satisfied with myself.
• − All in all, I am inclined to think that I am a failure.
• + I take a positive attitude toward myself.

These three items load similarly on a single factor across eight relationship types (CFI=.997, RMSEA=.014) and nine cultural regions (CFI=.992, RMSEA=.021). They are averaged to form a Self-Esteem Scale, which is correlated with having a Current Partner (r=.15***), and with Relationship Satisfaction (r=.28***) and Relationship Commitment (r=.14***). It is likely that having a partner promotes self-esteem, and self-esteem promotes establishing and maintaining a satisfying and committed relationship. The distinction between explicit and implicit self-esteem is discussed in the SPOTLIGHT on Implicit and Explicit Self-Esteem later in this chapter.

HOW DO EVALUATION RESPONSES COMBINE IN
SEM MODELS?

The General Life Satisfaction Scale, Job Satisfaction Scale, Appearance Satisfaction Scale, satisfaction with number of children, Life Fulfilling and Meaningful Scale, and Self-Esteem Scale are combined in SEM Structural Models to reveal links with Having a Current Partner. These models are similar across gender (CFI=.999, RMSEA=.018) and nine cultural regions (CFI=.996, RMSEA=.012). They reveal that Satisfaction with Number of Children is a Central Factor (γ=.14). What this means is that those with a current partner are more likely to be satisfied with their number of children, while those without a Current Partner are more likely to be dissatisfied with their number of children or not having children. Other evaluation responses add trivial explained variance.

The General Life Satisfaction Scale, Job Satisfaction Scale, Appearance Satisfaction Scale, number of children satisfaction, Life Fulfilling and Meaningful Scale, and Self Esteem Scale are combined in SEM Structural Models to reveal associations with Relationship Satisfaction, and with Relationship Commitment independent of Relationship Satisfaction. They are consistent across eight relationship types (CFI=.987, RMSEA=.019) and nine cultural regions (CFI=.987, RMSEA=.016).

These models reveal that the General Life Satisfaction Scale (γ=.21) and Life Fulfilling and Meaningful Scale (γ=.16) are Central Factors in links with Relationship Satisfaction. Associations of evaluative responses with Relationship Commitment independent of Relationship Satisfaction are trivial (r<.1), indicating that their associations with Relationship Commitment are through Relationship Satisfaction.

HOW WELL DID SELF-RATINGS PREDICT LIFE
SATISFACTION OVER TIME IN THE BCS?

In the 25-year follow-up of the Boston Couples Study, life satisfaction at age 45 was strongly correlated with self-esteem and the quality of the relationship with the current spouse or partner. In addition, high satisfaction with self in college at age 20 predicted life satisfaction 25 years later (Hill & Peplau, 2001).

Among those participating in the present study, 66 had participated in the Boston Couples Study either as a member of a couple (n=57) or in another group of students not in a couple at that time (n=9). For them, the current study was a 38-year follow-up at age 58 of their responses at age 20. Table 9.1 shows characteristics on which they rated themselves at age 20 and the correlations with their self-ratings on the same characteristics (labeled

TABLE 9.1 *Correlations between age 20 and age 58*

	Same	LifeSat
• Creativity	.37**	.21
• Physical Attractiveness	.37**	.33*
• Intelligence	.17	.38**
• Self-Confidence	.34**	.08
• Desirability as a dating partner#	.20	.43**
• Desirability as a marriage partner#	.21	.37**

#At age 58 there was just one question about desirability, which was worded "Desirable as a partner in a committed relationship."

Same) at age 58. Also shown are the correlations of those self-ratings at age 20 with the General Life Satisfaction Scale (labeled LifeSat), at age 58.

In other words, how college students rated themselves on creativity, physical attractiveness, and self-confidence at age 20 to some extent predicted how they rated themselves on these characteristics 38 years later. Rating the self as more physically attractive, more intelligent, and more desirable as a dating partner or marriage partner, at age 20, to some extent predicted general life satisfaction at age 58. How you evaluate yourself at age 20 may affect the choices you make, the opportunities you pursue, and how you respond to stressful situations, affecting your satisfaction with life decades later.

SELF-REFLECTION

How happy are you? How satisfied are you with various aspects of your life? Do you have people you can count on to provide social support? Do you have persistent feelings of sadness or anxiety? If so, have you considered seeking professional help?

IN SUMMARY, WHAT CENTRAL FACTORS HAVE BEEN IDENTIFIED IN THIS CHAPTER?

Having a Current Partner, Happiness, and Satisfaction with Number of Children are Central Factors. They capture the predictions of other factors. SEM models reveal that these Central Factors make similar predictions across gender and nine cultural regions.

For Relationship Satisfaction and Relationship Commitment, Happiness, the General Life Satisfaction Scale, and the Life Fulfilling and Meaningful

Scale, are Central Factors. These capture the predictions of other factors. SEM models reveal that these Central Factors make similar predictions across eight relationship types and nine cultural regions.

The predictions of these Central Factors are similar, even though the levels of these factors may vary. These Central Factors will be discussed further in Chapter 12 in relation to implications of the study for well-being.

SPOTLIGHT ON WELL-BEING OF PARTNERED VS. SINGLE PEOPLE

CLAUDIA C. BRUMBAUGH

In adulthood, romantic partners often fulfill an important role in people's lives. A partner is typically the "go-to" person for emotional support, intimacy, and providing a sense of security (Finkel et al., 2015). Romantic partners can also fulfill more practical functions such as contributing to each other's financial stability and caring for each other when physical health is at stake. Aside from these things, partners serve as a source of fun and entertainment, whether it's enjoying a new restaurant or going on an island vacation. For all of these reasons, romantic partners have the capacity to contribute to one's emotional and physical well-being.

To understand whether romantic relationships have positive effects on individuals, outcomes between coupled and single people have been assessed. Differences in numerous psychological variables have been found between single and romantically involved individuals. For instance, being married has been shown to relate to fewer reports of loneliness (Cacioppo & Hawkley, 2005). Partnered people are also more trusting and comfortable relying on others (Brumbaugh & Fraley, 2015). Finally, compared to single individuals, people in romantic relationships have greater attachment security (Brumbaugh, 2017). These findings all demonstrate that having a partner may increase one's sense of faith in others. The availability of a close romantic partner likely encourages people to have more positive feelings about their social world and safety net.

Aside from personal outcomes, feelings about dating and past partners also differ between partnered and single people. Brumbaugh and Fraley (2015) found that people who were in a current relationship reported more confidence in their romantic desirability and relational future. Because individuals who are dating have already demonstrated that they have the ability to attract another partner, their confidence may be higher than that of singles who might have more uncertainty about their romantic future and ability to find a mate. Brumbaugh and Fraley (2015) further found that partnered people reported fewer lingering feelings for their ex-partners, and partnered individuals had less contact with their ex-partners. This finding is congruent with other research findings showing that single people take longer to detach from ex-partners (Wang & Amato, 2000).

The broadest indicator of happiness in life is subjective well-being, and most research finds that people in relationships have higher well-being compared to those who are single (e.g., Brumbaugh & Fraley, 2015). However, not all relationships are equal, so other factors in the relationship must be considered. Not surprisingly, people who are more content in their romantic relationship tend to be happier in life than those in less satisfying relationships (Kamp Dush & Amato, 2005). Because romantic mates are so central to one's daily life, being less happy with the relationship may affect one's overall sense of well-being. Unhappy relationships seem to have a greater negative impact on women's happiness compared to men's (Levenson, Carstensen, & Gottman, 1993). This connection may stem from women's tendency to place a higher value on close relationships than men do (Rose & Rudolph, 2006). Emotional contagion can also occur within romantic relationships, wherein one person's unhappiness spreads to a spouse such that the spouse becomes unhappy (Tower & Kasl, 1996). Fortunately, however, the reverse is true and happiness can also spread between partners.

The exact status of the relationship matters as well, with married people having the highest well-being, followed by cohabiting, exclusively dating, and casually dating individuals (Kamp Dush & Amato, 2005). This pattern suggests that the commitment level and stability of the relationship is a moderating factor in how happy people feel. Various reasons for marriage's ability to provide happiness exist. One argument is that selection effects are at work, where people who are happier are more likely to get married and stay together. For instance, Lucas and colleagues (2003) found that people who would eventually divorce were already less happy prior to their wedding. Likewise, cheerful people may be more attractive as mates and thus find themselves more frequently initiating relationships that can lead to marriage. Thus, people who enter into relationships may already be happier even before they become involved in the relationship. However, support for selection effects in this domain is tenuous (Kamp Dush & Amato, 2005).

Another reason is that the social support provided by marriage makes people happier and healthier. It has also been proposed that people who are committed to relational roles (e.g., spouse) have a greater sense of identity and self-worth (Stryker & Burke, 2002). Finally, because society supports the institution of marriage, being married may make people feel more "normal" and thus happier. Indeed, most people idealize marriage and expect marriage to be a positive event in their lives (DePaulo & Morris, 2006). In sum, marriage appears to be a protective factor in maintaining well-being, regardless of the exact mechanisms.

Although an argument has been made here that relationships correspond to better psychological outcomes, this discussion would not be complete without some caveats. One issue that has been pointed out is that researchers cannot experimentally manipulate whether someone enters into a relationship, and so random assignment to relational status is impossible (DePaulo, 2016). Thus, the causality of some of these effects should be called into question. Another point is that the relational status of "single" can also mean *once*-married (and divorced). Some research may lump people of different backgrounds into the "single" category, which could cloud true effects.

Finally, some research demonstrates that the psychological benefits of being married may be fleeting. A longitudinal study conducted by Lucas and colleagues (2003) found an interesting long-term pattern regarding how marriage affects people's feelings of happiness. Specifically, around the wedding date, people had a small increase in happiness but then returned to their original pre-wedding baseline happiness about five years later. This same pattern of a boost in well-being immediately after the wedding, followed by a gradual decline, was also found by Luhmann and colleagues (2012). It should be noted that these longitudinal findings reflect how people react on average; however, there was still abundant variation in people's happiness trajectories.

Overall, the research on relationship status as it relates to psychological health points to a protective function of relationships, where having a romantic partner shields people from negative psychological states and feelings. Although the origins of this happiness can be debated, the general pattern of findings is that having a romantic partner correlates to better outcomes. Ideally, a romantic mate, whether it's a dating partner or spouse, lifts one to a higher place and gives a sense of security that they have someone to rely on and share their daily experiences.

SPOTLIGHT ON SPOUSES WITH A SPECIAL NEEDS CHILD

VERED SHENAAR-GOLAN AND OFRA WALTER

Subjective well-being has been strongly associated with social relationships (Kansky & Diener, 2017; Oishi, Diener, & Lucas, 2007). Previous studies considered supportive social relationships to be one of the strongest outcomes of subjective well-being (e.g., Kansky & Diener, 2017). Within social relationships, marriage is associated with higher levels of well-being and lower psychological distress (Diener, Gohm, Suh, & Oishi, 2000). Generally, married persons seem to have the highest levels of well-being, while the formerly married (widowed, divorced, separated) tend to have the lowest levels (see, for example, Dolan, Peasgood, & White 2008).

Studies indicate that happier people and those with high life satisfaction are more likely to get married, stay married, and report higher happiness and satisfaction with their partner (Luhmann, Lucas, Eid, & Diener, 2013). Based on frequent findings that point to the idea of a marriage benefit, Kansky and Diener (2017) recently suggested a possible mechanism for the link between well-being and romantic stability and success, in which happy people not just tend to report less negative conflict but are also better able to manage conflict when it arises.

The relationship between parenthood and well-being however, yielded conflicting findings, with some studies indicating that parenthood is associated with higher well-being (Aassve, Goisis, & Sironi, 2012; Nelson, Kushlev, & Lyubomirsky, 2014), and others suggesting the reverse (Evenson & Simon, 2005). Examination of these relationships among parents of children with special needs may yield an even more complex picture.

Caring for a child with special needs is often associated with challenging caregiving demands (Larson, 2010; McCann, Bull, & Winzenberg, 2012). In fact, research studies that examined parents of a child with special needs have described those parents as undergoing continuous coping experiences (Bernier, 1990). This caregiving situation causes financial hardship due to various treatments the child may require (Emerson et al., 2009; Lin et al., 2009), can disrupt the family balance and strains marital relationships (Fleischman, 2004; Hartley et al., 2010; Peer & Hillman, 2014), and entails a psychological and social burden that may strongly affect the subjective well-being of the parents (Isa et al., 2013; Resch, Mireles, Benz, Grenweldge, Peterson, & Zhang, 2010).

The parents' spousal relationship may be affected, as decisions surrounding a child with special needs may incur feelings of embarrassment, guilt, and conflict, leading to tension between the parents (Goldberg et al., 1990; Kazak & Christakis, 1994). One of the consequences of this situation is a higher rate of marriage dissatisfaction and divorce among those parents (Hartley et al., 2010).

Alongside studies that focused on the difficulties of parenting children with special needs, other studies have revealed the positive influences that raising a child with special needs can actually have on the family framework (Green, 2007; Peer & Hillman, 2014), such as greater cooperation between the parents (Scorgie & Sobsey, 2000). Moreover, these families maintain that their parenting for an exceptional child involves a constant learning process that preserves the marriage and deepens their commitment to the entire family unit. Parents may feel as if they are a team that stands together in the struggle to obtain community services and works together for the sake of the child's progress; this sense of teamwork surely strengthens the spousal connection (Fleischmann, 2004).

On the other hand, this ongoing coping effort can be expressed in a constant state of fatigue and in neglect of the spouse and other family members, all of which can contribute to an imbalanced homeostasis in the family framework and a decline in subjective well-being (Cummins et al., 2009a; Levy-Schiff & Schulman, 1997).

Generally, studies that examined variables predicting subjective well-being have found that social support from families (Garcia & Sison, 2012), and especially the individual's partner (Cummins, 2000), increases one's sense of subjective well-being. In the case of parents of a child with special needs, this type of social support is a source of existential security and provides a sense of control over their lives (Resch, Benz, & Elliott, 2012). Furthermore, a parent's perceived level of functioning in various areas, such as family, leisure time, and work, correlates to one's subjective well-being (Myers, Sweeney, & Witmer, 2000).

In our studies among parents of children with special needs and developmental disabilities in Israel (Shenaar-Golan, 2016, 2017), we found lower levels of subjective well-being than the average for Western populations (Cummins et al., 2014). Further to these findings of low subjective well-being, our study clarifies among other variables that being in a partnered relationship and perception of the child's disability as positively influencing central aspects of the parents' life, are significant contributors to raising parental subjective well-being (Shenaar-Golan, 2017).

An additional finding is that married parents have higher levels of subjective well-being than separated or divorced parents. And that parental positive appraisal of the disability's impact on family functioning and the couple's relationship resulted in a convergence of subjective well-being values higher than the mean range of values for the sample (Shenaar-Golan, 2016).

This finding is added to a long line of research studies that have documented that marriage correlates to higher subjective well-being values (Diener, 1984; Diener & McGavran, 2008), and that components of the partnered relationship such as intimacy of married life and the emotional support of the partner positively affect subjective well-being (Cummins et al.,

2009b; Smith, Greenberg, & Seltzer, 2012). Support of a life partner in situations of ongoing stress is preferred over all other types of support, as it is stable, effective, and readily available, lending various types of support that benefit subjective well-being (Garcia & Sison, 2012; Horlsey & Oliver, 2013).

It is important to note that most of the findings reviewed in this SPOTLIGHT are based on studies with Western, primarily North American samples. Moreover very few studies have directly examined culture as a moderator of parents' well-being. Views about parenthood and parental practices differ across cultures. Culture may play a role in parents' emotional experiences, norms for the timing of parenthood, number of children, centrality of children in parents' lives, and differences in gender roles (Krueger et al., 2009). Each of these cultural differences may have important implications for parents' well-being (Nelson, Kushlev, & Lyubomirsky, 2014). Many more studies are needed to understand these differences.

SPOTLIGHT ON IMPLICIT AND EXPLICIT SELF-ESTEEM

TAKAFUMI SAWAUMI AND TSUTOMU INAGAKI (FUJII)

As readers may already understand, intimate relationships affect well-being. But we point out a possibility that there is a bidirectional association between intimate relationships and well-being. We explore this in terms of "implicit" as compared with "explicit" self-esteem. Explicit self-esteem is the evaluation of self of which you are consciously aware. Implicit self-esteem is the evaluation of self that is not directly accessible to awareness.

In this SPOTLIGHT, we introduce two lines of research using implicit measurement of self-esteem: (a) how intimate relationships affect self-esteem and (b) how self-esteem affects intimate relationships. Before getting into more detail, we elaborate further on the measurement issue.

One popular way of measuring implicit self-esteem is the Implicit Association Test (IAT; Greenwald, McGhee, & Schwartz, 1998). In the IAT, all you need to do is sit at a computer and start a program (note that a standard program is provided for free on a company website, Millisecond). Then you are asked to categorize target words that will appear one after another at the center of the screen into a left or right category by pressing assigned keys on a keyboard. The target words are positive or negative attributes of the self. Your implicit self-esteem is based on your reaction time, with longer times indicating hesitancy in endorsing the term.

Another popular way of measuring implicit self-esteem is the Name-Letter Task (NLT; Nuttin, 1985). In the NLT, you are asked to answer your degree of liking for each letter of the alphabet. Your relative preference to letters matching your name, in comparison to other letters, determines your score of implicit self-esteem.

To consider how intimate relationships affect implicit self-esteem, we introduce one important study conducted by Dehart, Pelham, Fiedorowicz, Carvallo, and Gabriel (2011). In their study, the NLT and other scales were administered to participants who were recruited across a wide range of backgrounds (i.e., students, mothers, workers). The study revealed a positive relation between their own implicit self-esteem and their implicit evaluations of their significant others – romantic partners in this context. Highlighting the issue of causal direction, the authors suggested two possibilities to understand this phenomenon: (a) people may project their implicit self-regard onto their implicit evaluations of close others or (b) people's own implicit self-evaluation may be affected by their implicit evaluations of close others.

The latter explanation seems to have an important implication for romantic relationships: the more positive people's implicit attitude toward their romantic partner, the higher their own implicit self-esteem. Close attention has been directed toward research on how implicit attitudes change (e.g., Gawronski & Bodenhausen, 2006). It would be worthwhile to examine a possibility of changing people's implicit attitude toward their romantic partner for the better, perhaps leading to their own improved implicit self-esteem. Conversely, a negative change in implicit attitude toward the partner could decrease one's implicit self-esteem.

To explore people's own views of self-esteem and intimate relationships, we did a preliminary interview survey with ten Japanese university students in August 2017. Most interestingly, most of the informants mentioned the ambivalent nature of romantic relationships. On the one hand, they answered that intimate relationships can boost their own self-esteem or, more broadly, self-evaluation and self-confidence by attaining encouragement from their partner when they are in trouble, by being praised by others on the relationship, and by feeling a sense of superiority over others who are not in any intimate relationship. For example, one female informant said, "I would confirm my identity as a girlfriend of him while sitting behind him on a motorcycle," meaning a feeling of superiority over other females who do not have their boyfriend to allow them to do so. A male participant said, "I would feel glad if other people around me know about my intimate relationship," which again points to positive feelings.

On the other hand, as almost all participants recounted, intimate relationships can damage their self-esteem by comparing themselves with their partner who is better off and feeling a sense of inferiority, by experiencing a conflict of opinions and values, by hearing some stories about ex-partners of their partner, and by being worried at all times about how the relationship will go.

To show how implicit self-esteem can affect intimate relationships, we mention two of our own studies. Fujii, Sawaumi, and Aikawa (2014) showed, by using the IAT, that those who are discrepant between their level of implicit self-esteem and their level of explicit self-esteem are more likely to be less assertive. Discrepancy in this context can be defined in either way: those who are high in implicit self-esteem and low in explicit self-esteem and vice versa. Thus, it is fair to anticipate that in intimate relationships, people who understand their high self-esteem on a self-report basis but in actuality are low when measured at an implicit or unconscious level – namely, by means of the IAT or the NLT – would be less likely to express their own opinion.

In our interview study mentioned earlier, one male informant who was high in explicit self-esteem but low in implicit self-esteem answered, consistently with our prediction that he did not stick to his own way and was ready to follow what his partner said. More interestingly, he also responded that when the relationship seemed to get bitter, he would avoid the situation and go outside of his house by himself to calm down, suggesting the Japanese typicality of avoidance coping or secondary control (for more detail, see Ohbuchi, Fukushima, & Tedeschi, 1999; Sawaumi, Yamaguchi, Park, & Robinson, 2015).

In conclusion, there is evidence that self-esteem can affect intimate relationships, and intimate relationships can affect self-esteem.

10

How Do the Predictions Combine in Comprehensive Models?

To capture the complex predictions from the previous chapters, these predictions are summarized in this chapter and combined to create a *Comprehensive Partner Model* and a *Comprehensive Commitment Model*. The chapter discusses how well these models predict, what is surprising about the findings, and why the same factors make similar predictions across relationship types and cultural regions.

WHAT ARE COMPREHENSIVE FACTORS?

Chapter 1 noted that when predictor factors are correlated with each other, what they predict in common may be accounted for by the factor with the strongest effect, leaving little additional variance to be accounted for by other factors correlated with it. This may be reflected in low standardized regression coefficients for the other factors, even if they have sizable correlations with the dependent variable. The strongest predictor factors that are correlated with other predictor factors and capture what they predict in common, or have additional effects beyond what they have in common, are called Central Factors in this book.

For example, Chapter 5 identifies sexual satisfaction as a Central Factor in predicting relationship satisfaction. It captures positive effects of sexual frequency, ideal sexual frequency, and equal interest in having sex, as well as negative effects of having sex when you don't want to, since they are correlated with it.

Just as Central Factors capture effects of combining other factors in a chapter, Comprehensive Factors capture effects of combining Central Factors across chapters. When Central Factors are combined from several chapters, what they have in common may be accounted for by the Central Factors with the strongest effects, leaving little additional variance to be accounted for by other Central Factors correlated with them. This may be

TABLE 10.1 *Central Factors predicting Having a Current Partner*

Chapter 2. What are people seeking in intimate relationships?	
+ Having had a previous partner	(γ=.19)
− Difficulty finding a partner	(γ=−.16)
− Interested in finding a partner	(γ=−.12)
+ Desiring sexual activities	(γ=.11)
Chapter 3. How are intimate partners selected?	
+ Rating self desirable as a partner	(γ=.19)
+ Age	(γ=.16)
+Personality Important scale	(γ=.10)
Chapter 5. How do sexual attitudes and behaviors matter?	
+ Approve sex for unmarried man in love	(γ=.12)

reflected in low standardized regression coefficients for the other Central Factors.

The strongest Central Factors that are correlated with other Central Factors and capture what they have in common, or have additional effects beyond what they have in common, are called Comprehensive Factors in this chapter. It doesn't mean that the other Central Factors are not important, but that their effects are captured by the Comprehensive Factors that are correlated with them.

WHAT CENTRAL FACTORS PREDICT HAVING A CURRENT PARTNER?

Central Factors from each of the chapters that predict Having a Current Partner either positively (+) or negatively (−) are listed in Table 10.1, with their standardized regression coefficients from SEM Structural Models in those chapters.

WHAT COMPREHENSIVE FACTORS CAPTURE PREDICTIONS OF HAVING A CURRENT PARTNER?

To identify Comprehensive Factors that capture the effects of all of the Central Factors in predicting Having a Current Partner, these Central Factors are combined in SEM Structural Models. These models are similar across gender (CFI=1.00, RMSEA=.001) and nine cultural regions (CFI=.978, RMSEA=.015). Table 10.2 reveals the Comprehensive Factors in predicting Having a Current Partner.

The other Central Factors add trivial explained variance after those factors are taken into account. These Comprehensive Factors, and the other

TABLE 10.2 *Comprehensive Factors predicting Having a Current Partner*

+ Rating self desirable as a partner	(γ=.19)
+ Having had a previous partner	(γ=.13)
+ Age	(γ=.10)
− Difficulty finding a partner	(γ=−.15)
− Interested in finding a partner	(γ=−.12)

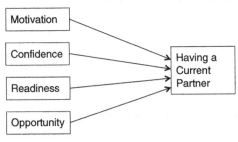

FIGURE 10.1 *Comprehensive Partner Model*

Central Factors that they capture, can be interpreted as reflecting the following theoretical concepts:

- **Motivation** – reflected in having had and desiring to replace a previous partner
- **Confidence** – reflected in rating self desirable as a partner
- **Readiness** – reflected in age
- **Opportunity** – reflected in less difficulty finding a partner

These concepts, and the factors reflecting them, constitute the *Comprehensive Partner Model* developed in this book, as shown in Figure 10.1.

These Comprehensive Factors make similar predictions of having a current partner, across both genders and nine cultural regions. This is in spite of any variations in the average levels of these factors, which will be discussed in Chapter 11. However, these factors together have a multiple correlation of R=.40, which when squared explains only 16 percent of the variation in Having a Current Partner. Hence there is a great deal of individual variation, with additional factors or better measures to be determined in further research.

WHAT CENTRAL FACTORS PREDICT RELATIONSHIP SATISFACTION OR RELATIONSHIP COMMITMENT?

Central Factors from Chapters 2 to 8 that predict Relationship Satisfaction, or Relationship Commitment regardless of Relationship Satisfaction, are listed

TABLE 10.3 *Central Factors predicting satisfaction or commitment*

	Satisfaction	Commitment
Chapter 2. What are people seeking in intimate relationships?		
+ Goal: Having a Committed Partner	(γ=.20)	(γ=.13)
+ Self-Transcendence Values	(γ=.10)	
+ Believing True Love Lasts Forever	(γ=.10)	
− Anxious Attachment	(γ=−.14)	
− Interested in Finding a Partner	(γ=−.12)	
Chapter 3. How are intimate partners selected?		
+ Personality Similarity Scale	(γ=.29)	
+ Intelligence Similarity Scale	(γ=.13)	
+ Similar on Willingness to Have Children	(γ=.21)	(γ=.15)
+ Rating Partner Desirable as Partner	(γ=.46)	(γ=.27)
+ Rating Self Desirable as Partner	(γ=.12)	
+ Rating Partner Intelligent Scale	(γ=.12)	
Chapter 4. What is love and how is intimacy expressed?		
+ Emotional Closeness	(γ=.30)	
+ Four Component Love Scale	(γ=.21)	(γ=.25)
+ Saying Both of Us Are in Love	(γ=.14)	(γ=.29)
+ Own Expression of Affection	(γ=.12)	
+ Eros (We Were Made for Each Other)		(γ=.20)
+ How Often Partners Communicate	(γ=.45)	(γ=.29)
+ Trusting Partner Not to Lie	(γ=.21)	
+ Never Lying to Partner	(γ=.12)	
+ How Well Know Partner	(γ=.12)	
+ Own Disclosure Scale	(γ=.13)	(γ=.35)
+ How Often Partners See Each Other		(γ=.20)
Chapter 5. How do sexual attitudes and behaviors matter?		
+ Sexual Satisfaction	(γ=.44)	
− Partner's Extra-Relationship Sex	(varies)	
− Approval of Partner's Outside Sex		(varies)
Chapter 6. What are the dynamics of exchange and power?		
+ Gained Benefits from the Relationship	(γ=.42)	
+ Equal Involvement in the Relationship	(γ=.30)	
+ Equal Power in the Relationship	(γ=.10)	
+ Invested in the Relationship		(γ=.16)
Chapter 7. How do couples cope with conflict?		
+ Positive Responses Scale	(γ=.28)	
+ Voice (Would Discuss and Fix Things Up)	(γ=.22)	
− Highest Sources of Conflict Scale	(γ=−.11)	
− Uncertainties Conflict Scale	(γ=−.12)	

Continued

TABLE 10.3 *(cont.)*

	Satisfaction	Commitment
– Expectations Conflict Scale	($\gamma=-.10$)	
– Exit (Would Break Up if Dissatisfied)	($\gamma=-.16$)	($\gamma=-.16$)
– Partner's Verbal Violence Scale	($\gamma=-.12$)	
– Partner Breaking Up and Coming Back	($\gamma=-.16$)	
+ Own Expression of Jealousy		($\gamma=.10$)
Chapter 8. How do external factors impact relationships?		
+ Parents Know Partner	($\gamma=.11$)	($\gamma=.15$)
+ Parents' and Others' Approval of Partner	($\gamma=.40$)	
+ Coping with Stress	($\gamma=.13$)	
– Impacts of Life Domains	($\gamma=-.11$)	

TABLE 10.4 *SEM indexes for predicting satisfaction and commitment*

	CFI	RMSEA
Chapters 2 & 3 across relationship types	.968	.022
Chapters 2 & 3 across cultural regions	.973	.016
Chapters 4 & 5 across relationship types	.976	.032
Chapters 4 & 5 across cultural regions	.987	.019
Chapter 6 across relationship types	.962	.027
Chapter 6 across cultural regions	.965	.020
Chapters 7 & 8 across relationship types	.975	.023
Chapters 7 & 8 across cultural regions	.980	.016

in Table 10.3, with their standardized regression coefficients from SEM Structural Models in those chapters. Only nontrivial coefficients are listed. Those factors with a coefficient for relationship satisfaction but not for relationship commitment have an indirect prediction of relationship commitment through relationship satisfaction, but not a direct prediction of relationship commitment independent of relationship satisfaction. The number of Central Factors is overwhelming and will be reduced to Comprehensive Factors that capture their effects in the next section.

WHAT COMPREHENSIVE FACTORS CAPTURE PREDICTIONS OF RELATIONSHIP SATISFACTION AND RELATIONSHIP COMMITMENT?

To identify Comprehensive Factors that capture the effects of all of these Central Factors, there are too many Central Factors to combine in single SEM Structural Models. So separate SEM models are analyzed for Central Factors from Chapters 2 and 3, Chapters 4 and 5 (omitting the two items about extra-relationship sex that vary), Chapter 6, and Chapters 7 and 8. These models are similar across eight relationships types and nine cultural regions as shown in Table 10.4.

These models reveal the following Comprehensive Factors in predicting Relationship Satisfaction and Relationship Commitment, which capture predictions they have in common with other Central Factors. They are grouped into Four Categories of Comprehensive Factors, as shown in Table 10.5.

The first Category of Comprehensive Factors refers to **partner suitability**, including similarity on the items in the Personality Similarity Scale (Personality, Attitudes and Values, and Sense of Humor); Overall Perceived Desirability of the Partner; and Approval of Parents, Friends, and Co-Workers or Classmates. The next set refers to **intimacy dimensions**, including Emotional Closeness, Mutual Love, Trust, Sexual Satisfaction, and Lack of Anxious Attachment. The third set refers to **exchange processes**, including Gained Benefits, Equal Involvement, Equal Power, and Investment in the Relationship. The fourth category refers to **conflict resolution**, Including Positive Responses in Dealing with Conflict, Discussing Areas of Dissatisfaction to Find Mutual Solutions, Lack of High Sources of Conflicts, and Lack of Willingness to End the Relationship if Dissatisfied.

While these Comprehensive Factors primarily have effects through Relationship Satisfaction, some have direct effects on Relationship Commitment independent of Relationship Satisfaction. Rating the Partner Desirable, Loving the Partner, Being Invested in the Relationship, and Not Breaking Up if Dissatisfied predict increased commitment to the relationship whether Relationship Satisfaction is high or low.

These Comprehensive Factors make similar predictions of Relationship Satisfaction and Relationship Commitment across eight relationship types and nine cultural regions. This is in spite of any variations in the average levels of these factors, which will be discussed in Chapter 11. Together these four categories of Comprehensive Factors that predict Relationship Satisfaction and Relationship Commitment constitute the *Comprehensive Commitment Model* developed in this book, which is shown in Figure 10.2.

HOW WELL DO THE COMPREHENSIVE FACTORS PREDICT RELATIONSHIP SATISFACTION AND RELATIONSHIP COMMITMENT?

- Together the factors in the four categories of the *Comprehensive Commitment Model* explain 76% of the variation in Relationship Satisfaction.
- Relationship Satisfaction explains 53% of the variation in Relationship Commitment.

TABLE 10.5 *Comprehensive Factors predicting satisfaction or commitment*

	Satisfaction	Commitment
1. Partner Suitability		
+ Personality Similarity Scale	(γ=.18)	
+ Rating Partner Desirable as a Partner	(γ=.41)	(γ=.27)
+ Parents and Others Approve of Partner	(γ=.25)	
2. Intimacy Dimensions		
+ Emotional Closeness	(γ=.30)	
+ Saying Both of Us Are in Love	(γ=.18)	(γ=.27)
+ Four Component Love Scale	(γ=.12)	(γ=.17)
+ Eros (We Were Made for Each Other)		(γ=.25)
+ Trusting Partner Not to Lie	(γ=.15)	
+ Sexual Satisfaction Scale	(γ=.12)	
− Anxious Attachment	(γ=−.10)	
3. Exchange Processes		
+ Gained Benefits from the Relationship	(γ=.42)	
+ Equal Involvement in the Relationship	(γ=.30)	
+ Equal Power in the Relationship	(γ=.10)	
+ Invested in the Relationship		(γ .16)
4. Conflict Resolution		
+ Positive Responses Scale	(γ=.21)	
+ Voice (Would Discuss and Fix Things Up)	(γ=.16)	
− Highest Sources of Conflict Scale	(γ=−.11)	
− Exit (Would Break Up if Dissatisfied)	(γ=−.12)	(γ=−.12)

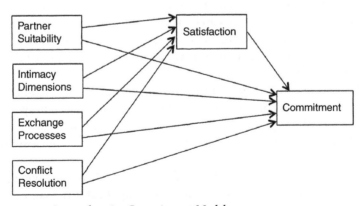

FIGURE 10.2 *Comprehensive Commitment Model*

- The four categories of the *Comprehensive Commitment Model* together with Relationship Satisfaction explain 77% of the variation in Relationship Commitment.

- This means that 77%–53%=24% of the variation in Relationship Commitment is explained by the four categories independent of Relationship Satisfaction.

The 76% prediction of Relationship Satisfaction and the 77% prediction of Relationship Commitment are very high for social science research. In addition, 77% is greater than the typical 61% of commitment explained by Rusbult's model (Le & Agnew, 2003), which is one of the theoretical bases of the *Comprehensive Commitment Model.*

At the same time, the 77% indicates that 23% of the variance in relationship commitment is determined by individual variation including other factors not in the *Comprehensive Commitment Model.* Possible other factors not compared cross-culturally are reviewed by Karney and Bradbury (1995).

SELF-REFLECTION

How well do the four categories of the *Comprehensive Commitment Model* (partner suitability, intimacy dimensions, exchange processes, and conflict resolution) reflect your own experience in relationship satisfaction and relationship commitment?

WHAT IS SURPRISING ABOUT THESE FINDINGS?

The finding that these four categories of the *Comprehensive Commitment Model* predict relationship satisfaction and relationship commitment is not surprising, given previous research. What is surprising is that these same factors make similar predictions across eight relationship types and nine cultural regions. This is in spite of variations in the average levels of the factors that will be discussed in Chapter 11.

Previous researchers have criticized generalizing findings across cultures without making explicit comparisons (Henrich, Heine, & Nerenzayan, 2010). The findings of the present study indicate the need to distinguish between **predictions** of factors and **average levels** of factors in making cross-cultural comparisons.

In particular, this study indicates that previous theories making predictions about intimate relationships have **wider applicability** than previously documented. This includes Rubin (1970), Berscheid and Walster (1969), Sternberg (1986), and Hendrick and Hendrick (1986), on love; Hazan and Shaver (1987) on attachment theory; Blau (1964) on social exchange theory; Rusbult (1980) on commitment; Gottman (1999) on responses to conflict; Rusbult et al. (1982) on responses to dissatisfaction; and many others.

Perhaps also surprising is the lack of explicit mention of Physical Attractiveness in the Partner Suitability Category of Comprehensive Factors, where items on the Personality Similarity Scale (personality, attitudes and values, and sense of humor) are more important. That is because measures of Physical Attractiveness are not among the Central Factors in Chapter 3 listed previously. Any predictions of Physical Attractiveness are captured along with intelligence and other characteristics in the Comprehensive Factor of the desirability of the partner as a partner in a committed relationship.

This lack of centrality of physical attractiveness in predicting relationship satisfaction and relationship commitment is consistent with findings of the Boston Couples Study mentioned in Chapter 3 of this book. The BCS found that physical attractiveness played a small role in initial attraction in terms of some matching between partners, along with matching on intelligence (Hill, Rubin, & Peplau, 1976). But ratings of physical attractiveness by the partner and by judges did not predict staying together over two years, or eventual marriage and staying married fifteen years later (Hill & Peplau, 1998). Other factors matter more.

The findings in the BCS that physical attractiveness had a small effect on initial attraction, and no effect on long-term bonding, indicate that evolutionary psychology theorizing provides just part of the answer to questions about intimate relationships. Other research has found that gender differences in the initiation and maintenance of intimate relationships are smaller than emphasized in evolutionary psychology theorizing (Marshall, 2010).

WHY DO THE SAME FACTORS MAKE SIMILAR PREDICTIONS?

Although cultures vary in their rules for appropriate intimate behavior, the physiological bases of emotions are similar across typically developing individuals. Biologically, there is only one race, the human race. This is documented in a series of posters produced by the Department of Genetic Anthropology in Geneva, Switzerland, that are on display at the Musée de l'Homme in Paris. A version in English was translated by Marc Segall and produced by Syracuse University, titled "All of us are related, each of us is unique," which has appeared online at http://allrelated.syr.edu/index.html.

These posters reveal that skin color varies gradually from the equator, where the sun is intense and dark skin is an advantage, to the North Pole, where there is less sunlight and light skin is an advantage. But under the skin, variations in physiological features are similar across skin tones. Differing races are a social construction, not a biological one. Our similarity to one another is further revealed in recent genetic research, which concludes that we share 99.9 percent of our DNA with all other humans (Smithsonian Museum of Natural History, no date).

In sum, all humans are members of the same species and have similar needs, even though cultures may vary in their ways of meeting those needs. SEM models reveal that the factors in the *Comprehensive Partner Model* make similar predictions across gender and cultural regions. And SEM models reveal that the factors in the *Comprehensive Commitment Model* make similar predictions across relationship types and cultural regions. Variations in the levels of those factors are analyzed in Chapter 11.

11

How Much Do the Levels of Factors Vary?

Variations in the levels of factors that predict Having a Current Partner, and variations in the levels of factors that predict Relationship Satisfaction and Relationship Commitment, are explored in this chapter. These variations are discussed in terms of overall means and standard deviations, and variations in means across relationship types and across cultural regions.

HOW MUCH DO THE LEVELS OF THE PREDICTORS OF HAVING A CURRENT PARTNER VARY?

The means (averages) and standard deviations ($s.d.$) of Having a Current Partner and of the Comprehensive Factors predicting Having a Current Partner are listed in Table 11.1. The standard deviations indicate the amount of individual variation in responses across all participants in the study. The possible responses for Having a Current Partner and for having had a previous partner are o=NO to 1=YES, hence those means indicate percentages expressed as decimals. Age varied from 18 to 84. The other factors have possible responses from o=NOT AT ALL to 8=EXTREMELY.

These standard deviations indicate a great deal of variation in individual responses. To determine variations across gender and cultural regions, multivariate analyses of variance are employed since this provides effect sizes (how much of an effect a factor has) in the form of R-squared. This indicates the percentage of variation (expressed as a decimal) in mean levels predicted by the independent variables of gender and cultural regions as shown in Table 11.2.

Overall, the variations in mean levels of Having a Current Partner and in the mean levels of the Comprehensive Factors that predict Having a Current Partner are negligible across gender, except for age. This is consistent with prior research findings that gender differences in the initiation of intimate relationships are small (Marshall, 2010).

TABLE 11.1 *Means for Having a Current Partner*

	Mean	(s.d.)
Having a Current Partner	0.71	0.45
+ Rating self desirable as a partner	5.99	2.03
+ Having had a previous partner	0.64	0.48
+ Age	25.6	8.19
− Difficulty finding a partner	4.91	2.53
− Interested in finding a partner	4.32	3.12

TABLE 11.2 *Percentage variation in means for Having a Current Partner*

	Gender R-squared	Regions R-squared
Having a Current Partner	.00	.05
+ Rating self desirable as a partner	.00	.07
+ Having had a previous partner	.00	.09
+ Age	.02	.07
− Difficulty finding a partner	.00	.02
− Interested in finding a partner	.00	.07

In addition, the variations in the factors are fairly small across cultural regions, with R-squared indicating that less than 10 percent of the variation in each factor is explained by cultural region. In other words, the difference in average levels across cultural regions is very small. This is in spite of any cultural variations in expectations concerning appropriate intimate behaviors. These variations are described in the next section.

IN WHAT WAYS DO THE LEVELS OF THE PREDICTORS OF HAVING A PARTNER VARY?

Having a Current Partner does not have a statistically significant gender difference (p>.05). In other words, the likelihood of having a current partner is similar for women and men in the study. Nor do the Comprehensive Factors that predicted Having a Current Partner have statistically significant gender differences in mean levels, except for age. On average, the men who participated are somewhat older (27.8) than the women (24.6, p<.001), but the effect of age on Having a Current Partner is similar for men and women.

To assess effect sizes of differences in levels across cultural regions, the previously mentioned Comprehensive Factors are correlated with each cultural region versus all other cultural regions. That is a simpler way to see how each region differs from the others instead of examining all possible comparisons of two regions at a time. The correlations squared also provide a measure of effect size. The probabilities are affected by the same countries appearing in multiple comparisons, which means that the small correlations that follow are less significant than indicated by asterisks.

A positive correlation indicates that the region has a higher mean level than the other regions combined, while a negative correlation indicates that the region has a lower mean level than the other regions combined. Only nontrivial correlations are reported:

- Having a current partner has lower rates in East Asia ($r=-.14^{***}$) and Southeast Asia ($r=-.15^{***}$).
- Similarly, having had a previous partner is also lower in East Asia ($r=-.11^{***}$) and Southeast Asia ($r=-.25^{***}$).
- Seeking a partner is higher in Southeast Asia ($r=.15^{***}$).
- Rating self desirable as a partner is lower in East Asia ($r=-.26^{***}$), but slightly higher in Latin America ($r=.12^{***}$).
- Difficulty finding a partner is only trivially correlated with cultural regions ($r<.10$).

Squaring the correlation indicates what percentage of the mean difference is due to being in that region. Since the highest correlation is $r=.26$, the highest percentage is r-squared$=.07=7\%$. This indicates that the mean difference from all other regions combined is relatively small for all of these factors. In other words, the difference in average levels among cultural regions is very small.

Note that the variations in the levels of these factors are primarily in East Asia and Southeast Asia, where individuals are less likely to have a current partner as discussed in Chapters 1 and 8. Having a current partner risks engaging in premarital intercourse, which reflects negatively on parenting in East Asia and is considered sinful among Muslim and other populations in Southeast Asia.

In spite of these small differences in the mean levels of Comprehensive Factors across cultural regions, they make similar predictions of Having a Current Partner across cultural regions as revealed in the previous SEM models.

SELF-REFLECTION

How well do the four categories of the *Comprehensive Partner Model* (motivation, confidence, readiness, and opportunity) reflect your own experience in seeking a current partner?

TABLE 11.3 *Means for satisfaction and commitment*

	Mean	(s.d.)
Relationship Satisfaction	6.46	1.69
Relationship Commitment	6.04	2.07
Partner Suitability		
+ Personality Similarity Scale	6.06	1.32
+ Rating Partner Desirable as a Partner	6.88	1.73
+ Parents and Others Approve of Partner	6.19	1.83
Intimacy Dimensions		
+ Emotional Closeness	6.45	1.91
+ Saying Both of Us Are in Love	6.16	2.30
+ Love Scale	6.09	1.65
+ Eros (We Were Made for Each Other)	5.50	2.59
+ Trusting Partner Not to Lie	6.26	2.12
+ Sexual Satisfaction	6.04	1.66
− Anxious Attachment	3.65	2.38
Exchange Processes		
+ Gained Benefits from the Relationship	6.37	1.92
+ Equal Involvement in the Relationship	2.50	0.68
+ Equal Power in the Relationship	2.45	0.67
+ Invested in the Relationship	6.00	2.15
Conflict Resolution		
+ Positive Responses	5.84	1.61
+ Voice (Would Discuss and Fix Things Up)	6.48	1.92
− Highest Sources of Conflicts Scale	2.87	1.92
− Exit (Would Break Up if Dissatisfied)	1.93	2.25

HOW MUCH DO THE LEVELS OF THE PREDICTORS OF SATISFACTION AND COMMITMENT VARY?

The means and standard deviations of Relationship Satisfaction and Relationship Commitment, and of the Comprehensive Factors predicting Relationship Satisfaction or Relationship Commitment independent of Relationship Satisfaction, are shown in Table 11.3. Equal involvement and equal power had possible responses of 1=ONE MUCH MORE, 2=ONE SOMEWHAT MORE, and 3=BOTH EQUAL. Possible responses for the other factors were from 0=NOT AT ALL to 8=COMPLETELY or 8=EXTREMELY.

In general, the means are fairly high, except for the three negative Comprehensive Factors. And the standard deviations indicate a fair amount of variation in individual responses. To determine variations across

TABLE 11.4 *Percentage variation in means for satisfaction and commitment*

	Rel. Type R-squared	Region R-squared
Relationship Satisfaction	.03	.02
Relationship Commitment	.07	.03
Partner Suitability		
+ Personality Similarity Scale	.01	.06
+ Rating Partner Desirable as a Partner	.02	.03
+ Parents and Others Approve of Partner	.05	.03
Intimacy Dimensions		
+ Emotional Closeness	.02	.01
+ Saying Both of Us Are in Love	.05	.01
+ Love Scale	.04	.01
+ Eros (We Were Made for Each Other)	.05	.04
+ Trusting Partner Not to Lie	.02	.05
+ Sexual Satisfaction	.02	.03
− Anxious Attachment	.01	.06
Exchange Process		
+ Gained Benefits from the Relationship	.04	.05
+ Equal Involvement in the Relationship	.03	.02
+ Equal Power in the Relationship	.00	.01
+ Invested in the Relationship	.03	.07
Conflict Resolution		
+ Positive Responses	.02	.05
+ Voice (Would Discuss and Fix Things Up)	.02	.04
− Highest Sources Of Conflicts Scale	.01	.04
− Exit (Would Break Up if Dissatisfied)	.03	.03

relationship types and cultural regions, multivariate analyses of variance (MANOVA) are employed since they provide effect sizes in the form of R-squared, which indicates the percentage of variation (expressed as a decimal) in mean levels predicted by the independent variables of relationship type and cultural region (Table 11.4).

Overall, the variations are not very large. None of the percentages of variation in these factors that are explained by relationship type or cultural region are larger than 7 percent, and many are as small as 1 percent or 2 percent. In other words, the difference in average levels among cultural regions is very small. This is in spite of any cultural variations in expectations concerning appropriate intimate behaviors. Variations in mean levels across relationship types are described in the next section, and variations across cultural regions are discussed later in this chapter.

HOW DO THE LEVELS OF THE PREDICTORS OF SATISFACTION
AND COMMITMENT VARY ACROSS RELATIONSHIP TYPES?

Previous research has found that gender differences in the maintenance of intimate relationships are small, for both opposite-sex and same-sex relationships (Marshall, 2010). In the present study, analyses of variance reveal that relationship satisfaction and relationship commitment are somewhat higher among men and women in same-sex marriages than in other relationship types. Since they had been recruited as newlyweds, they had been married a shorter time ($r=-.33^{***}$) on average than opposite-sex married participants who included both newlyweds and older marrieds. Overall, persons married a shorter time had somewhat greater relationship satisfaction ($r=.18^{***}$) and relationship commitment ($r=.17^{***}$). Kurdek (2005) had previously found greater satisfaction in early marriages, with no gender difference.

In addition, men and women in same-sex marriages are also somewhat higher on the Comprehensive Factors of the Personality Similarity Scale, Trusting the Partner Not to Lie, Gained Benefits, Equal Involvement, Invested, Positive Responses, and Voice, while lower on Anxious Attachment and Exit. Besides being newlyweds, it may be that same-sex couples need to be more committed in deciding to marry in spite of potential negative reactions from the wider society.

Not surprisingly men and women in both same-sex and opposite-sex marriages are somewhat higher than unmarried persons on rating the partner desirable as a partner in a committed relationship, parents and others approve of partner, emotional closeness, saying both are in love, the Four Component Love Scale, and Eros. But married persons have somewhat less sexual satisfaction than unmarried persons. And men and women in same-sex relationships, whether married or unmarried, report less conflict on the highest sources of conflict than those in opposite-sex relationships. In spite of these differences in the levels of these Comprehensive Factors, they make similar predictions of relationship satisfaction and relationship commitment across relationship types as revealed in the SEM models in Chapter 10.

WHICH FACTORS VARIED IN PREDICTING SATISFACTION AND
COMMITMENT ACROSS RELATIONSHIP TYPES?

The following factors are not included among potential Comprehensive Factors because their effects vary across relationship types:

- Living Together Conflict Scale
- Own disclosure of prior romantic or sexual activities
- Partner's disclosure of prior romantic or sexual activities
- Believing that the current partner had sex outside the relationship

• Own approval of current partner having outside sex

As reported in Chapter 7, the Living Together Conflicts Scale is slightly positively correlated with Relationship Commitment (r=.10***) because those actually living together have more of these conflicts (r=.34***) as well as more commitment (r=.37***). Among those not living together, the correlation between the Living Together Conflict Scale and Relationship Commitment is trivial (r<.10), while it is negative among those who say they were living together "some of the time" (r=−.13*) or "most or all of the time" (r=−.22**).

As reported in Chapter 4, own disclosure about prior sexual romantic or sexual activities has stronger positive correlations with Relationship Satisfaction for men in same-sex relationships (r=.53***) than for men and women in the other relationship types (r=.27***). Similar effects are found for partner's disclosure on this item (r=.46*** vs. r=29***). In other words, self and partner revealing prior romantic or sexual activities matter more for men in same-sex relationships.

As reported in Chapter 5, perceptions of partner's outside sex during the relationship has slightly less negative impact on relationship satisfaction for same-sex marriages (γ =−.15) than for other relationship types (γ=−.24). And approval of partner's outside sex has no impact on relationship commitment for same-sex marriages (γ=−.01), while having a slight negative effect for other relationship types (γ =−.12). In other words, approval of outside sex does not reduce relationship commitment among those who decided to marry their same-sex partners. But believing that the partner had outside sex still has at least some negative effect on relationship satisfaction among those in same-sex marriages.

The mean level of believing the partner had outside sex is 1.36 with a standard deviation of 2.52, with possible responses from 0 to 8, indicating that the average level is low, but individual responses were fairly variable. Analysis of variance (p<.001) reveals that the highest means are for men in same-sex relationships who are married (3.32) or unmarried (2.58). The mean level of approval of partner having outside sex is 1.13 with a standard deviation of 2.23, again indicating that the average is low, with a fair amount of individual variation. Again analysis of variance (p<.001) reveals that the highest mean levels of approval of partner having outside sex are for men in same-sex relationships who are married (3.50) or unmarried (2.73).

These are the primary ways in which the levels of the factors predicting relationship satisfaction and relationship commitment vary across relationship types. The other factors in this book have similar effects across relationship types.

HOW DO RELATIONSHIP TYPES VARY BY CULTURAL REGION?

Correlations are used to compare each cultural region with all other cultural regions. A positive correlation indicates that the percentage is higher in that cultural region than in other cultural regions combined, while a negative correlation indicates that the percentage is lower in that cultural region than in other cultural regions combined. Only nontrivial correlations are reported.

Due to the recruitment of married couples in Pakistan, there are relatively more married participants (r=.37***) in the cultural region of Central West South Asia that includes Pakistan. Due to the recruitment of newlyweds, including same-sex marriages, in the United States, there are relatively more married participants (r=.10***) and relatively more participants in same-sex relationships (r=.30***) in the cultural region of North America.

But there are fewer participants in same-sex relationships (r=−.17***) in the cultural region of Eastern Europe, where there are less favorable attitudes toward gay men and lesbians (Pew Research Center, 2013). And there are relatively fewer married participants in Latin America (r=−.15***) and in Western Europe (r=−.16***) due to variations in those who responded. In spite of these variations in relationship types across cultural regions, the predictors of relationship satisfaction and relationship commitment are similar across relationship types and cultural regions in SEM models provided earlier.

HOW DO THE LEVELS OF THE PREDICTORS OF SATISFACTION AND COMMITMENT VARY ACROSS CULTURAL REGIONS?

To assess effect sizes of differences in levels across cultural regions, the previously identified Comprehensive Factors are correlated with each cultural region versus the other cultural regions combined. A positive correlation indicates that the mean level is higher in that region, while a negative correlation indicates that the mean level is lower in that region. Only nontrivial correlations are reported.

Relationship satisfaction is slightly lower in East Asia (r=−.11***). Relationship commitment is slightly lower in Central West South Asia (r=−.11***), which includes parent choice marriages in Pakistan that have slightly lower relationship satisfaction than in own choice marriages, as indicated in the SPOTLIGHT on Parent-Choice vs. Own-Choice Marriages in Chapter 8.

Partner Suitability
- The Partner Similarity Scale is rated higher in North America (r=.15***), and lower in East Asia (r=−.19***).
- Rating partner desirable as a partner is lower in East Asia (r=−.15).
- Parents and others approve of partner is also lower in East Asia (r=−.16).

Intimacy Dimensions
- The love scale is lower in East Asia (r=−.11***).
- Eros (we were made for each other) is lower in East Asia (r=−.14***).

- Sexual satisfaction is also lower in East Asia ($r=-.15^{***}$).
- Eros is slightly higher in Eastern Europe ($r=.10^{***}$).
- Anxious attachment is higher in Southeast Asia ($r=.18^{***}$).
- Emotional closeness, saying both of us are in love, and trusting partner not to lie have trivial mean differences ($r<.10$) across cultural regions.

Exchange Processes

- Gained benefits is lower in Eastern Europe ($r=-.11^{***}$) and East Asia ($r=-.12$).
- Equal involvement is lower in Central West South Asia ($r=-.11^{***}$).
- Equal power has trivial mean differences across cultural regions ($r<.10$).

Conflict Resolution

- Positive responses are higher in North America ($r=.11^{***}$) and lower in East Asia ($r=-.20^{***}$).
- Voice (I would discuss and fix things up) is lower in Central West South Asia ($r=-.11^{***}$) and East Asia ($r=-.15^{***}$).
- Highest Sources of Conflict Scale is lower in North America ($r=-.21^{***}$) and higher in Southeast Asia ($r=.15^{***}$).
- Exit (I would break up if dissatisfied) is slightly higher in Latin America ($r=.11^{**}$).

Squaring the correlation indicates what percentage of the mean difference is due to being in that region. Since the highest correlation is $r=.21$, the highest percentage is r-squared=.04=4%. This indicates that the mean difference from all other regions combined is relatively small for all of these factors. In other words, there are more similarities than differences across cultural regions.

The most frequent mean differences among cultural regions are in East Asia, with slightly lower relationship satisfaction, and slightly lower levels of various Comprehensive Factors that predict relationship satisfaction. A recent study of marital satisfaction in 33 countries (Sorokowski et al., 2017) found the lowest average in Hong Kong (4.01), a somewhat low average in South Korea (4.36), but not a low average in China (4.49), in comparison with the total mean across all countries (4.47). One possible reason for these differences in East Asia is discussed in the SPOTLIGHT on Intimacy and Relational Mobility in Chapter 4. When there is more choice of potential partners, there is more need for reasons to keep partners in the relationship.

In sum, standard deviations reveal a fair amount of individual variation in the levels of factors in the *Comprehensive Partner Model*. Yet multiple analyses of variance reveal essentially no gender differences in these factors, and that less than 10 percent of the variation is prediction by cultural region. The differences that do occur are primarily in East Asia and Southeast Asia, where individuals are less likely to have a current partner. Similarly, there is a fair amount of individual variation in levels of the factors in the *Comprehensive Commitment Model*. Yet less than 8 percent of the variation is predicted by relationship type or cultural region.

In spite of these small differences in the mean levels of these Comprehensive Factors, they make similar predictions of Relationship Satisfaction and Relationship Commitment across relationship types and cultural regions as revealed in the SEM models in Chapter 10. As Maya Angelou (1994) says, "We are more alike, my friends, than we are unlike." Our intimate relationships are more similar than they are different across relationship types and cultural regions. This is true for the factors that predict relationship satisfaction and commitment, as well as for variations in the average levels of those factors, which are very small.

12

What Are the Implications of the Study?

This chapter discusses the limitations of the study, how the findings compare with the Boston Couples Study, and the implications of the study for self-reflection, couples' counseling, and well-being.

WHAT ARE THE LIMITATIONS OF THE STUDY?

Since the study is online (except in Pakistan), participants are limited to those who have access to the internet and to those willing to answer an extensive online questionnaire. They are likely to be younger, since older persons may be less familiar with computers. And they are likely to be better educated than the general public. Issues in using the internet for research are discussed by Gosling et al. (2004), Van Selm and Jankowski (2006), and Fraley (2007). Additional sampling issues in relationship research are discussed by Hill et al. (1979), de Jong Gieveld (1995), and Karney et al. (1995).

Although three-fourths of the participants in the present study are students, SEM Structural Models reveal that the Comprehensive Factors make similar predictions across students and non-students (CFI>.950, RMSEA<.05).

Few of the participants are from Africa or Oceana. Even fewer are from the Middle East, which this book includes in the Central West South Asia cultural region that includes Pakistan. Colleagues in the Middle East had agreed to provide translations and recruit participants but ultimately were unable to do so. It is hoped that more participants from the Middle East can be included in future supplementary reports on this study that is ongoing.

While the study investigates a comprehensive range of factors that matter in intimate relationships, there may be additional factors that need to be investigated cross-culturally in future research. And different measures of the same factors, such as scales with more items, may yield slightly different results. In particular, changing or omitting one of the Central Factors may result in another factor in the same category becoming a Central Factor and a Comprehensive Factor if it has a higher correlation with the predicted measures than other factors.

But it is likely that the same Four Categories of Comprehensive Factors (Partner Suitability, Intimacy Dimensions, Exchange Processes, and Conflict Resolution) are still likely to matter in predicting Relationship Satisfaction and Relationship Commitment. Hence the most important features of the *Comprehensive Commitment Model* are the Four Categories of Comprehensive Factors, and their prediction of both indirect effects on relationship commitment through relationship satisfaction and direct effects on relationship commitment independent of relationship satisfaction.

Not included in these analyses are forty participants whose gender differs from their sex. Among these, 68 percent describe Having a Current Partner. Correlations reveal that relationship satisfaction is correlated with all of the positive Comprehensive Factors identified in Chapter 10, except gained benefits, which is directly correlated with relationship commitment instead. As in Chapter 10, Relationship Commitment is positively correlated with rating the Partner Desirable as a Partner in a committed relationship, Emotional Closeness, Saying We Are Both in Love, the Four Components Love Scale, and negatively correlated with Willingness to Leave the Relationship. Hence it appears that the factors are similar, although further research is needed on the intimate relationships of those with nonbinary genders.

HOW DO THESE FINDINGS COMPARE WITH THE BOSTON COUPLES STUDY?

Unlike the Boston Couples Study, the present study is not longitudinal. That would require keeping track of thousands of participants for follow-up, instead of keeping participation anonymous. Hence the present study focuses on relationship satisfaction and commitment instead of who stays together and who breaks up. But it is interesting to compare the Comprehensive Factors that predict satisfaction and commitment in the present study with the predictors of relationship outcomes in the fifteen-year follow-up of the Boston Couples Study (BCS) (Hill & Peplau, 1998).

In the present study, rating the partner desirable as a partner in a committed relationship predicts relationship satisfaction and commitment in Comprehensive SEM models. In the BCS, rating the partner desirable as a marriage partner predicted initial dating relationship satisfaction, staying together on the two-year follow-up, and eventual marriage on the fifteen-year follow-up.

In the present study, saying both are in love predicts relationship satisfaction and commitment. In the BCS, the same measure predicted initial dating relationship satisfaction, staying together two years, and eventual marriage. Similarly, in the present study the Four Component Love Scale predicts relationship satisfaction and commitment. In the BCS, the Rubin Love Scale predicted initial dating satisfaction, staying together two years, and eventual marriage.

In the present study, the exchange factor of equal involvement predicts relationship satisfaction. In the BCS, the same measure predicted initial dating satisfaction, staying together two years, and eventual marriage. And in the present study the highest sources of conflicts scale predicts less relationship satisfaction. In the BCS, the problem index predicted less initial dating satisfaction, less staying together two years, and less eventual marriage.

Hence some of the factors that predicted relationship outcomes in the Boston Couples Study are the same as factors that predict relationship satisfaction and commitment similarly across eight relationship types and nine cultural regions in the present study. This indicates that findings of studies on intimate relationships that were conducted decades ago still have relevance today, in spite of the advent of the internet, which provides new ways of meeting partners and keeping in contact using social media, and other changes over time.

WHAT ARE THE IMPLICATIONS OF THIS STUDY FOR SELF-REFLECTION?

In general, the study implies that when thinking about a current or potential intimate relationship, you should consider the following Four Categories of the *Comprehensive Commitment Model*.

Partner suitability matters. In particular, how similar is the partner to you on personality, attitudes and values, and sense of humor? To what extent do characteristics of the partner make the person desirable as a partner in a committed relationship? To what extent do (or would) your parents, friends, classmates, or co-workers approve of the partner? When someone marries a person, one is also marrying the spouse's network of family and friends.

Intimacy dimensions matter. Do you feel emotionally close to the partner? To what extent are you in love with the partner, and to what extent is the partner in love with you? Do you trust the partner not to lie to you? Are your sexual activities with the person satisfying to you, or do you think they would be satisfying to you given the extent of the partner's consideration of your needs and desires? Are you anxious about establishing and maintaining intimate relationships?

Exchange processes matter. Do you believe you have gained benefits from the relationship? Are you equally involved in the relationship? Do you have equal say in the relationship? To what extent do you feel invested in the relationship?

Conflict resolution matters. How positively do you and the partner respond to conflict? Do you try to discuss issues and try to come to mutual understandings? Or are you willing to end the relationship if dissatisfied, instead of working together to improve the relationship or seek professional help? Do you have conflicts over the highest sources of conflicts – time management, poor communication, personalities, and leisure activities?

WHAT ARE THE IMPLICATIONS OF THIS STUDY FOR COUPLES' COUNSELING?

Therapists should help couples engage in the preceding questions for self-reflection. Even though the factors make similar predictions across relationship types and cultural regions, therapists need to be sensitive to possible cultural and individual differences in the average levels of those factors. There may be varying cultural expectations concerning appropriate intimate behaviors, including ways of communicating emotions. There may be individual differences in lifestyles, including preferred activities and desires. Sprenkle, Davis, and Lebow (2009) review principles of effective couples' therapy. Advice on multicultural counseling is provided by Ponterotto (2001) and Pedersen et al. (2015).

WHAT ARE THE IMPLICATIONS OF THIS STUDY FOR WELL-BEING?

Chapter 9 reveals that happiness and satisfaction with number of children, if any, are Central Factors in associations with having a current partner. In other words, those without a current partner are likely to be less happy, and less satisfied with the number of children they have.

Chapter 9 also reveals that happiness, general life satisfaction, and evaluating life as fulfilling and meaningful are Central Factors in associations with relationship satisfaction. In other words, those dissatisfied with their current relationship are less happy, have lower general life satisfaction, and evaluate their lives as less fulfilling and meaningful. These findings highlight the importance of the quality of intimate relationships for well-being.

Breakups of dating relationships and marriages are common. In the present study, 64 percent of the participants had had a previous intimate relationship that had ended. In the Boston Couples Study, 103 of the original 231 couples (45 percent) of the couples broke up by the two-year follow-up (Hill, Rubin, & Peplau, 1976), and only 73 (32 percent) eventually married the original partner (Hill & Peplau, 1998). In varying degrees, those whose relationships ended felt depressed, lonely, free, guilty, and less happy. Advice from a therapist for coping with a breakup is provided by Elliott (2009).

Ideally those who have had previous intimate relationships can learn more about themselves and how to have a more successful intimate relationship. But difficulty coping with a breakup can lead to depression, self-harm, and suicide attempts (Mirsu-Paun & Oliver, 2017). Hence it is important to seek social support from others after a breakup, and if the emotional turmoil persists, to seek professional help.

13

How Might the Findings Apply to Other Social Relationships?

Berscheid (1995) asked whether a grand, overarching theory of relationships can be developed. And Finkel, Simpson, and Eastwick (2017) called for greater integration across theories of close relationships. To pursue those goals, this chapter speculates on how factors found to matter in this study might also matter to some degree in other social relationships. This is explored in terms of the following:

- Factors found in early research on interpersonal attraction
- Dimensions of social relationships
- Commitment mechanisms in other social relationships
- How the *Comprehensive Partner Model* might apply to other social relationships
- How the *Comprehensive Commitment Model* might apply to other social relationships
- How these models might combine in a *Comprehensive Relationship Model*
- How the *Comprehensive Relationship Model* applies to social networks

WHAT FACTORS WERE FOUND IN EARLY RESEARCH ON INTERPERSONAL ATTRACTION?

Before Zick Rubin demonstrated that it was possible to measure love, psychologists spoke more generally about **interpersonal attraction** (Berscheid & Walster, 1969). It was assumed that the same kinds of factors might apply to various social relationships. Four of the kinds of factors found to be important were the following:

- Proximity
- Similarity
- Chance consequences
- Reciprocity of liking

Proximity refers to geographical and physical nearness that provides opportunities to meet and to interact. It often takes time to develop a relationship through processes of incremental exchange described in Chapter 1 of this book. Trust is gradually built when others reciprocate with actions as well as words. However, the internet has reduced distances between people, allowing people to meet and to interact in some ways while far apart.

Similarity can occur in terms of social characteristics, personal characteristics, and attitudes and values. Similarity is important because there needs to be something in common that brings individuals together and serves as a basis for interaction. How strong the similarity needs to be depends on the kind of social relationship, from strangers with little in common, to friends with some things in common, to lovers ideally with much in common. However, perceived similarity is often more important than actual similarity (Montoya, Horton, & Kirchner, 2008).

Chance consequences refer not only to chance encounters, but also to chance outcomes. It is said that everybody loves a winner. Rubin and Peplau (1975) found that winners were better liked even when they won by chance. They explained this by a belief in a just world, that good people are rewarded and bad people are punished.

Reciprocity of liking means that we generally like people who like us. And believing that someone likes you can lead to liking someone who is dissimilar (Aron, Kashdan, & Perez, 2006). But there are two major exceptions. One is ingratiation, when we think the other's expression of admiration is not sincere. If your sibling says something nice to you, you may wonder what they want. The other exception is when someone is "hitting on you" and it is not welcome. It may be perceived as sexual harassment.

It is likely that these factors found fifty years ago still apply in some degree to many kinds of social relationships, in many cultural contexts.

WHAT ARE SOME DIMENSIONS OF SOCIAL RELATIONSHIPS?

Roger Brown (1965) argued that there were two dimensions to relationships. One is **intimacy** and the other is **status**. These are reflected in the forms of address we use. If both persons use informal terms, like first names, that implies an intimate relationship. If both persons use formal terms, like titles, that implies a non-intimate relationship. But if one person addresses the other with a formal term while the other uses an informal term, that implies a status difference between them. The person called by title has a higher status than the person called by first name.

Kurth (1970) made a distinction between **friendship** and **friendly relations**, based on the following dimensions:

- Voluntary interaction – Friendly relations are limited to formal role relationships (such as a clerk you see all the time in the post office or grocery store), while friendship can occur in other places and at other times (although you may usually interact with the friend in certain environments).
- Sense of uniqueness – If a person with whom you have friendly relations is replaced by someone else, you have friendly relations with that new person. But friendships are not interchangeable in the same way.
- Level of intimacy – Usually we disclose more personal information in friendship than in friendly relations. Since the latter are often in networks, such as classmates or co-workers, information disclosed to one may be passed on to others. Friends should keep secrets.
- Obligations – We are more willing to become obligated in friendship than in friendly relations. Friendly relations normally reciprocate within the encounter, while friendship involves more trust that reciprocation will occur sometime in the future.

Kurth notes that we may engage in friendly relations with people that we don't even like, to facilitate interaction.

In regard to sense of uniqueness, recent research on **relational mobility** concerns how easy it is to replace social relationships. Thomson et al. (2018) explored this in thirty-nine countries. In some social environments, people have stable and long-lasting relationships. In other social environments, there are many options for relationships, so people can freely seek new partners and friends. When many alternatives are available, more intimacy behaviors are needed to keep people committed to relationships, such as self-disclosure and expressions of affection. This is discussed further in the SPOTLIGHT on Intimacy and Relational Mobility in Chapter 4 of this book.

WHAT COMMITMENT RITUALS AND MECHANISMS OCCUR IN OTHER SOCIAL RELATIONSHIPS?

Variations in commitment in intimate relationships are discussed in Chapter 1, which noted that there are commitment rituals and ceremonies, such as engagement and marriage, which increase public and private commitment. Friendships are less likely to have commitment rituals that are called that, but there may be other rituals that promote commitment, such as birthday parties, reunions, "boys' night out," and "girls' night out," or organizations that meet on a regular basis.

Groups often have commitment ceremonies. For example, Christians have baptism, in which parents and godparents commit to raise a baby in the faith; some Christian groups have Confirmation ceremonies for adolescents; Jews have male circumcision for babies and Bar Mitzvahs for adolescent boys and Bat Mitzvahs for girls. Other groups, such as fraternities, sororities,

TABLE 13.1 *Relevance of* Comprehensive Partner Model *for other relationships*

Motivation	
+ Having had a previous partner	motivation is relevant for all relationships
Confidence	
+ Rating self desirable as a partner	relevant on particular characteristics
Readiness	
+ Age	relevant for types of relationships
Opportunity	
− Difficulty in finding a partner	relevant for establishing relationships

and sports teams, may have commitment ceremonies called "initiation rituals."

Kanter (1972) identified commitment mechanisms in utopian communities that may be relevant to some degree in other groups. They free people from other commitments while committing the person to the given group. And they solve the system problems of continuance (keeping people in the group), cohesion (keeping the group from splitting up), and social control (obtaining obedience to group norms. These commitment mechanisms include the following:

- Sacrifice – giving up something considered valuable outside the group
- Investment – giving resources to the group such as money and time
- Renunciation – avoiding relationships deemed threatening to the group
- Communion – engaging in activities to promote identification with the group
- Mortification – using criticism to eliminate old identities outside the group
- Surrender – giving decision making to the group

While commitment rituals and mechanisms may take various forms in other social relationships, relationship satisfaction should be relevant to any kind of social relationship.

HOW MIGHT FACTORS THAT PREDICT HAVING A CURRENT PARTNER APPLY TO OTHER SOCIAL RELATIONSHIPS?

Table 13.1 lists categories of factors in the *Comprehensive Partner Model* that predict having a current partner in the current study, and their hypothesized relevance to having other social relationships.

Some social relationships are ascribed (assigned), such as kinship relationships that one is born into, while others need to be achieved, such as friendships. All of the categories of the *Comprehensive Partner Model* are relevant for having achieved relationships. They are also relevant for success

TABLE 13.2 *Relevance of* Comprehensive Commitment Model *for other relationships*

Partner Suitability	
+ Personality Similarity Scale	relevant on particular characteristics
+ Rating partner desirable as a partner	relevant for particular activities
+ Parents and others approve of partner	regarding joint activities or influence
Intimacy Dimensions	
+ Emotional closeness	varies in importance
+ Saying both of us are in love	feelings described as both liking
+ Love scale	feelings described as liking
+ *Eros (we were made for each other)*	*uniqueness varies in importance*
+ Trusting partner not to lie	extremely relevant
+ Sexual satisfaction	not relevant
− Anxious attachment	can result in dissatisfaction
Exchange Processes	
+ Gained benefits from the relationship	very relevant
+ Equal involvement in the relationship	varies with type of relationship
+ Equal power in the relationship	varies with status differences
+ *Invested in the relationship*	*varies with type of relationship*
Conflict Resolution	
+ Positive Responses	very relevant
+ Voice (would discuss and fix things up)	very relevant
− Highest Sources of Conflicts Scale	very relevant
− Exit (would break up if dissatisfied)	very relevant

in maintaining ascribed relationships. Motivation for establishing and maintaining relationships is relevant for all relationships. Confidence that one is desirable to others is relevant, but the relevant characteristics may vary across types of relationships. Similarly, age is relevant for different types of relationships, such as friendships, marriage, and work relationships. And opportunities for finding partners and interacting to maintain relationships are relevant for all social relationships.

HOW MIGHT FACTORS THAT PREDICT RELATIONSHIP SATISFACTION APPLY TO OTHER SOCIAL RELATIONSHIPS?

Table 13.2 lists categories of factors in the *Comprehensive Commitment Model* that predict relationship satisfaction or commitment in the current study, and their hypothesized relevance to satisfaction in other social relationships. The two factors in italics are relevant to commitment but not satisfaction in intimate relationships.

Note that personality similarity is relevant on some characteristics, such as honesty, for all social relationships, while other characteristics vary depending upon the activities in the relationship. Partner desirability again varies depending on the activities. Approval of parents and others depends on the extent to which they interact at the same time or are concerned about negative influence from the partner.

Emotional closeness varies in relevance depending on how intimate the relationship is. Feelings may be described as liking instead of love but are still relevant in being satisfied with a relationship. Teamwork or collaboration with others is more satisfying if you like the others. Sexual satisfaction is not likely to be relevant in other relationships, while anxious attachment can result in dissatisfaction.

Exchange processes can be relevant to any relationships. Gaining benefits is important for satisfaction. Equal involvement, equal power, and being invested in the relationship may vary with relationship type but are likely relevant to satisfaction depending on the acceptability of the status differences. And factors of conflict resolution are very relevant for satisfaction in any relationship.

In sum, partner desirability and emotional dimensions vary depending on the intimacy and activities of the relationship. But exchange processes and conflict resolution are likely relevant to any social relationship. An example of how some of the theories and factors important in this study might also apply in other social relationships is provided in the SPOTLIGHT on Workplace Relationships in Africa and Elsewhere later in this chapter.

HOW ARE THE PREVIOUSLY NOTED CATEGORIES COMBINED IN A *COMPREHENSIVE RELATIONSHIP MODEL*?

Chapter 9 noted that social relationships are important predictors of well-being, but that the quality of the relationships is more important than merely having the relationships (Saphire-Bernstein & Taylor, 2013). Chapter 9 also reported that General Life Satisfaction is associated with Relationship Satisfaction, but there is a trivial direct association between General Life Satisfaction and Relationship Commitment. These findings suggest that the predictors of Having a Current Partner and the predictors of Relationship Satisfaction can be combined into a *Comprehensive Relationship Model* as shown in Figure 13.1.

In this model, factors representing motivation, confidence, readiness, and opportunity predict having a social relationship. And partner suitability, intimacy dimensions, exchange process, and conflict resolution predict relationship satisfaction. These are combined in this model so that relationship satisfaction mediates between having a social relationship and life satisfaction. Relationship commitment is omitted from this model since its association with life satisfaction is due to relationship satisfaction.

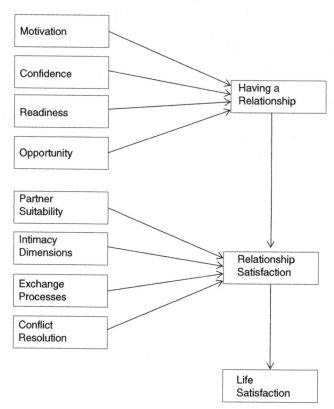

FIGURE 13.1   *Comprehensive Relationship Model*

HOW DOES THE *COMPREHENSIVE RELATIONSHIP MODEL* RELATE TO SOCIAL NETWORKS?

Social relationships are often embedded in social networks (Borgatti et al., 2009), which vary in the number of persons and in the number of relationships among them. As noted in Chapter 10, approval of parents and others is important for relationship satisfaction with a romantic or sexual partner. But approving of each other in a network should be important for relationship satisfaction and life satisfaction as well, to the extent that network members interact with each other.

Just as it takes a village to raise a child, as noted in Chapter 2, it takes a network of relationships to meet the various needs of an adult. These networks of relationships provide **circles of support** to help people cope with life. The term "circles of support" has primarily been used in regard to helping persons with disabilities (Kreutzer, Deluca, & Caplan, 2011) and helping persons reentering society after prison (Elliot & Zajac, 2015). But it

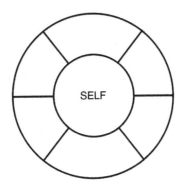

FIGURE 13.2 Inner circle of support

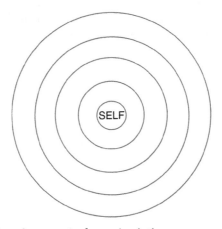

FIGURE 13.3 Circles of support in decreasing intimacy

is a useful concept for predicting life satisfaction for anyone. The inner circle of closest intimate relationships can be visualized as a life ring that buoys a person up. In Figure 13.2, the lines represent relationships surrounding the self, like the ropes to hang onto on a life ring.

Additional circles are shown in Figure 13.3, where they range from the partner and most intimate family members and friends, to moderately intimate relatives and friends, to acquaintances and friendly relations like those described earlier by (Kurth, 1970) and may include mentors and mental health professionals.

Each relationship in the circles can be described in terms of the *Comprehensive Relationship Model* (CRM). Since multiple CRMs occur in a network, the factors affecting one CRM may interact with factors affecting others. For example, approval or disapproval of a relationship by one network member may influence others' approval or disapproval of that relationship or other relationships in the network. Network members often provide opportunities to meet partners and other network members and may include or exclude other members in activities. They may be sources of conflict in other relationships or mediators to resolve conflict. In other words, the interactions are complex. It is proposed that the comprehensive models identified in this book could be building blocks in creating the overarching and integrative theory that has been called for by Berscheid (1995) and Finkel, Simpson, and Eastwick (2017).

SELF-REFLECTION

How well do members of your social network know one another? Do they get along? Do your parents know your friends? Do your closest friends know one another? Have your parents approved or disproved of your friends? Have some of your friends approved or disapproved of other friends or acquaintances?

SPOTLIGHT ON WORKPLACE RELATIONSHIPS IN AFRICA AND ELSEWHERE

OLUFEMI A. LAWAL

Despite the enormous speed at which the nature of work and workplaces is changing in our contemporary world, most work tasks and work environments are still handled by humans. The advent of internet and communications technology (ICT) and ICT-enhanced automation has not only made the pace and speed of work faster; it has made for higher-quality products and services to be achievable by fewer workers in much less time than before. For example, virtual work teams, whose members may not have met one another physically before, meet more easily and frequently and may be more productive than work teams whose members have to physically meet for useful decision making or productive efforts to be deployed. Either way, it still takes humans to put things to work no matter their number in various organizations.

For active, paid employed people, the most productive hours of every workday are spent in the workplace. And spending the better part of the day at work is typically not a daily routine that any worker goes through all alone. It is usually shared with other workers, as the workplace itself is a daily meeting point for all kinds of people who are working in the same organization, departments, sections, groups, units, or teams. It is, therefore, natural that different forms of relationships develop among people in such environments. Because their developments may be largely influenced by diverse factors, these interpersonal relationships can also vary in strength, intensity, or intimacy, meaning that they can be formal, informal, casual, emotional, romantic, or professional.

Interpersonal relationships at work can stem from circumstances that may be under the control of or well beyond the individuals involved in it. This SPOTLIGHT is a theoretical analysis of the factors underpinning the development, maintenance, and adaptability of workplace interpersonal relationships. While there are many such factors, explanations will be discussed in terms of a biological factor (oxytocin), Attachment Theory, a cultural factor (collectivism), leader-follower relationships, paternalism, and two types of trust.

A BIOLOGICAL FACTOR (OXYTOCIN)

The tendency and ability to relate and bond intimately with certain people but not with others are under the coordination of the brain, and trust is understood to mediate the process. *Trust* is commonly defined as the process by which a person (the trustor) willingly renders oneself vulnerable to another person (the trustee) on the belief that the trustee will behave or act as the trustor expects. A number of brain structures (e.g., the amygdala) and hormones (e.g., oxytocin and dopamine) are known to be more involved than others in brain-behavior relationships. But oxytocin stands out regarding its centrality to trust. Several experiments that have attempted to understand how the hormone oxytocin influences interpersonal bonding found that it actually impacts trust, which, in turn, largely influences whom to relate or get intimate with (e.g., Insel & Young, 2001; Kosfeld, Heinrichs, Zak, Fischbacher, & Fehr, 2005). Specifically, the experiments reveal that by increasing levels of oxytocin, the tendency or readiness to trust is also increased.

Oxytocin is generally understood to be the catalyst that drives the regulatory functions of the brain on social behavior. According to Shalev and Ebstein (2013), among other behaviors regulated by oxytocin are the quality of pair bonding, parenting, social stress, in-group and out-group relationships, and social communications. Two major trajectories appear to be common in the outcomes of the research on the relationship between oxytocin and behavior: either that higher levels of oxytocin are found in humans who invest more in relationships requiring trust, including economic, romantic, and filial, or that these humans tend to invest more in such relationships after receiving infusions of oxytocin (Anacker & Beery, 2013).

However, research also shows that the effect of oxytocin on bonding and intimacy is always direct only when individuals in relationships are well adjusted mentally, are happy to be involved in the relationships, or are finding the relationships rewarding. Where they are maladjusted (e.g., anxious or personality disordered) or find their relationships unsatisfactory/unrewarding, the effect of oxytocin on intimacy can be indirect in that increased levels of it generate opposite behaviors (Scheele et al., 2012). For example, people with borderline personality disorder are understood to trust and cooperate far less when infused with oxytocin (Bartz et al., 2011; Shamay-Tsoory et al., 2009).

The effect of oxytocin on interpersonal relationships provides a basis for its relevance to the maintenance of relationships between and among members of a group or a team. Pro-social and agnostic behaviors, which oxytocin also influence, help to strengthen group cohesion and intragroup relations (Anacker & Beery, 2013). These happen, sometimes through enhancing in-group favoritism and ethnocentrism with oxytocin being the driver of affiliation and intimacy among in-group members (Shalev & Ebstein, 2013). For example, in a prisoner's dilemma experiment, some participants, who were making financial decisions on behalf of a group under the influence of oxytocin (administered to them), report being better protected, trusting their in-group members more, and making more decisions that would benefit them but punish out-group members at the same time, all in response to a threat of a noncooperative out-group member (De Dreu et al., 2010).

ATTACHMENT THEORY

The intimacy in some interpersonal or intragroup relationships can be better understood from the standpoint of Attachment Theory, which views the quest for attachment or intimacy as something driven by the need to maximize our chances of survival as humans (Labek et al., 2016; Wichmann, 2015). Accordingly, survival is better assured when humans are attached to one another because attachment brings about personal or shared sense of protection against harm as well as access to physical and psychological events that guarantee the continuity of the bond and survival of the parties involved in it. For example, a child is said to be inextricably bonded to a caregiver, usually the mother, because this intimacy guarantees the provision of the child's needs for care by way of protection against dangers, support, and provision of food (Bowlby, 1969, 1973, 1980; Labek et al., 2016; Wichmann, 2015).

While Attachment Theory appears to sufficiently explain why certain people engage in intimate relationships, it does not explain why the same people are attached to certain categories of people but not to others; neither does it explain why several other people do not engage in intimate relationships at all. The fact that humans differ in the manner in which they are wired for relationships significantly clarifies what Attachment Theory does not explain. For example, oxytocin – where significantly present or increased – impacts a single man differently from a man in a relationship. When they both encounter an attractive female, it may predispose the single man to engage the female in a relationship, while it inclines the man in a relationship to distance himself from her (Grillon et al., 2013; Scheele et al., 2012; Striepens et al., 2012).

A CULTURAL FACTOR (COLLECTIVISM)

Collectivism can be defined as a cultural inclination of individuals to relate to members of a group they closely identify with as people who are crucial to their existence or survival just because they are co-members of the same group that they hold in so much importance. In the workplace, collectivism requires that a worker subordinate personal goals for group goals and exhibit an already cultivated sense of harmony and interdependence, and concern for others (Hofstede, 2001). In both theory and research, individuals in society and employees in the workplace who are highly collectivistic, known as "collectivists," are also strongly disposed toward the interdependent self-construal that is a perception of oneself not only as an important member of a group but also as one whose existence and survival are dependent on the plight of the group (Markus & Kitayama, 1991). It is also known as the "interdependent relational self-concept," suggesting that a person's self-definition or self-concept is predicated on the nature and quality of their relationships with others (Lam & Zane, 2004; Markus & Kitayama, 1991).

In the workplace, interdependent self-construal can be seen as employees' views as to who and how important they are, which derives from their understanding of the purpose and importance of their work group in the organization. Being high on interdependent self-construal should predispose an employee to forgo personal interests and goals for the work group's interests and goals. The implication of this is that an average Nigerian worker would be expected, and therefore feel culturally bound, to relate with their coworkers as closely as possible. This being an expectation, employees who – for one reason or the other – are "distant" from members of their work group would not be comfortable with this state of affairs. Therefore, the cultural pressure to always defer to their work group, which employees experience on account of their collectivist orientation, has implications for their interpersonal relationships.

Levels of collectivism and interdependent self-construal may vary in employees with implications for the strength of their identities with and commitments to their groups. The gains of working in groups in terms of productivity and industrial harmony are enormous in organizations. Early research evidence of this comes from the Hawthorne Experiments by Elton Mayo and his colleagues, who found that while physical factors like working equipment and work environment were crucial to a successful work delivery, social needs that may be met by treating workers humanely are more important. And when the humane treatment was extended to giving workers freedom to organize themselves into groups to undertake group work assignments and be rewarded as groups, workers spent fewer days to complete their weekly assignments, rested more, interacted more, and shared the reward meant for a week after a few days. The qualities of goods produced were also judged to be better than when employees worked alone as individuals.

However, in most African cultures where collectivism is prevalent, sufficiently high levels of both collectivism and interdependent self-construal would certainly be required for interpersonal and intragroup relationships to be intimate or cohesive. Whether being highly intimate with one another or working together in a cohesive work team would constitute an advantage for productivity and industrial harmony remains hypothetical: in individualistic societies, where independent self-construal is rather prevalent, work group or team members do not necessarily have to be in intimate relationships to be productive. There are certainly several other factors that are bases for intimate relationships among members of a work group.

That members of a work group relate intimately probably on account of being highly collectivistic or strongly interdependence oriented as seems common in Africa may not always be an unlimited blessing to organizations.

One major problem associated with groups of highly collectivistic and very interdependent workers, that is, cohesive work groups, is their high suscept- ibility to the decision-making error known as "groupthink." Groupthink can be defined as a distorted style of thinking that renders group members incapable of making a rational decision (Kassin, 2008). Groupthink occurs when workers in a cohesive work group, in an attempt to make a decision, begin to strive for unanimity because their motivation to maintain the unanimity of the group overrides their motivation to realistically appraise . alternative courses of actions before the decision is made. To ensure that the highest priority is remaining intimate with one another and that their group is cohesive, members become desperate to agree with one another, thereby committing errors that could easily be avoided (Plotnik, 2002). Through suppression of dissent and self-imposed conviction that the group's position is correct, they strive to maintain group harmony (Baron, 2002; Baron & Byrne, 2004; Baron & Kalsher, 2002).

Given the nature of groupthink, it is a common feature of minority social influence, notably leadership, and explains why decision making is the biggest problem in African leadership. It leads groups across societies and organizations in Africa to defy ethnic and religious barriers to be cohesive, especially when exposed to an out-group made up of opposi- tion, rivals, rebels, or recalcitrant followers. The consequence is usually radical decisions that become worse and usually inhumane as decision makers become more desperate to remain united and committed to one another. So to fortify their common front, they crush real, imagined, perceived, and envisaged opposition, uprising, insurrection, insurgencies, and rebellion, which may be inevitable. These, taking place usually at societal levels, are some of the major reasons Africa has been so turbu- lently in conflict for decades, which have also caused many indigenous and multinational work organizations to fail, and millions of people to fall into poverty.

LEADER-FOLLOWER RELATIONSHIPS

"Leader-follower relationships," also commonly known as leader-member exchange (LMX), can be defined as the nature and quality of the dyadic (one-on-one) relationship existing between organizational leaders and each of their subordinates in the workplace. The quality and intimacy of these relationships can vary widely. In terms of quality, the relation- ship can be good or bad. Intimacy can range from "very formal" to "very informal" or "very cordial." The adoption of these two extremes is premised on the nature of LMX as a construct that views the relationship between superiors and each of their subordinates as one that can range on a continuum of very formal to very cordial or very intimate, such that the superior relates with each of the subordinates at different points on the continuum.

A major concern with LMX being defined as good or bad is that of the erroneous assumption that once LMX is cordial, it is taken for granted that it is good. But the "good" in some LMXs is questionable on the ground that they are premised on a relationship-based trust rather than character-based trust, which suggests that the underlying relationship can be anything from "healthy and pure" to "compromised and corrupt." The trust factor underpinning this will be discussed later in this SPOTLIGHT.

A cordial LMX presupposes an intimate leader-follower relationship. Here, leader-follower relationship means more than just implementing what is contained in the formal employment contract of the subordinate involved; superiors go out of their way to demonstrate preference and support for the subordinate, and giving the subordinate greater freedom and work responsibility. As alluded to earlier, a formal LMX is not a foreclosure of a relationship between a leader and subordinates. It only points to the fact that the relationship is restrictive and strictly about implementation of the terms of employment in an employee's contract. Employees in this category usually perform only routine tasks (Krone, 1991), and their leaders rarely try to motivate them beyond the call of duty.

According to Dansereau et al. (1975), leaders in cordial or intimate LMXs usually have a special relationship with close and trusted subordinates, to whom they give high levels of responsibility, decision influence, and access to resources. These subordinates who, by their intimacy with the leader, are in-group members to the leader, usually work harder, are usually tasked with more administrative duties, and are expected to be fully committed and loyal to their leader. The subordinates who are not in this category are regarded as out-group members to the leader, are either less trusted or not trusted at all, and are given low levels of choice or influence, all because their relationships with the leader are not intimate.

Exploring the roots of these relationships, Classical LMX Theory (Graen & Cashman, 1975; Dansereau et al., 1975) stresses that they start as soon as individuals join the organization and assume work responsibilities with their work group or team. They are said to typically follow the three stages of:

1. **Role taking:** The members join the team and the leader assesses their abilities and talents. Based on this, the leader may offer them opportunities to demonstrate their capabilities. But beyond work-related capabilities that this theory addressed, it is instructive to note that the leader also tries to establish how, in terms of personality dispositions, attitudes, and mannerisms, similar or dissimilar the leader is with each employee.

2. **Role making:** In this second phase, the leader and member engage in an informal negotiation whereby a role is created for the member and the

promise of benefit and power in return for dedication and loyalty is made at least informally. Trust building is important in this stage. And since the goal of the leader is to co-opt the member into the leader's in-group, any betrayal felt, especially by the leader, can result in the member being relegated to the out-group.

Given that the informal negotiation is inclusive of relationship factors as well as pure work-related ones, a member who is *similar* to the leader in various ways is more likely to succeed. As evidence of the important place of similarity of leader and follower in determining the outcome of the informal negotiation, mixed gender, ethnic, and racial relationships are said to be less successful than same-gender, -ethnic, and -racial ones – in terms of their chances of becoming intimate.

3. **Routinization:** The indicators that a successful work group or team of largely in-group members would emerge become rife at this stage as a pattern of ongoing social exchange between the leader and each member becomes established. First, successful members are similar in many ways to the leader (which perhaps explains why many senior teams are all White, male, middle-class, and middle-aged). Next, together, leader and followers work hard at building and sustaining trust and respect. They are also empathetic, patient, reasonable, sensitive, and good at seeing the viewpoint of other people (especially of the leader).

PATERNALISM

"Paternalism" may best be understood as a variant of LMX in collectivist societies. It refers to situations in which an organizational leader assumes parental roles and obligations over some subordinate employees in the workplace, and the affected employees look up to the leader for such a responsibility (Aycan, 2002; Pellegrini & Scandura, 2008). The organizational leader, who is usually older than the subordinate with whom they are engaged in a paternalistic relationship, regards the subordinate as one under their care whom they are obliged to protect and care for (Triandis, 1993). The subordinate involved, in turn, reciprocates such care and protection of the "father figure at work" by being loyal to them, deferring to them completely, and complying with their directives (Pellegrini & Scandura, 2008). Typically, the follower "voluntarily" depends on the leader.

Looking at paternalism as a variant of LMX is quite instructive in that it may be suggestive of even a more intimate superior-subordinate relationship than may be found in LMX: all forms of paternalism necessitate that the two parties involved (the leader and the follower) are intimate. This is not farfetched considering that paternalism appears to be more widespread in collectivistic cultures where power distance, people's belief about the how more powerful leaders are than followers, is very high (Hofstede, 1980, 1998). In Africa, where power distance is at an all-time high, with most people deifying their leaders, followers are usually given to deferring to leaders completely. Work organizations in this part of the world are characterized with strong bonds between leaders and subordinates who see those leaders as next only to God. As such, while bosses in such relationships take it for granted that the subordinates with whom they are in paternalistic relationships are completely loyal to them, the subordinates involved continue to ascribe more powers to them.

The fear that the "halo" with which they are being treated by the bosses may turn to "horns" that can be used to crush them if they defy the bosses' authorities indefinitely keeps many subordinates in the relationships. Such fears and associated behaviors of subordinates can be understood to be borne out of "Uncertainty Avoidance" (Hofstede, 1980, 2001). Therefore, not all paternalistic relationships in the workplace are consensual despite that all appear to be intimate.

Research evidence that seems to corroborate this theory is that of Harris and Kacmar (2006). In their investigation of whether the leader-follower relationship can be too intimate, they found that this relationship can become so intimate that it can adversely affect the well-being of subordinate employees involved in it. Specifically, they discovered that as this relationship becomes more intimate, the leader comes to trust and count on the follower more and more to the point of delegating virtually all their own responsibilities to the follower. Job stress sets in for the subordinate when they continue to combine these with their own responsibilities, which increases as the burden of work increases. Although the research was an LMX research, it appears as a classic case of paternalism in developing societies.

TWO TYPES OF TRUST

Perhaps seeing trust as a willingness to "risk" one's intimacies in the hands of another person(s) would be more appropriate at this stage of discussing workplace relationships. Trust theory (Dirk & Ferrin, 2002) instructs that this risk is of two types. The first is character-based trust that is trust that an individual gives another individual on the strength of the "real" attributes of the person being trusted. In leader-follower relationships, for example, character-based trust is usually given because the trustor has experienced/interacted with the trustee and ascertained their competence, integrity, fairness, intelligence, skills, knowledge, doggedness, and resilience. The basis or reason for character-based trust is always the perception of the leader's character, in terms of several attributes, and how the character influences a follower's sense and feeling of vulnerability in a leader-follower relationship (Mayer, Davis, & Schoorman, 1995). Closely related to Dirk and Ferrin's (2002) character-based trust perspective is McAllister's (1995) typology of cognitive trust, which, similar to character-based trust, reflects issues such as the reliability, integrity, honesty, and fairness of a trustee.

In the light of the previous discussion, character-based trust applies more to formal relationships that are usually guided by rules, regulations, and ethics and, therefore, characterized by less intimacy compared to informal relationships. One can in fact view character-based trust, where present and high, as the driver of business and organizations in the contemporary world order where state-of-the-art technologies have significantly reduced human interactions in business.

The second type of trust is relationship-based trust that, according to Dirks and Ferrin (2002), thrives on existing relationships and the commitments of parties involved in the LMX, paternalism, and other forms of leader-follower relationships at work. Compared to character-based trust, relationship-based trust is not necessarily based on objectivity but purely on social exchange processes whereby parties involved build trust by simply obeying the norm of reciprocity (Blau, 1964) – by striving to return good for good, help for help, favor for favor, goodwill for goodwill, support for support, etc. In leader-follower contexts, followers see their relationship with their leader as something transcending what is specified by rules, laws, or the formal employment contract.

Also similar to relationship-based trust is McAllister's (1995) typology of affective trust in which wanting to take so much risk as to become vulnerable depends on the perception that the trustee will not hurt the trustor, owing to the cordial relationship between them. In the workplace, affective trust is usually found between co-workers who also are in a cordial relationship with one another. The trust is premised on the special relationship between the two workers on the strength of which one will trust the other regardless of whether the trusted co-worker has integrity, is reliable, is consistent, is honest, is fair, or is predictable. In fact these important attributes are not required for affective trust and, as such, may not be necessary in intimate relationships that are driven by such trust.

With this background in mind, relationship-based trust is the oil and driver of intimate relationships in organizations, and without which no organization can survive. The reason is that the workplace thrives not only on formal relationships but also on various degrees of intimate interpersonal and intragroup relationships. For example, it is common knowledge that organizational citizenship behavior and co-worker support, both of which thrive on relationships, oftentimes very intimate ones, are two important factors without which no organization can survive. What is important in affective or relationship-based trust is mutual agreements, beliefs, understanding, etc. It is essentially an emotional kind of trust with the implication of a "perceptual" set (or readiness) to always find the trusted partner "trustworthy" no matter the situation. Thus, another way of referring to relationship-based trust is to call it a "blind trust."

Although relationship-based trust holds a lot of advantages for work organizations, the other implications of sharing this emotional or blind trust by some people in organizations may be more disadvantageously far-reaching than may be imagined. The behaviors and events that may signal that intimate relationships, driven by relationship-based trust, have caused problems in the workplace are many. One is ingratiation, which refers to a set of related political tactics that are aimed at portraying oneself as likable to one's targets, especially where it is undeserved. It is a kind of behavior that pervades all workplaces, occurring exclusively between subordinates and superiors whereby subordinates target their ingratiatory behaviors, such as opinion conformity and favor doing, at their superiors with sole aim of distorting the superiors' perceptions of them. Where successful, and subordinates are liked by their superiors, ingratiation would bias and corrupt the relationships between those subordinates and their superiors at work.

Another source of problems is organizational romance, which can be found among co-workers but more commonly in a superior-subordinate relationship. The romance can be heterosexual or homosexual but has one of the greatest potentials to bias and corrupt processes in organizations. The intimacy between partners who are usually involved in workplace romance can be so strong that there is no room for any formality or objectivity again when it comes to performance evaluation, recommendations, and discipline.

Finally, and perhaps the events with the strongest possible form of relationship intimacy in the workplace, are caucuses and cultism. Different forms and dimensions of caucuses and cultism trouble today's workplace. Some are formed in the workplace while others are peopled by workers from all cadres who had been members of such groups before getting to the organization – in fact, some get their jobs because their "godfathers" or senior members of a cult are big shots in the organization. Opinions and accounts of people in organizations go a long way to suggest that members of these groups display the strongest forms of intimacies toward one another wherever they find themselves, including work organizations. It is also a common belief that members of these groups would leave no stone unturned to favor one another, including covering up crimes.

Epilogue: What Future Research Is Needed?

As noted in the Introduction to this book, there has been a great deal of research on relationships, but very little of it has been cross-cultural. Even less has involved relationships other than marriage. A notable exception is a recent anthology about grandparents in various cultures (Schwalb & Hossain, 2017). Also of interest is a one-year longitudinal study that found that Rusbult's Investment Theory predicted staying best friends among adolescents in the Netherlands (Branje et al., 2007). Another study explored social support among siblings (brothers or sisters) in the Netherlands (Voorpostel & Blieszner, 2008).

Chapter 1 introduced the **statistical tools** and **conceptual tools** used in this book. Future research is needed using these tools in the following ways.

RESEARCH USING THE STATISTICAL TOOLS

- Comparing predictions of factors, not just average levels of factors.
- Paying attention to effect sizes, and noting when effects are trivial.
- Emphasizing similarities as well as differences.
- Grouping factors into categories, and noting which factors are Central Factors that capture effects of other factors, while realizing that which factors are central may vary from study to study depending on the measures used.

RESEARCH USING THE CONCEPTUAL TOOLS

- Exploring other measures of the categories of the *Comprehensive Partner Model* (motivation, confidence, readiness, opportunity) and other potential predictors of having a current partner.
- Exploring other measures of the categories of the *Comprehensive Commitment Model* (partner suitability, intimacy dimensions, exchange

processes, conflict resolution) and other potential predictors of relationship satisfaction and relationship commitment.

- Exploring both direct effects and indirect effects of factors that predict relationship commitment and other aspects of intimate relationships.
- Exploring in couples how the factors for one partner relate to the factors for the other partner and vice versa.
- Exploring longitudinally how the factors interact and the comprehensive models predict over time.
- Exploring how the *Comprehensive Partner Model* and the *Comprehensive Commitment Model* apply to the romantic or sexual relationships of persons with nonbinary gender identities.
- Exploring how the *Comprehensive Partner Model* and the *Comprehensive Commitment Model* might apply to other social relationships.
- Exploring how the factors that predict one social relationship interact with the factors that predict other social relationships in one's social network. For example, social relationships provide opportunities to meet potential partners, and partners introduce other social relationships. Approval by parents and friends affect partner suitability, and approval by partner affects suitability of other social relationships.
- Exploring how the *Comprehensive Relationship Model* might interact with other predictors of life satisfaction identified by Diener and his colleagues (e.g., Diener & McGavran, 2008).
- Exploring all of these factors across relationship types and cultures, making explicit comparisons of cultures, not just anthologies of cultures.

In summary, this book demonstrates the usefulness of these statistical tools and conceptual tools for understanding intimate relationships and suggests ways in which these tools may be useful for future research on both intimate relationships and other social relationships.

GLOSSARY OF STATISTICAL TERMS

All of these terms are introduced in Chapter 1, except Comprehensive Factor, which is introduced in Chapter 10.

- $*$ = $p<.05$, $**$ = $p<.01$, $***$ = $p<.001$, probability that the result could have been due to chance (less than 5%, less than 1%, and less than 0.1%, respectively)
- γ = standardized regression coefficient in SEM models, range 0 to 1 or 0 to -1; $\gamma<.10$ adds trivial explained variance in R-squared
- **Alpha** = how closely items in a scale are associated with one another, range 0 to 1, Alpha=.7 or above is desired
- **Analysis of Variance (ANOVA)** = for conducting F-tests comparing means of more than two groups
- **Central Factor** = factor that captures effects that it has in common with other factors in making predictions in this book
- **Confirmatory Factor Analysis** = for testing consistency of factor loadings across groups
- **Comparative Fit Index (CFI)** = measure of consistency of links across groups, range 0 to 1, CFI>.95 is desired
- **Comprehensive Factor** = Central Factor that captures effects that it has in common with other Central Factors in this book
- **Correlation (r)** = measure of association between two variables (see **r**)
- **Effect size** = indicator of how strong an effect is, r-squared in this book
- **Explained variance (r-squared)** = percentage of variation in one variable predicted by variation in one or more other variables
- **F-test** = for comparing means of more than two groups
- **Factor analysis** = for telling which items "load" on separate factors
- **Factor loading** = how closely the item is associated with the factor, range 0 to 1, loading .4 or above is desired
- **Mean** = average of a group
- **Multiple Regression** = prediction based on multiple predictor variables
- *ns* = not statistically significant
- $p<.05$ = less than 5% probability of being due to chance (1 chance in 20)
- **Point-biserial correlation** = r when a variable has only two values
- **r** = (Pearson) correlation, range 0 to 1 or 0 to -1
- **r-squared** = percentage of variation in one variable predicted by another variable

- **R-squared** = percentage of variation in one variable predicted by multiple variables in Multiple Regression
- **Reliability analysis (Alpha)** = how closely items in a scale are associated with each other, range 0 to 1, Alpha=.7 or above is desired
- **Repeated Measures ANOVA** = for conducting F-tests comparing responses to different questions answered by the same group
- **Replication** = finding the same result again
- **RMSEA (Root Mean Squared Error of Approximation)** = measure of consistency of links across groups, range 0 to 1, RMSEA <.05 is desired
- **SEM Measurement Models** = for conducting Confirmatory Factor Analysis, to see if factor loadings are consistent across groups
- **SEM Structural Models** = used to test consistency of links across groups in this book
- *s.d.* **(standard deviation)** = measure of individual variability
- **Standard score (normalized score)** = converted to mean of 0 and *s.d.* of 1 by subtracting the group mean and dividing by the *s.d.*, so scores are independent of mean and *s.d.*
- **Standardized regression coefficient in SEM models (γ)** = measure of link, range 0 to 1 or 0 to −1, γ<.10 adds trivial explained variance in R-squared
- **Statistically significant** = unlikely to be due to chance variations in variables
- **Structural Equation Modeling (SEM)** = for testing links among variables
- **T-test** = for comparing means of two groups
- **Trivial correlation** = r<.10 so r-squared <.01 explaining <1%
- **Variance** = the square of the standard deviation (*s.d.*), which is the square root, of the sum of the squared difference, between each score and the group mean

BOSTON COUPLES STUDY PUBLICATIONS

ORIGINAL STUDY

Hill, C. T., Rubin, Z., & Peplau, L. A. (1976). Breakups before marriage: The end of 103 affairs. *Journal of Social Issues, 32*(1), 147–168.
Reprinted in A. Skolnick & J. Skolnick (Eds.). (1977). *Family in transition: Rethinking marriage, sexuality, childrearing and family organization* (2nd ed.). Boston: Little, Brown & Co.
Reprinted in G. Levinger & O. C. Moles (Eds.). (1979). *Divorce and separation: A survey of causes and consequences.* New York: Basic Books.
Hill, C. T., Peplau, L. A., & Rubin, Z. (1981). Differing perceptions in dating couples. *Psychology of Women Quarterly, 5*(3), 418–434.
(1983). Use of contraceptives by college dating couples. *Population and Environment: Behavioral and Social Issues, 6*(1), 60–69.
& Willard, S. (1979). The volunteer couple: Sex differences, couple commitment, and participation in research on interpersonal relationships. *Social Psychology Quarterly, 42*(4), 415–420.
Peplau, L. A. (1976). Impact of fear of success and sex-role attitudes on women's competitive achievement. *Journal of Personality and Social Psychology, 34,* 561–568.
(1976). Fear of success in dating couples. *Sex Roles, 2,* 249–258.
(1979). Power in dating relationships. In J. Freeman (Ed.), *Women: A feminist perspective,* 2nd ed. (pp. 106–121). Palo Alto, CA: Mayfield Publishing. Reprinted in the 3rd ed. (l984) and revised for the 4th ed. (l989).
Rubin, Z., & Hill, C. T. (1976, November). The sexual balance of power. Psychology Today (pp. l42 ff.).
Reprinted in C. Gordon & G. Johnson (Eds.). (1979). *Readings in human sexuality: Contemporary perspectives* (2nd ed.). New York: Harper & Row.
(1977). Sexual intimacy in dating couples. *Journal of Social Issues, 33*(2), 86–109.
Pleck, J. H. (1976). Male threat from female competence. *Journal of Consulting and Clinical Psychology, 44*(4), 608–613.
Risman, B. J., Hill, C. T., Rubin, Z., & Peplau, L. A. (1981). Living together in college: Implications for courtship. *Journal of Marriage and the Family, 43,* 77–83.
Rubin, Z. (1974). Lovers and other strangers: The development of intimacy in encounters and relationships. *American Scientist, 62,* 182–190.

Hill, C. T., Peplau, L. A., & Dunkel-Schetter, C. (1980). Self-disclosure in dating couples: Sex roles and the ethic of openness. *Journal of Marriage and the Family*, 42(2), 305–318.

& Mitchell, C. (1976). Couples research as couples counseling: Some unintended effects of studying close relationships. *American Psychologist, 31*, 17–25.

Peplau, L. A., & Hill, C. T. (1981). Loving and leaving: Sex differences in romantic attachments. *Sex Roles, 7*(8), 821–835.

Stewart, A. J., & Rubin, Z. (1976). The power motive in dating couples. *Journal of Personality and Social Psychology, 34*, 305–309.

15-YEAR FOLLOW-UP OF PARTICIPANTS

Bui, K. T., Peplau, L. A., & Hill, C. H. (1996). Testing the investment model of relationship commitment and stability in a 15-year study of heterosexual couples. *Personality and Social Psychology Bulletin, 22*, 1244–1257.

Hill, C. T., & Peplau, L. A. (1998). Premarital predictors of relationship outcomes: A 15-year follow-up of the Boston Couples Study. In T. N. Bradbury (Ed.), *The developmental course of marital dysfunction*. New York: Cambridge University Press.

Peplau, L. A. (1994). Men and women in love. In D. L. Sollie & L. S. Leslie (Eds.), *Gender, families, and close relationships: Feminist research journeys* (pp. 19–49). Thousand Oaks, CA: Sage Publications.

Hill, C. T., & Rubin, Z. (1993). Sex-role attitudes in dating and marriage: A 15-year followup of the Boston Couples Study. *Journal of Social Issues, 40*(3), 31–52.

Vincent, P., Peplau, L.A., & Hill, C. T. (1998). A longitudinal application of the theory of reasoned action to women's career behavior. *Journal of Applied Social Psychology, 28*(9), 761–778.

25-YEAR FOLLOW-UP OF PARTICIPANTS

Hill, C. T., & Peplau, L. A. (2001). Life Satisfaction: A 25-year follow-up of the Boston Couples Study. VIIth European Congress of Psychology, London, England.

(2002). Romantic beliefs and marital outcomes: A 25-year study. Southeastern Psychological Association, New Orleans.

(2003). Sources of Self-Esteem: A 25-year Study. 29th Congreso Inter-Americano de Psicologia, Lima, Peru.

REFERENCES

Aassve, A., Goisis, A., & Sironi, M. (2012). Happiness and childbearing across Europe. *Social Indicators Research, 108,* 65–86.

Abma, J. C., & Martinez, G. M. (2017). Sexual activity and contraceptive use among teenagers in the United States, 2011–2015. *National Health Statistics Reports, 104,* 1–23.

Acevedo, V. E., de Giraldo, Restrepo L., & Tovar, J. R. (2007). Parejas satisfechas de larga duración en la ciudad de Cali. *Pensamiento Psicológico, 3*(8), 85–107.

Adair, J. G., & Huynh, C.-L. (2012). Internationalization of psychological research: Publications and collaborations of the United States and other leading countries. *International Perspectives in Psychology: Research, Practice, Consultation, 1*(4), 252–267. doi:10.1037/a0030395

Puhan, B. N., & Vohra, N. (1993). Indigenization of psychology: Empirical assessment of progress in Indian research. *International Journal of Psychology, 28*(2), 149–169. doi:10.1080/00207599308247182

Adams, A. E., Tolman, R. M., Byee, D., Sullivan, C. M., & Kennedy, A. C. (2012). The impact of intimate partner violence on low-income women's economic well-being: The mediating role of job stability. *Violence Against Women, 18*(12), 1345–1367.

Adams, D. (1988). Counseling men who batter: A profeminist analysis of five treatment models. In M. Bograd & K. Yllo (Eds.). *Feminist perspectives on wife abuse* (pp. 176–199). Beverly Hills, CA: Sage.

Adams, G., Anderson, S. L., & Adonu, J. K. (2004). The cultural grounding of closeness and intimacy. In D. J. Mashek & A. Arons (Eds.), *Handbook of closeness and intimacy* (pp. 321–339). Abbington, UK: Routledge.

Agnew, C. R. (2016). *Social Influences on romantic relationships: Beyond the dyad.* Cambridge: Cambridge University Press.

Agudelo, O., Castro, V., Estrada, L., Forero, H., Lizcano, C., López, J., . . . & Vargas, A. (2005). *Crisis de la pareja: variables del contexto, estrategias de afrontamiento y bienestar marital* (Tesis de grado). Chía, Colombia: Universidad de la Sabana.

Ali, P. A., Dhingra, K., & McGarry, J. (2016). A literature review of intimate partner violence and its classifications. *Aggression and Violent Behavior, 31,* 16–25.

Allendorf, K., & Ghimire, D. J. (2013). Determinants of marital quality in an arranged marriage society. *Social Science Research, 42*(1), 59–70.

Alley, T. R., & Cunningham, M. R. (1991). Averaged faces are attractive, but very attractive faces are not average. *Psychological Science, 2*(2), 123–125. doi:10.1111/j.1467-9280

American Psychiatric Association. (2013). *Diagnostic and statistical manual of mental disorders,* 5th ed. Arlington, VA: American Psychiatric Publishing.

Anacker, A. M. J., & Beery, A. K. (2013). Life in groups: The roles of oxytocin in mammalian sociality. *Frontiers in Behavioral Neuroscience, 17*(185), 29–39.

Anagnostopoulos, D. C., & Soumaki, E. (2013). The state of child and adolescent psychiatry in Greece during the international financial crisis: A brief report. *European Child & Adolescent Psychiatry, 22*(2), 131–134.

Anderson, K. L. (2009). Book review: A typology of domestic violence: Intimate terrorism, violent resistance, and situational couple violence. Contemporary Sociology: *A Journal of Reviews, 38*(6), 532–533.

Angelou, M. (1994). *The complete collected poems of Maya Angelou.* New York: Random House.

Apostolou, M. (2013). Do as we wish: Parental tactics of mate choice manipulation. *Evolutionary Psychology, 11*(4), 795–813.

Arbucle, J. L. (2016). IBM SPSS Amos 24 User's Guide. Retrieved from ftp://public .dhe.ibm.com/software/analytics/spss/documentation/statistics/24.0/en/amos/ Manuals/IBM_SPSS_Amos_User_Guide.pdf.

Archer, J. (2000). Sex differences in aggression between heterosexual partners: A meta-analytic review. *Psychological Bulletin, 126,* 651–680.

Argyle, M., Henderson, M., Bond, M., Iizuka, Y., & Contarello, A. (1986). Cross-cultural variations in relationship rules. *International Journal of Psychology, 21*(3), 287–315.

Arif, N., & Fatima, I. (2015). Marital satisfaction in different types of marriage. *Pakistan Journal of Social and Clinical Psychology, 13*(1), 36–40.

Ariza, A. L., & Guevara, L. M. (2002). *El desempleo en la relación de pareja como generador de crisis y conflicto: factores protectores y estrategias de afrontamiento* (Tesis de grado). Chía, Colombia: Universidad de la Sabana.

Aron, A., Steele, J. L., Kashdan, T. B., & Perez, M. (2006). When similars do not attract: Tests of a prediction from the self-expansion model. *Personal Relationships, 13*(4), 387–396.

Arriaga, X. B., & Agnew, C. R. (2001). Being committed: Affective, cognitive, and conative components of relationship commitment. *Personality and Social Psychology Bulletin, 27,* 1190–1203. https://doi.org/10.1177/0146167201279011

Asch, S. E. (1946). Forming impressions of personality. *Journal of Abnormal and Social Psychology, 41,* 1230–1240.

Aycan, Z. (2002). Leadership and teamwork in developing countries: Challenges and opportunities. *Online Readings in Psychology and Culture.* Retrieved from https://scholarworks.gvsu.edu/orpc/vol7/iss2/1/

Babalis, T., Tsoli, K., Nikolopoulos, V., & Maniatis, P. (2014). The effect of divorce on school performance and behavior in preschool children in Greece: An empirical study of teachers' views. *Psychology, 5*(1), 20.

Barber, N. (2018). Cross-national variation in attitudes to premarital sex: Economic development, disease risk, and marriage strength. *Cross-Cultural Research, 52*(3), 259–273.

Baron, R. A. (2002). *Introduction to psychology* (Custom edition). Boston: Allyn & Bacon.

   & Byrne, D. (2004). *Social psychology* (10th ed.). Boston: Allyn & Bacon.

& Kalsher, M. J. (2002). *Essentials of psychology* (3rd ed.). Boston: Allyn & Bacon.

Barrett, D. W. (2017). *Social psychology: Concepts and emerging trends*. New Delhi: SAGE.

Bartz, J., Simeon, D., Hamilton, H., Kim, S., Crystal, S., Braun, A., . . . & Hollander, E. (2011). Oxytocin can hinder trust and cooperation in borderline personality disorder *Social Cognitive & Affective Neuroscience, 6*, 556–563. doi:10.1093/scan/nsq085

Baumeister, R., & Leary, M. R. (1995). The need to belong: Desire for interpersonal attachments as a fundamental human motivation. *Psychological Bulletin, 117*, 497–529.

Baumrind, D. (1967). Child care practices anteceding three patterns of preschool behavior. *Genetic Psychology Monographs, 75*(1), 43–88.

Beaumont, K., & Maguire, M. (2013). Policies for sexuality education in the European Union. European Parliament, manuscript completed in January 2013. Brussels, © European Union, 2013. Retrieved from www.europarl.europa.eu/RegData/etudes/note/join/2013/462515/IPOL-FEMM_NT(2013)462515_EN.pdf

Beck, A. T., Ward, C. H., Mendelson, M., Mock, J., & Erbaugh, J. (1961). An inventory for measuring depression. *Archives of. General Psychiatry, 4*(6), 561–571.

Beck, C. J., Anderson, E. R., O'Hara, K. L., & Benjamin, G. A. H. (2013). Patterns of intimate partner violence in a large, epidemiological sample of divorcing couples. *Journal of Family Psychology, 27*(5), 743.

Benagiano, G., Carrara, S., & Filippi, V. (2012). Social and ethical determinants of sexuality: 4. Sexuality and families. *The European Journal of Contraception and Reproductive Health Care, 17*(5), 329–339.

Benito, E. (2012, April). Psychological science around the world: Latin America. *APS Observer, 25*(4). Retrieved from www.psychologicalscience.org/observer/psychological-science-around-the-world-latin-america

Bernier, J. C. (1990). Parental adjustment to a disabled child: A family-system perspective. *Families in Society, 71*, 589–596.

Berry, J. W. (1980). Acculturation as varieties of adaptation. In A. Padilla (Ed.), *Acculturation: Theory, models and findings* (pp. 9–25). Boulder: Westview.

(2005). Acculturation: Living successfully in two cultures. *International Journal of Intercultural Relations, 29*, 697–712.

Berscheid, E. (1995). Help wanted: A grand theorist of interpersonal relationships, sociologist or anthropologist preferred. *Journal of Social and Personal Relationships, 12*(4), 529–533.

& Reis, H. T. (1998). Attraction and close relationships. In D. T. Gilbert, S. T. Fiske, & G. Lindzey (Eds.), *The handbook of social psychology*, 4th ed. (pp. 193–281). New York: McGraw-Hill.

& Walster, E. H. (1969). *Interpersonal attraction*. Boston: Addison Wesley.

& Walster, E. H. (1978). *Interpersonal attraction*, 2nd ed. Reading, MA: Addison Wesley.

Birditt, K. S., Wan, W. H., Orbuch, T. L., & Antonucci, T. C. (2017). The development of marital tension: Implications for divorce among married couples. *Developmental Psychology, 53*(10), 1995–2006.

Black, M. C., Basile, K. C., Breiding, M. J., Smith, S. G., Walters, M. L., Merrick, M. T., . . . & Stevens, M. R. (2011). *The National Intimate Partner and Sexual Violence Survey (NISVS): 2010 summary report*. Centers for Disease Control and Prevention. Atlanta, GA: National Center for Injury Prevention and Control.

Blake, R. R., & Mouton, J. S. (1985). *The managerial grid*. Houston, TX: Gulf.

Blau, P. M. (1964). *Exchange and power in social life*. New York: John Wiley & Sons.

Blood, R. O. (1967). *Love match and arranged marriage: A Tokyo-Detroit comparison*. New York: Free Press.

Blumstein, P., & Schwartz, P. (1983). *American couples*. New York: William Morrow & Company.

Bochevar, K. A. (Бочевар К. А.) (2012). Romantic relations in pre-adult age: Notions of difficulties coping [Романтические отношения в юношеском возрасте: представления о преодолении трудностей] (Kandidatskaya dissertation, Moscow, 2012).

Boguszewski, R. (2014). *Religijność a zasady moralne. Komunikat z badań CBOS nr 15/2014*. Warszawa: CBOS. [online] http://cbos.pl/

Bonache, H., Ramírez-Santana, G., & Gonzalez-Mendez, R. (2016). Estilos de resolución de conflictos y violencia en parejas de adolescentes. *International Journal of Clinical and Health Psychology, 16*(3), 276–286.

Bonomi, A. E., Thompson, R. S., Anderson, M., Reid, R. J., Carrell, D., Dimer, J. A., & Rivera, F. P. (2006). Intimate partner violence and women's physical, mental, and social functioning. *American Journal of Preventive Medicine, 30*, 458–466.

Booth, A., & Johnson, D. (1988). Premarital cohabitation and marital success. *Journal of Family Issues, 9*(2), 255–272.

Borgatti, S. P., Mehra, A., Brass, D. J., & Labianca, G. (2009). Network analysis in the social sciences. *Science, 323*(5916), 892–895.

Bossard, J. H. S. (1932). Residential propinquity as a factor in marriage selection. *American Journal of Sociology, 38*(2), 219–224.

Bőthe, B., Tóth-Király, I., Demetrovics, Z., & Orosz, G. (2017). The pervasive role of sex mindset: Beliefs about the malleability of sexual life is linked to higher levels of relationship satisfaction and sexual satisfaction and lower levels of problematic pornography use. *Personality and Individual Differences, 117*, 15–22.

Tóth-Király, I., Zsila, Á., Griffiths, M. D., Demetrovics, Z., & Orosz, G. (2017). The development of the Problematic Pornography Consumption Scale (PPCS), *The Journal of Sex Research, 55*(3), 395–406.

Bowlby, J. (1969). *Attachment*. New York: Basic Books.

(1973). *Separation: Anxiety and anger*. New York: Basic Books.

(1980). *Loss*. New York: Basic Books.

Bradbury, T. N., & Karney, B. R. (2013). *Intimate relationships*, 2nd ed. New York: W. W. Norton.

Fincham, F. D., & Beach, S. R. H. (2000). Research on the nature and determinants of marital satisfaction: A decade in review. *Journal of Marriage and the Family, 62*, 964–980.

Branje, S. J. T., Frijns, T., Finkenauer, C., Engels, R., & Meeus, W. (2007). You are my best friend: Commitment and stability in adolescents' same-sex friendships. *Personal Relationships, 14*, 587–603.

Broman, C. L. (1993). Race differences in marital well-being. *Journal of Marriage and the Family, 55*(3), 724–732.

Brown, R. (1965). *Social psychology*. London: Collier Macmillan.

Browning, E. (1850). *Sonnets from the Portuguese and other love poems* (Reissue 1990). New York: Doubleday.

Brumbaugh, C. C. (2017). Transferring connections: Friend and sibling attachments' importance in the lives of singles. *Personal Relationships, 24*(3), 534–550. doi:10.1111/pere.12195

Brumbaugh, C. C., & Fraley, R. C. (2015). Too fast, too soon? An empirical investigation into rebound relationships. *Journal of Social and Personal Relationships, 32,* 99–118.

Buchmann, M. (1989). *The script of life in modern society: Entry into adulthood in a changing world.* Chicago: University of Chicago Press.

Bui, K. T., Peplau, L. A., & Hill, C. T. (1996). Testing the Rusbult model of relationship commitment and stability in a 15-year study of heterosexual couples. *Personality and Social Psychology Bulletin, 22*(12), 1244–1257.

Bulanda, J. R., & Brown, S. L. (2007). Race-ethnic differences in marital quality and divorce. *Social Science Research, 36*(3), 945–967.

Burgess, E. W., Wallin, P., & Schultz, G. D. (1954). *Courtship, engagement, and marriage.* Philadelphia: J. B. Lippincott & Company.

Buss, D. (1985). Human mate selection: Opposites are sometimes said to attract, but in fact we are likely to marry someone who is similar to us in almost every variable. *American Scientist, 73*(1), 47–51.

(1989). Sex differences in human mate preferences: Evolutionary hypotheses tested in 37 cultures. *Behavioral and Brain Sciences, 12,* 1–49. doi:10.1017/S0140525X00023992

(1995). *The evolution of desire: Strategies of human mating.* New York: Basic Books.

Buunk, A. P., Dijkstra, P., & Mass, K. (2018). The universal threat and temptation of extradyadic affairs. In A. L. Vangelisti & D. Perlman (Eds.), *Cambridge handbook of personal relationships,* 2nd ed., (pp. 199–210). New York: Cambridge University Press.

Park, J. H., & Dubbs, S. L. (2008). Parent-offspring conflict in mate preferences. *Review of General Psychology, 12*(1), 47–62.

Park, J. H., & Duncan, L. A. (2010). Cultural variation in parental influence on mate choice. *Cross-Cultural Research, 44*(1), 23–40. doi:10.1177/1069397109337711

Buunk, B. P., & Bakker, A. B. (1997). Commitment to the relationship, extradyadic sex, and AIDS prevention behavior. *Journal of Applied Social Psychology, 27*(14), 1241–1257. doi:10.1111/j.1559-1816.1997.tb01804.x

Cacioppo, J. T., & Hawkley, L. C. (2005). People thinking about people: The vicious cycle of being a social outcast in one's own mind. In K. D. Williams, J. P. Forgas, & W. von Hippel (Eds.), *The social outcast: Ostracism, social exclusion, rejection, and bullying* (pp. 91–108). New York: Psychology Press.

Campbell, A., Converse, P. E., & Rodgers, W. L. (1976). *The quality of American life: Perceptions, evaluations, and satisfactions.* New York: Russell Sage Foundation.

Campbell, K., & Ponjetti, J., Jr. (2007). The moderating effects of rituals on commitment in premarital involvements. *Sexual and Relationship Therapy, 22*(4), 415–428.

Canaval, G., González, M.C., Humphreys, J., De Leóne, N., & González, S. (2009). Violencia de pareja y salud de las mujeres que consultan a las comisarías de familia, Cali, Colombia. *Investigación y Educación en Enfermería, 27*(2), 209–217.

Cannon, W. (1927). The James-Lange Theory of Emotions: A critical examination and an alternative theory. *The American Journal of Psychology, 39,* 106–124. doi:10.2307/1415404

Capaldi, D., & Owen, L. D. (2001). Physical aggression in a community sample of at-risk young couples: Gender comparisons for high frequency, injury, and fear. *Journal of Family Psychology, 15,* 425–440.

Casadiego, J. G., Martínez, C. L., Riatiga, A. Y., & Vergara, E. (2015). *Habilidades de comunicación asertiva como estrategia en la resolución de conflictos familiares que permite contribuir al desarrollo humano integral en la familia* (Tesis de grado). Universidad Nacional, Abierta y a Distancia, Bogotá.

Castiglioni, M., Hărăguș, M., Faludi, C., & Hărăguș, P. T. (2016). Is the family system in Romania similar to those of Southern European countries? *Comparative Population Studies–Zeitschrift für Bevölkerungswissenschaft, 41*(1), 57–86.

Catalano, S. (2007). *Intimate partner violence in the United States.* U.S. Department of Justice, Bureau of Justice Statistics. Available at www.ojp.usdoj.gov/bjs/intimate/ipv.htm

Caughlin, J. P., Huston, T. L., & Houts, R. M. (2000). How does personality matter in marriage? An examination of trait anxiety, interpersonal negativity, and marital satisfaction. *Journal of Personality and Social Psychology, 78*(2), 326–336.

Chatzichristou C. (1992). *Parents separation, divorce and children,* 5th ed. Athens: Ellinika Grammata.

Chen, S. X., Bond, M. H., & Tang, D. (2007). Decomposing filial piety into filial attitudes and filial enactments. *Asian Journal of Social Psychology, 10,* 213–223.

Cheung, I., Campbell, L., LeBel, E. Contributing authors: Ackerman, R.A., Aykutog˘lu, B., Bahník, Š., . . . & Yong, J. C. (2016). Registered Replication Report: Study 1 from Finkel, Rusbult, Kumashiro, & Hannon (2002). *Perspectives on Psychological Science, 11*(5), 750–764.

Chinanews.com. (2016). Survey indicates a greater need for sexual education. Retrieved from www.ecns.cn/2016/09-27/228066.shtml

Chinasage. (2017). Three character classic: San Zi Jing. Retrieved from www.chinasage.info/lang3characters.htm

Ciecieląg, P., & Boryszewski, P. (2017). Zaangażowanie religijne, [in]: *Jakość Życia w Polsce w 2015 r. Wyniki badania spójności społecznej.* Warszawa: Główny Urząd Statystyczny Studia i Analizy Statystyczne, (pp. 113–142). [online] http://stat.gov.pl/

Cieciuch, J., & Davidov, E. (2012). A comparison of the invariance properties of the PVQ-40 and the PVQ-21 to measure human values across German and Polish samples. *Survey Research Methods 6*(1), 37–48.

Clark, E. M., Harris, A. L., Hasan, M., Votaw, K. B., & Fernandez, P. (2015). Concluding thoughts: Interethnic marriage through the lens of interdependence theory. *Journal of Social Issues, 71*(4), 821–833.

Cohen, A. B. (2011). Religion and culture. *Online Readings in Psychology and Culture, 4*(4). http://dx.doi.org/10.9707/2307-0919.1108

Coker, A. L., Smith, P. H., Bethea, L., King, M. R., & McKewon, R. E. (2000). Physical health consequences of physical and psychological intimate partner violence. *Archives of Family Medicine, 9,* 451–457.

Cole, J. (1996). *Geography of the world's major regions.* New York: Routledge.

Coltrane, S., & Adams, M. (2013). *Gender and families,* 2nd ed. Lanham: Rowman & Littlefield Publishers.

Contreras, R., Hendrick, S. S., & Hendrick, C. (1996). Perspectives of marital love and satisfaction in Mexican American and Anglo-American couples. *Journal of Counseling & Development, 74*(4), 408–415.

Corra, M., Carter, S. K., Carter, J. S., & Knox, D. (2009). Trends in marital happiness by gender and race, 1973 to 2006. *Journal of Family Issues, 30*(10), 1379–1404.

Crawford, D. W., Houts, R. M., Huston, T. L., & George, L. J. (2002). Compatibility, leisure, and satisfaction in marital relationships. *Journal of Marriage and Family*, 64(2), 433–449.

Crenshaw, T. L. (1996). *The alchemy of love and lust*. New York: Putnam.

Chronbach, L. J. (1951). Coefficient alpha and the internal structure of tests. *Psychometrika*, 16(3), 297–334.

Crowne, S. S., Juon, H., Ensminger, M., Burrell, L., McFarlane, E., & Duggan, A. (2011). Concurrent and long-term impact of intimate partner violence on employment stability. *Journal of Interpersonal Violence*, 26(6), 1282–1304.

Csikszentmihályi, M. (1990). *Flow: The psychology of optimal experience*. New York: Harper & Row.

Cummins, R. A. (2000). Personal income and subjective well-being: A review. *Journal of Happiness Studies*, 1, 133–158. doi:10.1023/A:1010079728426

Li, N., Wooden, M., & Stokes, M. (2014). A demonstration of set-points for subjective wellbeing. *Journal of Happiness Studies*, 15, 183–206. doi:10.1007/s10902-013-9444-9

Mellor, D., Stokes, M., & Lau, A. L. D. (2009a), Measures of subjective wellbeing. In E. Mpofu & T. Oakland (Eds.), *Rehabilitation and health assessment: Applying ICF guidelines* (pp. 409–426). New York: Springer.

Woerner, J., Gibson, A., Lai, L., Weinberg, M., & Collard, J. (2009b). Australian Unity Wellbeing Index: Report 20.0. *The Wellbeing of Australians – Money, debt and loneliness*. Australian Centre on Quality of Life, School of Psychology, Deakin University. Retrieved from www.deakin.edu.au/research/acqol/index_wellbeing/index.htm

Cunningham, M. R., Roberts, A. R., Barbee, A. P., Druen, P. B., & Wu, C.-H. (1995). "Their ideas of beauty are, on the whole, the same as ours": Consistency and variability in the cross-cultural perception of female physical attractiveness. *Journal of Personality and Social Psychology*, 68(2), 261–279. doi:10.1037/0022-3514.68.2.261

Dainton, M. (2015). An interdependence approach to relationship maintenance in interracial marriage. *Journal of Social Issues*, 71(4), 772–787.

Dansereau, F. Jr., Graen, G., & Haga, W. J. (1975). A vertical dyad linkage approach to leadership within formal organizations: A longitudinal investigation of the role-making process. *Organizational Behavior and Human Performance*, 13, 46–78.

Davila, J., Karney, B. R., Hall, T. W., & Bradbury, T. N. (2003). Depressive symptoms and marital satisfaction: Within-subject associations and the moderating effects of gender and neuroticism. *Journal of Family Psychology*, 17(4), 557.

Davis, D. S. (2014). Privatization of marriage in post-socialist China. *Modern China*, 40, 551–577. doi:10.1177/0097700414536528

De Dreu, C. K., Greer, L. L., Handgraaf, M. J., Shalvi, S., Van Kleef, G. A., Baas, M., . . . & Feith, S. W. (2010). The neuropeptide oxytocin regulates parochial altruism in intergroup conflict among humans. *Science*, 328, 1408–1411. doi:10.1126/science.1189047

de Jong, G. J. (1995). Research into relationship research designs: Personal relationships under the microscope. *Journal of Social and Personal Relationships*, 12(4), 583–588.

De la Puerta, S., & Fossa, P. (2013). Narrativas del Amor de Pareja en una Muestra Multicultural: Un estudio exploratorio. *Revista de Psicología GEPU*, 4(2), 74–98.

Dec-Pietrowska, J., Paprzycka, E., Walendzik-Ostrowska, A., Gulczyńska, A., Jankowiak, B., & Waszyńska, K. (2016). Sposoby obrazowania kobiecości i męskości w podręcznikach do przedmiotu wychowanie do życia w rodzinie. Analiza ilościowa form wizualnych. In I. Chmura-Rutkowska, M. Duda, M. Mazurek, & A. Sołtysiak-Łuczak (Eds.), *Gender w podręcznikach. Projekt badawczy. Raport. t. 3: Raporty przedmiotowe i rekomendacje* (pp. 130–139). Warszawa: Fundacja Feminoteka.

Dehart, T., Pelham, B., Fiedorowicz, L., Carvallo, M., & Gabriel, S. (2011). Including others in the implicit self: Implicit evaluation of significant others. *Self and Identity, 10*, 127–135.

Deol, S. S. (2014). Honour killings in India: A study of the Punjab State. *International Journal of Social Sciences, 3*(6), 7–16.

DePaulo, B. M. (2006). *Singled out: How singles are stereotyped, stigmatized, and ignored, and still live happily ever after.* New York: St. Martin's Press.

(2016). Singles and mental health. In H. Friedman (Ed.), *Encyclopedia of mental health*, 2nd ed. (Vol. 4, pp. 158–163). Oxford: Elsevier.

& Morris, W. L. (2006). The unrecognized stereotyping and discrimination against singles. *Current Directions in Psychological Science, 15*, 251–254.

Devries, K. M., Mak, J. Y., García-Moreno, C., Petzold, M., Child, J. C., Falder, G., . . . & Rosenfeld, L. (2013). The global prevalence of intimate partner violence against women. *Science, 340*(6140), 1527–1528.

Dhar, R. L. (2013). Intercaste marriage: A study from the Indian context. *Marriage and Family Review, 49*(1), 1–25. doi:10.1080/01494929.2012.714720

Diamond, J. (1997). *Guns, germs, and steel: The fates of human societies.* New York: W. W. Norton.

Diamond, L. M., & Blair, K. L. (2018). The intimate relationships of sexual and gender minorities. In A. L. Vangelisti & D. Perlman (Eds.), *Cambridge handbook of personal relationships*, 2nd ed. (pp. 199–210). New York: Cambridge University Press.

Díaz, K., & Porras, K. (2011). *Identificación de los principales estilos comunicativos para la resolución de conflictos en un grupo de parejas, y los niveles de satisfacción familiar en sus hijos adolescentes* (Tesis de grado). Universidad Pontificia Bolivariana, Bucaramanga.

Díaz, Y. P., Jaramillo, M. M., Silva, S., & Cerón, A. (2015). *La resolución de conflictos como herramienta de prevención en la violencia intrafamiliar (VIF) en las familias de los municipios de Ibagué Tolima* (Tesis de grado). Universidad Nacional Abierta y a Distancia, Mariquita, Tolima.

Diaz-Loving, R., & Sánchez Aragón, R. (2004). *Psicologia del amor: Una vision integral de la relacion de pareja.* Ciudad de México: Miguel Angel Porrua.

(2010). *Antologia psicosocial de la pareja. Clasicos y contemporaneos.* Ciudad de México: Miguel Angel Porrua.

Diener, E. (1984). Subjective well-being. *Psychological Bulletin, 95*(3), 542–575. doi:10.1037/0033-2909.95.3.542

Gohm, C. L., Suh, E., & Oishi, S. (2000). Similarity of the relations between marital status and subjective well-being across cultures. *Journal of Cross-Cultural Psychology, 31*, 419–436.

Oishi, S., & Lucas, R. E. (2002). Subjective well-being: The science of happiness and life satisfaction. In C. R. Snyder & S. J. Lopez (Eds.), *Handbook of positive psychology.* Oxford and New York: Oxford University Press.

Diener, M. L., & McGavran, M. B. (2008). What makes people happy? A developmental approach to the literature on family relationships and well-being. In R. Larsen & M. Eid (Eds.), *The science of subjective well-being* (pp. 345–347). New York: Guilford Press.

Dion, K. K., & Dion, K. K. (1997). Individualistic and collectivist perspectives on gender and the cultural context of love and intimacy. In L. A. Peplau & S. E. Taylor (Eds.), *Sociocultural perspectives in social psychology* (pp. 314–329). Englewood Cliffs, NJ: Prentice Hall.

Dirks, K. T., & Ferrin, D. L. (2002). Trust in leadership: Meta-analytic findings and implications for research and practice. *Journal of Applied Psychology, 87,* 611–628.

DiTommaso, E., & Spinner, B. (1997). Social and emotional loneliness: A re-examination of Weiss' typology of loneliness. *Personality and Individual Differences, 22*(3), 417–427.

Dolan, P., Peasgood, T., & White, M. (2008). Do we really know what makes us happy? A review of the economic literature on the factors associated with subjective well-being. *Journal of Economic Psychology, 29*(1), 94–122.

Domański, H., & Przybysz, D. (2007). *Homogamia małżeńska a hierarchie społeczne.* Warszawa: Wydawnictwo IFiS PAN.

Dong, M. C., & Li, S. Y. (2007). Conflict resolution in Chinese family purchase decisions: The impact of changing female roles and marriage duration. *International Journal of Conflict Management, 18,* 308–324.

Dubbs, S. L., Buunk, A. P., & Taniguchi, H. (2013). Parent-offspring conflict in Japan and parental influence across six cultures. *Japanese Psychological Research, 55*(3), 241–253. doi:10.1111/jpr.12003

Elliott, I. A., & Zajac, G. (2015). The implementation of circles of support and accountability in the United States. *Aggression and Violent Behavior, 25,* 113–123. doi:10.1016/j.avb.2015.07.014

Elliott, S. J. (2009). *Getting past your breakup: How to turn a devastating loss into the best thing that ever happened you.* Boston: Da Capo Lifelong Books.

Ellsberg, M., Arango, D. J., Morton, M., Gennari, F., Kiplesund, S., Contreras, M., & Watts, C. (2014). Prevention of violence against women and girls: What does the evidence say? *The Lancet, 385*(9977), 1555–1566.

ELTE. (2016). Study on sex life. https://444.hu/2017/03/19/itt-vannak-az-elte-eddigi-legnagyobb-online-szexkutatasanak-eredmenyei

Emerson, E., Graham, H., McCulloch, A., Blacher, J., Hatton, C., & Llewellyn, G. (2009). The social context of parenting 3-year-old children with developmental delay in the UK. *Child: Care, Health, and Development, 35*(1), 63–70.

Emerson, R. M. (1962). Power-dependence relations. *American Sociological Review, 27,* 31–41.

(1976). Social exchange theory. *Annual Review of Sociology, 2,* 335–362.

Erol, R. Y., & Orth, U. (2016). Self-esteem and the quality of romantic relationships. *European Psychologist, 21*(4), 274–283. doi:10.1027/1016-9040/a000259

Eurostat. (2017). *Marriage and divorce statistics.* Available at http://ec.europa.eu/euro stat/statistics-explained/index.php/Marriage_and_divorce_statistics

Evenson, R. J., & Simon, R. W. (2005). Clarifying the relationship between parenthood and depression. *Journal of Health and Social Behavior, 46,* 341–358.

Fernández-Fuertes, A. A., & Fuertes, A. (2010). Physical and psychological aggression in dating relationships of Spanish adolescents: Motives and consequences. *Child Abuse and Neglect, 34,* 183–191.

Ferraro, K. J. (2006). *Neither angels nor demons: Women, crime, and victimization.* Boston: Northeastern University Press.

Ferrer, V., Bosch, E., Navarro, C., Ramis, M., & García, E. (2008). El concepto del amor en España. *Psicothema, 20*(4), 589–595.

Figueroa, J., & González, E. y Solís, V. (1981). Una aproximación al problema del significado: Las redes semánticas. *Revista Latinoamericana de Psicología, 13*(3), 447–458.

Finkel, E. J., Cheung, E. O., Emery, L. F., Carswell, K. L., & Larson, G. M. (2015). The suffocation model: Why marriage in America is becoming an all-or-nothing institution. *Current Directions in Psychological Science, 24*, 238–244.

Rusbult, C. E., Kumashiro, M., & Hannon, P. A. (2002). Dealing with betrayal in close relationships: Does commitment promote forgiveness? *Journal of Personality and Social Psychology, 82*, 956–974. doi:10.1037/0022-3514.82.6.956

Simpson, J. A., & Eastwick, P. W. (2017). The psychology of close relationships: Fourteen core principles. *Annual Review of Psychology, 68*, 383–411.

Fleischmann, A. (2004). Narratives published on the internet by parents of children with autism: What do they reveal and why is it important? Retrieved from http://foa.sagepub.com/cgi/cotent/abstract/19/1/35

Fletcher, G. J. O., Simpson, J. A., Campbell, L., & Overall, N. (2013). *The science of intimate relationships.* Hoboken, NJ: Wiley-Blackwell.

Foa, U. G., & Foa, E. B. (1980). Resource theory: Interpersonal behavior as exchange. In K. J. Gergen, M. S. Greenberg, & R. H. Willis (Eds.), *Social exchange: Advances in theory and research* (pp. 77–94). New York: Plenum.

Follingstad, D. R., & DeHart, D. D. (2000). Defining psychological abuse of husbands toward wives: Contexts, behaviors, and typologies. *Journal of Interpersonal Violence, 15*(9), 891–920.

Fox, G. L. (1975). Love match and arranged marriage in a modernizing nation: Mate selection in Ankara, Turkey. *Journal of Marriage and the Family, 37*(1), 180–193.

Fraley, R. C. (2007). Using the Internet for personality research: What can be done, how to do it, and some concerns. In R. W. Robins, R. C. Fraley, & R. F. Krueger (Eds.), *Handbook of research methods in personality psychology* (pp. 130–148). New York: Guilford.

French, J., & Raven, B. (1959). The bases of social power. In D. Cartwright (Ed.), *Studies in social power* (pp. 150–167). Ann Arbor: Institute for Social Research.

Friedman, M. A., Dixon, A. E., Brownell, K. D., Whisman, M. A., & Wilfley, D. E. (1999). Marital status, marital satisfaction, and body image dissatisfaction. *International Journal of Eating Disorders, 26*(1), 81–85.

Fujii, T., Sawaumi, T., & Aikawa, A. (2014). Discrepancy between explicit/implicit self-esteem and narcissism. *Japanese Journal of Research on Emotions, 21*, 162-168.

Furstenberg, F. F. (2000). The sociology of adolescence and youth in the 1990s: A critical commentary. *Journal of Marriage and Family, 62*(4), 896–910.

Gaines, S. O., Jr. (1997). *Culture, ethnicity and personal relationship processes.* New York: Routledge.

Clark, E. M., & Afful, S. E. (2015). Interethnic marriage in the United States: An introduction. *Journal of Social Issues, 71*(4), 647–658.

& Hardin, D. P. (2013). Interdependence revisited: Perspectives from cultural psychology. In L. Campbell & J. A. Simpson (Eds.), *Oxford handbook of close relationships* (pp. 553–572). Oxford: Oxford University Press.

& Ketay, S. (2013). Positive psychology, culture, and personal relationship processes. In M. Hojjat, & D. Cramer (Eds.), *Positive psychology of love* (pp. 218–231). Oxford: Oxford University Press.

Garcia, J. A., & Sison K. J. (2012). Locus of hope and subjective well-being. *International Journal of Research Study in Psychology*, 1(3), 53–58.

García-Moreno, C., Jansen, H. A. F. M., Ellsberg, M., Heise, L., & Watts, C. (2005). *WHO multi-country study on women's health and domestic violence against women: Initial results on prevalence, health outcomes and women's responses.* Geneva: World Health Organization.

Garrido-Macías, M., Valor-Segura, I., & Expósito, F. (2017). ¿Dejaría a mi pareja? Influencia de la gravedad de la transgresión, la satisfacción y el compromiso en la toma de decisión. *Psychosocial Intervention*, 26(2), 111–116.

Gawronski, B., & Bodenhausen, G. V. (2006). Associative and propositional processes in evaluation: An integrative review of implicit and explicit attitude change. *Psychological Bulletin*, 132, 692-731.

Georgas, J. (1989). Changing family values in Greece: From collectivist to individualist. *Journal of Cross-Cultural Psychology*, 20, 80–91.

(1991). Intrafamily acculturation of values in Greece. *Journal of Cross-Cultural Psychology*, 22, 445–457.

(2003). Family: Variations and Changes Across Cultures. *Online Readings in Psychology and Culture*, 6(3). http://dx.doi.org/10.9707/2307-0919.1061

Berry, J. W., van de Vivjer, F., Kagitçibasi, C., & Poortinga Y. H. (2006). *Families across cultures: A 30 nation psychological study*. New York: Cambridge University Press.

& Dragona, T. (1988). Social support and its relation with psychosocial stress, psychosomatic symptoms and anxiety. *Psichologika Themata*, 1(2), 5–22.

Van der Vijver, F., & Berry, J. W. (2004). The ecocultural framework, ecosocial indicators and psychological variables in cross-cultural research. *Journal of Cross-Cultural Psychology*, 35(1), 74–102.

Gesselman, A. N., Webster, G. D., & Garcia, J. R. (2017). Has virginity lost its virtue? Relationship stigma associated with being a sexually inexperienced adult. *The Journal of Sex Research*, 54(2), 202–213.

Ghebrea, G. (1999). Factori care afectează stabilitatea cuplului marital. Probleme şi politici sociale (Factors affecting marital stability), *Revista Calitatea Vieții*, 1/2, 3–41.

Gilligan, C. (1982). *In a different voice: Psychological theory and women's development.* Cambridge, MA: Harvard University Press.

Giotsa, A. (2003). Values and emotional closeness among the Greek family's members: Empirical data. In V. Riga (Ed.), *The Pandora's box*. Athens: Ellinika Grammata (in Greek).

(2007). Values and the family. A cross-cultural research. *Psychology*, 13(4), 111–128.

(2012). Children's creative expression through drawing: The Family Drawing Projective Techniques. In A. V. Rigas (Ed.), *Creativity. Psychology of art and literature in social clinical perspectives*, pp. 122–132. Gutenberg.

Anifanti, I. Lampaki, K., Mouzou, I. Xylagras, D., & Kastriotis, D. (2015). *Towards unemployment we found the family*. Cyprus, Nicosia: Congress of the Hellenic Psychological Society.

& Mitrogiorgou, E. (2014a). Representations of families through the children's drawings in times of crisis in Greece. *International Journal of Education and Culture*, 3(2).

& Mitrogiorgou, E. (2014b). Economic Crisis crisis in Greece: Impact on Different different Fieldsfields. In A. Giotsa (Ed.), *Psychological and Educational Approaches in Times of Crises - Exploring New Data*. New York: Untested Ideas Research Center.

& Mitrogiorgou, E. (2016). Representations of families through the children's drawings in parental divorce incidents in Greece. *Journal of Childhood and Developmental Disorders,* 2(4), 29.

& Touloumakos, A. (2014a). Perceived parental acceptance and psychological adjustment. *Cross Cultural Research,* 48(3), 250–258.

& Touloumakos, A. (2014b). They accept me, they accept me not. *Journal of Family Issues,* 37(9), 1226–1243.

& Zergiotis, A. (2010, July). Father love in Greece: Children's perceptions of their parents' acceptance-rejection. Paper presented at the Third International Congress on Interpersonal Acceptance and Rejection, Padua, Italy.

Goldberg, S., Morris, P., Simmons, R. J., Fowler, R. S., & Levinson, H. (1990). Chronic illness in infancy and parenting stress: A comparison of three groups of parents. *Journal of Pediatric Psychology,* 15, 347–358.

Goodwin, R. (1999). *Personal relationships across cultures.* New York: Routledge.

(2008). *Changing relations: Achieving intimacy in a time of social transition.* Cambridge: Cambridge University Press.

Google Scholar. (2018). Retrieved from https://scholar.google.com/citations?user=9KkOxOYAAAAJ&hl=en&oi=ao

Gosling, S. D., Vazire, S., Srivastava, S., & John, O. P. (2004). Should we trust web-based studies? A comparative analysis of six preconceptions about internet questionnaires. *American Psychologist,* 59(2), 93.

Gottman, J. M. (1999). *The Marriage Clinic: A scientifically based marital therapy.* New York: Norton.

Graen, G., & Cashman, J. F. (1975). A role-making model of leadership in formal organizations: A developmental approach. In J. G. Hunt & L. L. Larson (Eds.), *Leadership frontiers* (pp. 143–165). Kent, OH: Kent State University Press.

Gravetter, F. J., & Wallnau, L. B. (2016). *Statistics for the behavioral sciences,* 10th ed. Belmont, CA: Wadsworth Publishing.

Gray-Little, B., & Burks, N. (1983). Power and satisfaction in marriage: A review and critique. *Psychological Bulletin,* 93(3), 513–538.

Green, S. E. (2007). "We're tired, not sad": Benefits and burdens of mothering a child with a disability. *Social Science and Medicine,* 64, 150–163. doi:10.1016/j.socscimed.2006.08.025

Greenwald, A. G., McGhee, D. E., & Schwartz, J. L. K. (1998). Measuring individual differences in implicit cognition: The Implicit Association Test. *Journal of Personality and Social Psychology,* 74, 1464–1480.

Greve, B. (2010). *Happiness and social policy in Europe.* Cheltenham, UK: Edward Elgar Publishing.

Grillon, C., Krimsky, M., Charney, D. R., Vytal, K., Ernst, M., & Cornwell, B. (2013). Oxytocin increases anxiety to unpredictable threat. *Molecular Psychiatry,* 18, 958–960. doi:10.1038/mp.2012.156

Guo, Q., Feng, L., & Wang, M. (2017). Chinese undergraduates' preferences for altruistic traits in mate selection and personal advertisement: Evidence from Q-sort technique. *International Journal of Psychology,* 52(2), 145–153.

Gutiérrez de Pineda, V. (1976). *Estructura, función y cambio de la familia en Colombia.* Bogotá: Asociación Colombiana de Facultades de Medicina.

Hadden, B. W., Agnew, C. R., & Tan, K. (2018). Commitment readiness and relationship formation. *Personality and Social Psychology Bulletin,* 44(8).

Hallock, S. (1988). An understanding of negotiation styles contributes to effective reality therapy for conflict resolutions with couples. *Journal of Reality Therapy,* 8(1), 7–12.

Hamberger, L. K., Larsen, S. E., & Lehrner, A. (2017). Coercive control in intimate partner violence. *Aggression and Violent Behavior, 37*, 1–11.

Hamon, R. R., & Ingoldsby, B. B. (Eds.). (2003). *Mate selection across cultures.* Thousand Oaks, CA: Sage.

Harris, K. J., & Kacmar, K. M. (2006). Too much of a good thing: The curvilinear effect of leader-member exchange on stress. *Journal of Social Psychology, 146*(1), 65–84.

Hartley, S. L., Barker, E. T., Seltzer, M. M., Floyd, F., Greenberg, J., Orsmond, G., & Bolt, D. (2010). The relative risk and timing of divorce in families of children with an autism spectrum disorder. *Journal of Family Psychology, 24*(4), 449–457.

Hatfield, E., & Rapson, R. L. (2005). *Love and sex: Cross-cultural perspectives.* New York: University Press of America.

Hazan, C., & Shaver, P. R. (1987). Romantic love conceptualized as an attachment process. *Journal of Personality and Social Psychology, 52*, 511–524.

He, J., & van de Vijver, F. (2012). Bias and equivalence in cross-cultural research. *Online Readings in Psychology and Culture, 2*(2). http://dx.doi.org/10.9707/2307-0919.1111

Heine, S. J. (2016). Interpersonal attraction and close relationships. In *Cultural Psychology*, 3rd ed., chap. 11. New York: W.W. Norton and Company.

Hellenic Statistical Authority. 2017). *Population and housing census.* Available at www.statistics.gr/en/statistics/pop.

Hendrick, C. (Ed.). (1989). *Close relationships.* Newbury Park, CA: Sage.

(1986). A theory and method of love. *Journal of Personality and Social Psychology, 50*, 392–402.

(2000). *Close relationships: A sourcebook.* Thousand Oaks: Sage.

Hendrick, S. S. (1981). Self-disclosure and marital satisfaction. *Journal of Personality and Social Psychology, 40*(6), 1150–1159.

Henrich, J., Heine, S. J., & Norenzayan, A. (2010). The weirdest people in the world? *Behavioral and Brain Sciences, 33*(2–3), 61–83. doi:10.1017/S0140525X0999152X

Hernández González, E., & González Méndez, R. (2009). Coerción sexual, compromiso y violencia en las relaciones de pareja de los universitarios. *Escritos de Psicología, 2*(3), 40–47.

Hill, C. T. (2001a). Identity arithmetic: A multi-dimension view of ethnic identity. Paper presented at the Western Psychological Association, Maui, Hawaii.

(2001b). A three-dimensional view of sexual identity. Paper presented at the Western Psychological Association, Maui, Hawaii.

(2010). Distinguishing effects of culture and religion on sexual attitudes and behavior. Paper presented at the International Association for Cross-Cultural Psychology, Melbourne, Australia.

(2015). Loss of parents' religious identities among college students. Paper presented at the Society of Personality and Social Psychology, Long Beach.

(2016, August). Ethnic and gender differences in sexual behaviors among college students. Paper presented at the International Association for Cross-Cultural Psychology, Nagoya, Japan.

Barros, M. R., Boehnke, K., Boer, D., Brumbaugh, C., Rodriguez J. E. C., . . . & Torres, C. (2014, July). More than just sex: Correlates of sexual satisfaction across gender, marital status, sex of partner, and cultures. Paper presented at the International Congress of Applied Psychology Paris, France.

Barros, M. R., Boehnke, K., Boer, D., Brumbaugh, C., Rodriguez J. E. C., . . . & Torres, C. (2015, July). Correlates of personal values in a cross-cultural study of intimate relationships. Paper presented at the European Congress of Psychology, Milan, Italy.

Barros, M. R., Boehnke, K., Boer, D., Brumbaugh, C., Rodriguez J. E. C., ... & Torres, C. (2016, July). Basic human values, well-being, and intimate relationships. Paper presented at the International Congress of Psychology, Yokohama, Japan.

& Peplau, L. A. (1998). "Premarital predictors of relationship outcomes: A 15-year follow-up of the Boston Couples Study." In T. N. Bradbury (Ed.), *The developmental course of marital dysfunction* (pp. 237–278). New York: Cambridge University Press.

& Peplau, L. A. (2001). Life satisfaction: A 25-year follow-up of the Boston Couples Study. Paper presented at the VIIth European Congress on Psychology, London, England.

& Peplau, L. A. (2002). Romantic beliefs and marital outcomes: A 25-year study. Paper presented at the Southeastern Psychological Association, New Orleans

& Peplau, L. A. (2003). Sources of self-esteem: A 25-year study. Paper presented at the 9th Congreso Inter-Americano de Psicologia, Lima, Peru.

Peplau, L. A. & Rubin, Z. (1981). Differing perceptions in dating couples. *Psychology of Women Quarterly, 5*(3), 418–434.

Peplau, L. A., & Rubin, Z. (2008). Is love blind? Attractiveness ratings by self, partner, and others, and the outcome of dating relationships 25 years later. Paper presented at the International Congress of Psychology, Berlin, Germany.

Rubin, Z., & Peplau, L. A. (1976). Breakups before marriage: The end of 103 affairs. *Journal of Social Issues, 32*(1), 147–168.

Rubin, Z., Peplau, L. A., & Willard, S. G. (1979). The volunteer couple: Sex differences, couple commitment, and participation in research on interpersonal relationships. *Social Psychology Quarterly, 42*(4), 415–420.

Hines, D. A., & Malley-Morrison, K. (2001). Psychological effects of partner abuse against men: A neglected research area. *Psychology of Men and Masculinity, 2,* 75–85.

Ho, D. Y. F. (1996). Filial piety and its psychological consequences. In M. H. Bond (Ed.), *The handbook of Chinese psychology* (pp. 155–165). Hong Kong: Oxford University Press.

Hofstede, G. (1980). *Culture's consequences: International differences in work-related values.* London: Sage.

(1984). The cultural relativity of the quality of life concept. *Academy of Management Review, 9*(3), 389–398.

(1998). Attitudes, values and organizational culture: Disentangling the concepts. *Organization Studies, 19*(3), 477–493.

(2001). *Culture's consequences: Comparing values, behaviors, institutions, and organizations across nations.* Thousand Oaks, CA: Sage.

(2002). Dimensions do not exist – a reply to Brendan McSweeney. *Human Relations, 55*(11), 1355–1361.

(2011). Dimensionalizing cultures: The Hofstede model in context. Online Readings in Psychology and Culture, 2(1). Retrieved from https://doi.org/10.9707/2307-0910.1014

Hogg, M. A. (1992). *The social psychology of group cohesiveness: From attraction to social identity.* New York: Harvester Wheatsheaf.

Holt-Lunstad, J. (2018). Relationships and physical health. In A. L. Vangelisti & D. Perlman (Eds.), *Cambridge handbook of personal relationships,* 2nd ed. (pp. 449–463). New York: Cambridge University Press.

Holt-Lunstad, J., Smith, T. B., Baker, M., Harris, T., & Stephenson, D. (2015). Loneliness and social isolation as risk factors for mortality: A meta-analytic review. *Perspectives on Psychological Science, 10*(2), 227–237. doi:10.1177/1745691614568352

Holtzworth-Munroe, A., & Stuart, G. L. (1994). Typologies of male batterers: Three subtypes and the differences among them. *Psychological Bulletin, 116*, 476–497.

Horsley, S., & Oliver, C. (2013). Positive impact and its relationship to well-being in parents of children with intellectual disability: A literature review. *International Journal of Developmental Disabilities, 61*(1), 1–19.

House, J. S., Landis, K. R., & Umberson, D. (1988). Social relationships and health. *Science, 241*(4865), 540–545. doi:10.1126/science.3399889

Hu, L., & Bentler, P. M. (1999). Cutoff criteria for fit indexes in covariance structure analysis: Conventional criteria versus new alternatives. *Structural Equation Modeling, 6*(1), 1–55.

Huesmann, L. R., & Levinger, G. (1976). Incremental Exchange Theory: A formal model for progression in dyadic social interaction. *Advances in Experimental Social Psychology, 9C*, 191–229.

Hunt, M. (1959). *The natural history of love.* New York: Grove Press.

Hunter, S. (2012). *Lesbian and gay couples: Lives, issues, and practice.* Oxford: Oxford University Press.

Hurtado, F., Ciscar, C., & Rubio, M. (2004). El conflicto de pareja como variable asociada a la violencia de género contra la mujer: Consecuencias sobre la salud sexual y mental. *Revista de Psicopatología y Psicología Clínica, 9*(1), 49–64.

Ilchenko,V. V. (Ильченко В.В.) (2010). Ethnic peculiarities of psychosexual development of females in multicultural environment: By the example of the Republic of North Ossetia-Alania [Этнические особенности психосексуального развития девушек в поликультурной среде: на примере Республики Северная Осетия-Алания] (Kandidatskaya dissertation, Saint Petersburg, 2010).

& Sanakoeva F. G. (Ильченко В.В., Санакоева Ф.Г.) (2017). Psychological aspects of romantic relationships and intimate attitudes of youth [Психологические аспекты романтических отношений и интимно-личностных установок молодежи]. Development of the child in the family, series: Family and children in the modern world. Collective monograph / Under the general and scientific editorship of PhD, Professor V. L. Sitnikov, PhD S. A. Burkova, PhD E. B. Dunaevskaya. V. 1. – St. Petersburg: "Social and Humanitarian Knowledge," 2017. – 454 p. (pp. 411–416).

Sanakoeva, F. G. (Ильченко В.В., Санакоева Ф.Г.) (2015, November). Psychological determinants of sexual behavior and intimate attitudes of youth [Психологические детерминанты полового поведения и интимно-личностных установок молодежи] Paper presented at the Proceedings of Russian scientific conference: Karmin's meetings (pp. 159–163). Saint Petersburg, Emperor Alexander I St. Petersburg State Transport University.

Imamoglu, E. O., & Seluk, E. (2018). Cultural and self-related considerations in relationship well-being. In C. C. Weisfeld, G. E. Weisfeld, & L. Dhillon (Eds.), *The psychology of marriage: An evolutionary and cross-cultural view.* Lanham: Lexington Books.

Impett, E. A., & Peplau, L. (2002). Why some women consent to unwanted sex with a dating partner: Insights from attachment theory. *Psychology of Women Quarterly, 26*(4), 360–370.

Inchley, J., Currie, D., Young, T., Samdal, O., Torsheim, T., Augustson, L., ... & Barnekow, V. (Eds.). (2016). Growing up unequal: Gender and socioeconomic differences in young people's health and well-being. Health Behaviour in School-Aged Children (HBSC) Study: International report from the 2013/2014 Survey. Retrieved from www.euro.who.int/__data/assets/pdf_file/0003/303438/HSBC-No.7-Growing-up-unequal-Full-Report.pdf?ua=1

Ingoldsby, B. B., & Smith, S. D. (2006). *Families in global and multicultural perspective*, 2nd ed. Thousand Oaks: Sage.

Insel, T. R., & Young, L. J. (2001). The neurobiology of attachment. *Nature Reviews Neuroscience, 2*, 129–136.

Isa, S. N., Aziz, A. A., Rahman, A. A., Ibrahim, M. I., Ibrahim, W. P., Mohamad, N., ... & Van Rostenberghe, H. (2013). The impact of disabled children on parent health-related quality of life and family functioning in Kelantan and its associated factors. *Journal of Developmental and Behavioral Pediatrics, 34*, 262–268.

Isaza, L. (2011). Causas y estrategias de solución de conflictos en las relaciones de pareja formadas por estudiantes universitarios. *Psicogente, 14*(26), 336–351.

Izdebski, Z. (2006). *Ryzykowna dekada. Seksualność Polaków dobie HIV/AIDS. Studium porównawcze 1997-2001-2005.* Zielona Góra: Oficyna Wydawnicza Uniwersytetu Zielonogórskiego.

(2012). *Seksualność Polaków na początku XXI wieku. Studium Badawcze.* Kraków: Wydawnictwo Uniwersytetu Jagiellońskiego.

Jankowiak, B. (2010). *Aktywność seksualna nauczycieli a jakość i trwałość ich związków partnerskich.* Poznań. Poznań: Wydawnictwo Naukowe UAM.

(2018). *Zachowania ryzykowne młodzieży. Studium teoretyczno-empiryczne* Poznań: Wydawnictwo Naukowe UAM

Jaramillo-Vélez, D. E., Ospina-Muñoz, D. E., Cabarcas-Iglesias, G., & Humphreys, J. (2005). Resiliencia, Espiritualidad, Aflicción y Tácticas de Resolución de Conflictos en Mujeres Maltratadas. *Revista de Salud Pública, 7*(3), 281–292.

Johnson, M. P. (1995). Patriarchal terrorism and common couple violence: Two forms of violence against women. *Journal of Marriage and Family, 57*(2), 283–294.

(2008). *A typology of domestic violence: Intimate terrorism, violent resistance and situational couple violence.* Lebanon, NH: Northeastern University Press.

(2010). Langhinrichsen-Rolling's confirmation of the feminist analysis of intimate partner violence: Comment on "controversies involving gender and intimate partner violence in the United States. *Sex Roles, 62*(3–4), 212–219.

& Leone, J. M. (2005). The differential effects of intimate terrorism and situational couple violence: Findings from the national violence against women survey. *Journal of Family Issues, 26*(3), 322–349.

Jones, G. W. (2017). Changing marriage patterns in Asia. In Z. Zhao & A. C. Hayes (Eds.), *Routledge handbook of Asian demography* (pp. 351–369). New York: Taylor and Francis.

Kagitcibasi, C. (2002). A model of family change in cultural context. *Online Readings in Psychology and Culture, 6*(3). http://dx.doi.org/10.9707/2307-0919.1059

(2007). *Family self and human development across cultures.* Mahwah, NJ: Lawrence Erlbaum Associates.

Kakabadse, A., & Kakabadse, N. (2004). *Intimacy: International survey of the sex lives of people at work.* Basingstoke, UK: Palgrave Macmillan.

Kamp Dush, C. M., & Amato, P. R. (2005). Consequences of relationship status and quality for subjective well-being. *Journal of Social and Personal Relationships, 22*, 607–627.

Kansky, J., & Diener, E. (2017). Benefits of well-being: Health, social relationships, work, and resilience. *Journal of Positive Psychology and Wellbeing, 1*(2), 129–169.

Kanter, R. M. (1972). *Commitment & community: communes and utopias in sociological perspective.* Cambridge, MA: Harvard University Press.

Kapoor, S., Hughes, P. C., Baldwin, J. R., & Blue, J. (2003). The relationship of individualism–collectivism and self-construals to communication styles in India and the United States. *International Journal of Intercultural Relations, 27*, 683–700. doi:10.1016/j.ijintrel.2003.08.002

Karandashev, V. (2015). A cultural perspective on romantic love. *Online Readings in Psychology and Culture, 5*(4). http://dx.doi.org/10.9707/2307-0919.1135

Karanikolos, M., Mladovsky, P., Cylus, J., Thomson, S., Basu, S., Stuckler, D., . . . & Mackenbach, J. P. (2013). Financial crisis, austerity, and health in Europe. *Lancet, 13*(9874), 1323–1331.

Karney, B. R., & Bradbury, T. N. (1995). The longitudinal course of marital quality and stability: A review of theory, methods, and research. *Psychological Bulletin, 118*(1), 3–34. http://dx.doi.org/10.1037/0033-2909.118.1.3

Davila, J., Cohan, C. L., Sullivan, K. T., Johnson, M. D., & Bradbury, T. N. (1995). An empirical investigation of sampling strategies in marital research. *Journal of Marriage and the Family, 57*, 909–920.

Kassin, S. (2008). *Social psychology.* Microsoft® Student [DVD]. Redmond, WA: Microsoft Corporation.

Kataki, C. (2012). *The purple liquid* (in Greek). Athens: Pedio Publications.

Kazak, A. E., & Christakis, D. A. (1994). Caregiving issues in families of children with chronic medical conditions. In E. Kahana, D. E. Biegel, & M.D. Wykle (Eds.), *Family caregiving applications across the life span* (pp. 331–356). Thousand Oaks, CA: Sage.

Kelley, H. H., Berscheid, E., Christensen, A., Harvey, J. H., Huston, T. L., Levinger, G., . . . & Peterson, D. R. (1983). *Close relationships.* New York, W. H. Freeman and Company.

Kelly, J. B., & Johnson, M. P. (2008). Differentiation among types of intimate partner violence: Research update and implications for interventions. *Family Court Review, 46*(3), 476–499.

Kenrick, D. T., Griskevicius, V., Neuberg, S. L., & Schaller, M. (2010). Renovating the pyramid of needs: Contemporary extensions built upon ancient foundations. *Perspectives on Psychological Science, 5*, 292.

Khaleque, A. (2018). *Intimate relationships across the lifespan: Formation, development, enrichment, and maintenance.* Santa Barbara, CA: Preager.

Kiefer, A. K., & Sanchez, D. T. (2007). Scripting sexual passivity: A gender role perspective. *Personal Relationships, 14*, 269–290.

Kinsey, A. C., Pomeroy, W. B., & Martin, C. E. (1948). *Sexual behavior in the human male.* Philadelpia: W. B. Saunders.

Kito, M., Yuki, M., & Thomson, R. (2017). Relational mobility and close relationships: A socioecological approach to explain cross-cultural differences. *Personal Relationships, 24*, 114–130.

Kitson, G. C., & Sussman, M. B. (1982). Marital complaints, demographic characteristics, and symptoms of mental distress in divorce. *Journal of Marriage and the Family, 44*(1), 87–101.

Klevens, J. (2001). Violencia física contra la mujer en Santa Fe de Bogotá: prevalencia y factores asociados. *Revista Panameña de Salud Pública, 9*(2), 78–83.

Knafo, A., Roccas, S., & Sagiv, L. (2011). The value of values in cross-cultural research: A special issue in honor of Shalom Schwartz. *Journal of Cross-Cultural Psychology*, 42(2), 178–185.

Knee, C. R., & Petty, K. N. (2013). Implicit theories of relationships: Destiny and growth beliefs. In J. A. Simpson & L. Campbell (Eds.), *The Oxford handbook of close relationships* (pp. 183–198). New York: Oxford University Press.

Knox, D. & Schacht, C. (2015). *Choices in relationships: An introduction to marriage and the family*, 12th ed. Boston: Cengage Learning.

Koh, C., & Matsuo, H. (2016). Current situations and challenges concerning sexual health among unmarried couples composed of a mix of Japanese, South Korean nationals, and ethnic Koreans born in Japan (Zainichi): A qualitative study. *Health*, 9(01), 14–24.

Kosfeld, M., Heinrichs, M., Zak, P J. U., & Fischbacher, F. E. (2005). Oxytocin – A biological basis for trust. *Nature*, 435(2), 673–676. doi10.1038/nature03701

Krause, S., Pokorny, D., Schury, K., Doyen-Waldecker, C., Hulbert, A., Karabatsiakis, A., ... & Buchheim, A. (2016). Effects of the Adult Attachment Projective Picture System on oxytocin and cortisol blood levels in mothers. *Frontiers in Human Neuroscience*, 10(254), 154–166.

Kreutzer, J. S., DeLuca, J., & Caplan, B. (Eds.). (2011). *Encyclopedia of clinical neuropsychology*. New York: Springer.

Krone, K. J. (1991). Effects of leader-member exchange on subordinates' upward influence attempts. *Communication Research Reports*, 8(1), 9–18.

Krueger, A. B., Kahneman, D., Fischler, C., Schkade, D., Schwarz, N., & Stone, A. A. (2009). Time use and subjective well-being in France and the U.S. *Social Indicators Research*, 93, 7–18.

Kumar, V. A. (2016). 81 honour killings in three years in Tamil Nadu. Retrieved from www.deccanchronicle.com/nation/crime/150316/81-honour-killings-in-three-years-in-tamil-nadu.html

Kurdek, L. A. (1997). The link between facets of neuroticism and dimensions of relationship commitment: Evidence from gay, lesbian, and heterosexual couples. *Journal of Family Psychology*, 11(4), 503.

 (2005). Gender and marital satisfaction early in marriage: A growth curve approach. *Journal of Marriage and the Family*, 67, 68–84.

Kurth (1970), Friendships and friendly relations. In G. J. McCall, M. M. McCall, & N. K. Denzin (Eds.), *Social relationships* (pp. 136–170). Chicago: Aldine Publishing Co.

Kushlev, K., Dunn, E. W., & Ashton-James, C. (2012). Does affluence impoverish the experience of parenting? *Journal of Experimental Social Psychology*, 48, 1381–1384.

Kwak, A. (2005). *Rodzina w dobie przemian. Małżeństwo i kohabitacja*. Warszawa: Wydawnictwo Akademickie „Żak."

Labek, K., Viviani, R., Gizewski, E.R., Verius, M., & Buchheim, A. (2016). Neural correlates of the appraisal of attachment scenes in healthy controls and social cognition – An fMRI study. *Frontiers in Human Neuroscience*, 10(231), 22–31.

Lalonde, R. N., Cilia, J., Lou, E., & Crobbie, R. A. (2015). Are we really that different from each other? The difficulties of focusing on similarities in cross-cultural research. *Peace and Conflict: Journal of Peace Psychology*, 21(4), 525–534.

Lam, A. G., & Zane, N. W. S. (2004). Ethnic differences in coping with interpersonal stressors: A test of self-construals as cultural mediators. *Journal of Cross-Cultural Psychology*, 35(4), 446–459.

Lamanna, M. A., Riedmann, A., & Stewart, S. D. (2014). *Marriage, families, and relationships: Making choices in a diverse society*, 12th ed. Boston: Cengage Learning.

Larson, E. (2010). Psychological well-being and meaning-making when caregiving for children with disabilities: Growth through difficult times or sinking inward. *OTJR: Occupation, Participation and Health*, *30*(2), 78–86.

Laursen, B., & Hafen, C. A. (2010). Future directions in the study of close relationships: Conflict is bad (except when it's not). *Social Development*, *19*, 858–872.

Lawrence, E., & Bradbury, T. N. (2007). Trajectories of change in physical aggression and marital satisfaction. *Journal of Family Psychology*, *21*(2), 236–247.

Orengo, R., Langer, A., & Brock, R. L. (2012). Consequences of psychological and physical abuse for victims: Review and critique of the literature. Special Series: Partner Abuse State of Knowledge. *Partner Abuse*, *3*(4).

Le, B., & Agnew, C. R. (2003). Commitment and its theorized determinants: A meta-analysis of the investment model. *Personal Relationships*, *10*(1), 37–57. doi:10.1111/1475-6811.00035

& Emery, L. F. (2015). Relationships. *Oxford Bibliographies*. Retrieved from www.oxfordbibliographies.com/view/document/obo-9780199828340/obo-9780199828340-0084.xml

Lee, J. A. (1973). *The colors of love*. Englewood Cliffs, NJ: Prentice Hall.

Lee, W., Nakamura, S., Chung, M., Chun, Y., Fu, M., Liang, S., & Liu, C. (2013). Asian couples in negotiation: A mixed-method observational study of cultural variations across five Asian regions. *Family Process*, *52*, 499–518. doi:10.1111/famp.12040

Lefkowitz, E. S., Gillen, M. M., Shearer, C. L., & Boone, T. L. (2004). Religiosity, sexual behaviors, and sexual attitudes during emerging adulthood. *Journal of Sex Research*, *41*(2), 150–159.

Levenson, R. W., Carstensen, L. L., & Gottman, J. M. (1993). Long-term marriage: Age, gender, and satisfaction. *Psychology and Aging*, *8*, 301–313.

Levy-Shiff, R., & Shulman, S. (1997). Families with a developmentally disabled child: Parent-child marital and family relations. In I. Duvdevany, M. Hovav, A. Rimmerman, & A. Ramot (Eds.), *Parents and persons with developmental disabilities* (pp. 15–34) [in Hebrew]. Jerusalem, Israel: Magnes Press.

Li, L. M. W., Adams, G., Kurtis, T., & Hamamura, T. (2015). Beware of friends: The cultural psychology of relational mobility and cautious intimacy. *Asian Journal of Social Psychology*, *18*, 124–133.

Li, Y. J., & Cohen, A. B. (2014). Religion, sexuality, and family. In V. Saraglou (Ed.), *Religion, personality, and social behavior* (pp. 213–229). New York: Psychology Press.

Lin, J. D., Hu, J., Yen, C. F., Hsu, S. W., Lin, L. P., Loh, C. H., . . . & Wu, J. L. (2009). Quality of life in caregivers of children and adolescents with intellectual disabilities: Use of WHOQOL-BREF survey. *Research in Developmental Disabilities*, *30*, 1448–1458.

Londoño, B., Giraldo, S., Montoya, A. M., Moadie, V., Victoria, M. I., Goyes, I, & Montezuma, S. (2014). Violencia contra las mujeres en tres ciudades de Colombia: Pasto, Cartagena y Cali. 2005–2009. *Opinión Jurídica*, *13*(25), 35–50.

Londoño, C. (2014). *Factores que permiten a las parejas permanecer unidas y satisfechas. Un Estudio en la ciudad de Medellín* (Tesis de maestría). Universidad Pontifica Bolivariana, Medellín.

Londoño, D. A. (2005). *Funcionamiento de la pareja y estrategias de afrontamiento ante crisis causadas por problemas económicos* (Tesis de grado). Universidad de la Sabana, Chía.

Lucas, R. E., Clark, A. E., Georgellis, Y., & Diener, E. (2003). Reexamining adaptation and the set point model of happiness: Reactions to changes in marital status. *Journal of Personality and Social Psychology, 84*, 527–539.

Luhmann, M., Hofmann, W., Eid, M., & Lucas, R. E. (2012). Subjective well-being and adaptation to life events: A meta-analysis. *Journal of Personality and Social Psychology, 102*, 592–615.

Lucas, R. E., Eid, M., & Diener, E. (2013). The prospective effect of life satisfaction on life events. *Social Psychological and Personality Science, 4*, 39–45.

Ma, X., Luo, L., Geng, Y., Zhao, W., Zhang, O., & Kendrick, K. M. (2014). Oxytocin increases liking for a country's people and national flag but not for other cultural symbols or consumer products. *Frontiers of Behavioral Neuroscience, 8*(21), 97–107.

Maddox Shaw, A. M., Rhoades, G. K., Allen, E. S., Stanley, S. M., & Markman, H. J. (2013). Predictors of extradyadic sexual involvement in unmarried opposite-sex relationships. *Journal of Sex Research, 50*(6), 598–610. doi:10.1080/00224499.2012.666816

Maio, G. R. (2017). *The psychology of human values.* New York: Routledge.

Mannarini, S., Balottin, L., Munari, C., & Gatta, M. (2017). Assessing conflict management in the couple: The definition of a latent dimension. *The Family Journal, 25*(1), 13–22.

Markova, E. Y. (Маркова Е.Ю.) (2014). Gender peculiarities of ideas about love in pre-adult age [Гендерные особенности представлений о любви в юношеском возрасте]. *Theory and Practice of Social Development, 21*, 318–322.

Markus, H. R., & Kitayama, S. (1991). Culture and the self: Implications for cognition, emotion, and motivation. *Psychological Review, 98*(2), 224–253.

(2003). Culture, self, and the reality of the social. *Psychological Inquiry, 14*, 277–283. doi:10.1207/S15327965PLI1403&4_17

Marshall, T. C. (2008). Cultural differences in intimacy: The influence of gender-role ideology and individualism-collectivism. *Journal of Social and Personal Relationships, 25*, 143–168.

(2010). Gender, peer relations, and intimate romantic relationships. In J. C. Chrisler & D. R. McCrear (Eds.), *Handbook of gender research in psychology* (pp. 281–310). New York: Springer.

Martínez-Álvarez, J. L., Carcedo, R. J., Fuertes, A., Vicario-Molina, I., Fernández-Fuertes, A. A., & Orgaz, B. (2012). Sex education in Spain: Teachers' views of obstacles. *Sex Education, 12*(4), 425–436.

Martínez Íñigo, D. (2005). Contrastación del modelo de inversión de Rusbult en una muestra de casados y divorciados. *Psicothema, 12*(1), 65–69.

Maslow, A. H. (1943). A theory of human motivation. *Psychological Review, 50*(4), 370–396.

(1971). *Farther reaches of human nature,* New York: The Viking Press.

Masser, B., & Abrams, D. (1999). Contemporary sexism: The relationships among hostility, benevolence, and neosexism. *Psychology of Women Quarterly, 23*, 503–517.

Mastekaasa, A. (1992). Marriage and psychological well-being: Some evidence on selection into marriage. *Journal of Marriage and the Family, 54*, 901–91I.

Mayer, R. C., Davis, J. H., & Schoorman, F. D. (1995). An integrative model of organizational trust. *Academy of Management Review, 20,* 709–734.

McAdoo, H. P. (1999). *Family ethnicity: Strength in diversity,* 2nd ed. Thousand Oaks: Sage.

McAllister, D. J. (1995). Affect and cognition-based trust as foundations for inter-personal cooperation in organizations. *Academy of Management Journal, 38,* 24–59.

McCann, D., Bull, R., & Winzenberg, T. (2012). The daily patterns of time use for parents of children with complex needs: A systematic review. *Journal of Child Health Care, 16*(1), 26–52.

McCrae, R. R., & Costa, P. T. (1987). Validation of the five-factor model of personality across instruments and observers. *Journal of Personality and Social Psychology, 52,* 81–90.

McHugh, M. C., & Frieze, I. H. (1997). The measurement of gender-role attitudes. *Psychology of Women Quarterly, 21,* 1–16.

Medián. (2007). Translation from Polish: Median Public Opinion and Market Research Institute. Sex test. Retrieved from www.median.hu/object.27b47266 -b3c1-4520-a710-db51f2d25b50.ivy

Meltzer, A. L., & McNulty, J. K. (2010). Body image and marital satisfaction: Evidence for the mediating role of sexual frequency and sexual satisfaction. *Journal of Family Psychology, 24*(2), 156–164.

Mikulincer, M., & Shaver, P. R. (2017). *Attachment in adulthood: Structure, dynamics, and change,* 2nd ed. New York: Guilford Press.

Miller, R. (2017). *Intimate relationships,* 8th ed. New York: McGraw-Hill Higher Education.

Mirsu-Paun, A., & Oliver, J. A. (2017). How much does love really hurt? A meta-analysis of the association between romantic relationship quality, breakups and mental health outcomes in adolescents and young adults. *Journal of Relationships Research, 8,* 1–12. http://dx.doi.org/10.1017/jrr.2017.6

Moberg, K. U. (2003). *The oxytocin factor: Tapping the hormone of calm, love, and healing.* Boston: De Capo Press.

    (2013). *The hormone of closeness: The role of oxytocin in relationships.* London: Pinter & Martin.

Mogollón, O. M., & Villamizar, D. J. (2013). Análisis de las relaciones de pareja de los estudiantes de la Universidad de Pamplona. *Cuidado y Ocupación Humana, 1*(1), 108–120.

Mollenhorst, G., Völker, B., & Flap, H. (2008). Social contexts and personal relation-ships: The effect of meeting opportunities on similarity for relationships of different strength. *Social Networks, 30*(1), 60–68.

Montoya, R. M., Horton, R. S., & Kirchner, J. (2008). Is actual similarity necessary for attraction? A meta-analysis of actual and perceived similarity. *Journal of Social and Personal Relationships, 25*(6), 889–922.

Mooney, T. B., & Williams, J. N. (2016). The Confucian filial duty to care (xiao 孝) for elderly parents. In J. T. Ozolinš (Ed.), *Religion and culture in dialogue* (pp. 111–127). Switzerland: Springer.

Morrison, T., & Conaway, W. A. (2006). *Kiss, bow, or shake hands: The bestsel-ling guide to doing business in more than 60 countries.* Avon, MA: Adams Media.

Mousourou, L. M. (1999). *Crisis of family and values.* Report of Social Research.

Murray, S. L., Holmes, J. G., & Griffin, D. W. (1996). The benefits of positive illusions: Idealization and the construction of satisfaction in close relationships. *Journal of Personality and Social Psychology, 70*(1), 79–98.

Murstein, B. I. (1976). *Who will marry whom?* New York: Springer.

Myers, J. E., Sweeney, T. J., & Witmer, M. (2000). Counseling for wellness: A holistic model for treatment planning. *Journal of Counseling and Development, 78*(3), 251–266.

Mylonas K., Gari A., Giotsa A., Pavlopoulos V., & Panagiotopoulou P. (2006). Greece. In J. Georgas, J. W. Berry, F. van de Vivjer, C. Kagitçibasi, & Y. H. Poortinga (Eds.), *Families across cultures: A 30 nation psychological study* (pp. 344–352). New York: Cambridge University Press.

National Center for Injury Prevention and Control. (2003). *Costs of intimate partner violence against women in the United States.* Atlanta: Centers for Disease Control and Prevention.

Nauck, B. (2007). Value of children and the framing of fertility: Results from a cross-cultural comparative survey in 10 societies. *European Sociological Review, 23*, 615–629.

Nelson, S. K., Kushlev, K., & Lyubomirsky, S. (2014). The pains and pleasures of parenting: When, why, and how is parenthood associated with more or less well-being?. *Psychological Bulletin, 140*(3), 846.

Nichols, R. (2013). The origins and effects of filial piety (Xiao 孝): How culture solves an evolutionary problem for parents. *Journal of Cognition and Culture, 13*(3–4), 201–230.

Niño, D., & Abaunza, N. (2015). Relación entre dependencia emocional y afrontamiento en estudiantes universitarios. *Psiconex Psicología, Psicoanálisis y Conexiones, 7*(10), 1–27.

NIPSSR. (2017). *The Fifteenth Japanese National Fertility Survey in 2015.* Retrieved from www.ipss.go.jp/ps-doukou/e/doukou15/Nfs15R_points_eng.pdf

Notarius, C. I., & Markman, H. (1993). *We can work it out: Making sense of marital conflict.* New York: Putnam.

Nuttin, J. M. (1985). Narcissism beyond Gestalt and awareness: The name letter effect. *European Journal of Social Psychology, 15*, 353-361.

Ohbuchi, K., Fukushima, O., & Tedeschi, J. T. (1999). Cultural values in conflict management: Goal orientation, goal attainment, and tactical decision. *Journal of Cross-Cultural Psychology, 30*, 51-71.

Oishi, A., Diener, E., & Lucas, R. E. (2007). The optimum level of well-being: Can people be too happy? *Perspectives on Psychological Science, 2*, 346–360.

Palacio, M. C. (2009). Los cambios y transformaciones en la familia. Una paradoja entre lo sólido y lo líquido. *Revista Latinoamericana de Estudios de Familia, 1*, 46–60.

Panuzio, J., & DiLillo, D. (2010). Physical, psychological, and sexual intimate partner aggression among newlywed couples: Longitudinal prediction of marital satisfaction. *Journal of Family Violence, 25*(7), 689–699.

Paprzycka, E., Dec-Pietrowska, J., & Walendzik-Ostrowska, A. (2016). Difference versus diversity – the contexts of defining femininity and masculinity in textbooks for the subject Education for Family Life: Qualitative analysis. In I. Chmura-Rutkowska, M. Duda, M. Mazurek, & A. Sołtysiak-Łuczak (Eds.), *Gender in textbooks. Research project. Report,* Vol. 3: *Subject reports and recommendations* (pp. 140–165). Warsaw: Feminoteka Foundation.

    & Izdebski, Z. (2016). *Single i singielki. Intymność i seksualność osób żyjących w pojedynkę.* Warszawa: Difin.

Parks, M. R. (2006). *Personal relationships and personal networks*. New York: Routledge.

    & Eggert, L. L. (1991). The role of social context in the dynamics of personal relationships. In W. H. Jones & D. Perlman (Eds.), *Advances in personal relationships: A research annual* (Vol.2, pp. 1–34). Oxford, UK: Jessica Kingsley.

Pedersen, P. B., Lonner, W. J., Draguns, J. G., Trimeble, J. E., & Scharrón-del Rio, M. R. (2015). *Counseling across cultures*, 7th ed. Thousand Oaks, CA: Sage.

Peer, J. W., & Hillman, S. B. (2014). Stress and resilience for parents of children with intellectual and developmental disabilities: A review of key factors and recommendations for practitioners. *Journal of Policy and Practice in Intellectual Disabilities*, 11(2), 92–98.

Pellegrini, E. K., & Scandura, T. A. (2008). Paternalistic leadership: A review and agenda for future research. *Journal of Management*, 34, 566–593.

Pence, E., & Paymar, M. (1993). *Education groups for men who batter: The Duluth model*. New York: Springer.

Peplau, L. A. (1979). Power in dating relationships. In J. Freeman (Ed.), *Women: A feminist perspective*, 2nd ed. (pp. 106–121). Palo Alto, CA: Mayfield Publishing. Reprinted in the 3rd ed. (1984) and revised for the 4th ed. (1989).

    & Garnets, L. D. (2000). A new paradigm for understanding women's sexuality and sexual orientation. *Journal of Social Issues*, 56(2), 330–350.

    & Perlman, D. (1982). *Loneliness: A sourcebook of current theory, research and therapy*. New York: John Wiley and Sons.

Hill, C. T., & Rubin, Z. (1993). Sex-role attitudes in dating and marriage: A 15-year followup of the Boston Couples Study. *Journal of Social Issues*, 49(3), 31–52.

Rubin, Z., & Hill, C. T. (1976, November). The sexual balance of power. Psychology Today, pp. 142 ff.

Rubin, Z., & Hill, C. T. (1977). *Sexual intimacy in dating couples. Journal of Social Issues*, 33(2), 86–109.

Perlman, D., Duck, S., & Hengstebeck, N. D. (2018). The seven seas of the study of personal relationships research: Historical and recent currents. In A. L. Vangelisti & D. Perlman (Eds.), *Cambridge handbook of personal relationships*, 2nd ed. (pp. 9–27). New York: Cambridge University Press.

Pew Research Center. (2013). Eastern and Western Europe divided over gay marriage, homosexuality. Retrieved from www.pewresearch.org/fact-tank/2013/12/12/east ern-and-western-europe-divided-over-gay-marriage-homosexuality

    (2014). *Premarital sex*. Retrieved from www.pewglobal.org/2014/04/15/global-morality/table/premarital-sex/

Pietrowska-Dec, J., Walendzik-Ostrowska, A., & Gulczyńska, A. (2016). Recommendation. In I. Chmura-Rutkowska, M. Duda, M. Mazurek, & A. Sołtysiak-Łuczak (Eds.), *Gender in textbooks. Research project. Report*, Vol. 3: *Subject reports and recommendations* (p. 170). Warsaw: Feminoteka Foundation.

Pimentel, E. E. (2000). Just how do I love thee? Marital relations in urban China. *Journal of Marriage and Family*, 62, 32–47. doi:10.1111/j.1741-3737.2000.00032.x

Plotnik, R. (2002). *Introduction to psychology*, 6th ed. Pacific Grove, CA: Wadsworth Group.

Ponterotto, J. G. (Ed.). (2001). *Handbook of multicultural counseling*. Thousand Oaks, CA: Sage.

Popescu, R. (2010). Profilul familie contemporane (The profile of contemporary families in Romania). *Revista Calitatea Vieţii*, 21(1–2), 5–29.

Przybył, I. (2017). *Historie przedślubne. Przemiany obyczajowości i instytucji zaręczyn.* Poznań: Wydawnictwo Naukowe UAM.

Queen, S. S., Habenstein, R. W., & Adams, J. B. (1961). *The family in various cultures.* Chicago: J. B. Lippincott Company.

Raina, P., & Maity, M. T. (2018). An empirical study on marital satisfaction between arranged and self-marriage couples in Bangalore. *International Journal of Indian Psychology, 6,* 101–108.

Ratajczak, Ł. P. (2016). *Ojcostwo w doświadczeniach niepełnoletnich chłopców.* Poznań: Wydawnictwo Naukowe UAM.

Raymo, J. M., Park, H., Xie, Y., & Yeung, W.-J. J. (2015). Marriage and family in East Asia: Continuity and change. *Annual Review of Sociology, 41*(1), 471–492. doi:10.1146/annurev-soc-073014-112428

Regan, P. C., Lakhanpal, S., & Anguiano, C. (2012). Relationship outcomes in Indian-American love-based and arranged marriages. *Psychological Reports, 110* (3), 915–924.

Reis, H. T., & Franks, P. (1994). The role of intimacy and social support in health outcomes: Two processes or one? *Personal Relationships, 1,* 185–197.

Resch, J. A., Benz, M. R., & Elliott, T. R. (2012). Evaluating a dynamic process model of wellbeing for parents of children with disabilities: A multi-method analysis. *Rehabilitation Psychology, 57*(1), 61–72.

Mireles, G., Genz, M. R., Grenwelge, C., Peterson, R., & Zhang, D. (2010). Giving parents a voice: A qualitative study of the challenges experienced by parents of children with disabilities. *Rehabilitation Psychology, 55*(2), 139–150.

Rice, R. W., Near, J. P., & Hunt, R. G. (1980). The job-satisfaction/life-satisfaction relationship: A review of empirical research. *Basic and Applied Social Psychology, 1*(1), 37–64.

Rivera, A. S. (2000). Conceptualización, medición y correlatos de poder y pareja: una aproximación etnopsicológica. (Tesis doctoral inédita). UNAM. México, D.F.

& Díaz-Loving, R. (1999). Estrategias de poder en la pareja. In R. Díaz-Loving (Ed.), *Antología Psicosocial de la pareja* (pp. 183–214). México: Miguel Angel Porrúa.

& Díaz- Loving, R. (2002). *La cultura del poder en la pareja.* México: Facultad de Psicología. UNAM.

Díaz- Loving, R., & Cruz del Castillo, C. (2005). Escala de Conflicto. Documento Inédito. Facultad de Psicología. Universidad Nacional Autónoma de México.

Díaz-Loving, R., Sánchez, A., & Alvarado, H. (1996). Estilos y estrategias del poder en la relación de pareja. Revista de Psicología Social y Personalidad, 3(1), 17–26.

Robinson, B. E., Carroll, J. J., & Flowers, C. (2001). Marital estrangement, positive affect, and locus of control among spouses of workaholics and spouses of non-workaholics: A national study. *American Journal of Family Therapy, 29*(5), 397–410.

Robinson, K. J., & Cameron, J. J. (2012). Self-esteem is a shared relationship resource: Additive effects of dating partners' self-esteem levels predict relationship quality. *Journal of Research in Personality, 46,* 227–230.

Rogers, S. J., & May, D. C. (2003). Spillover between marital quality and job satisfaction: Long-term patterns and gender differences. *Journal of Marriage and Family, 65*(2), 482–495.

Rohner, R. P. (1986). *The warmth dimension: Foundations of parental acceptance-rejection theory.* Beverly Hills, CA: Sage.

(2004). Extended parental acceptance-rejection bibliography. Retrieved from http://csiar.uconn.edu/bibliography/

(2017). *The Warmth Dimension* (A. Giotsa, Ed). Athens: Gutenberg Editions.

& Khaleque A. (2005). *Handbook for the study of parental acceptance and rejection.* Storrs, CT: Rohner Research.

Khaleque A., & Cournoyer D. E. (2012). Introduction to parental acceptance-rejection theory. Retrieved from http://csiar.uconn.edu/bibliography/

Rokeach, M. (1973). *The nature of human values.* New York: Free Press.

Rose, A. J., & Rudolph, K. D. (2006). A review of sex differences in peer relationship processes: Potential trade-offs for the emotional and behavioral development of girls and boys. *Psychological Bulletin, 132,* 98.

Rosemont, H. (1991). Rights-bearing individuals and role-bearing persons. In M. Bockover (Ed.), *Rules, rituals, and responsibility: Essays dedicated to Herbert Fingarette* (pp. 71–102). La Salle, IL: Open Court.

Rosenberg, M. (1965). *Society and the adolescent self-image.* Princeton: Princeton University Press.

Rosenblatt, P. C., & Weiling, E. (2015). *Knowing and not knowing in intimate relationships.* Cambridge: Cambridge University Press.

Rostosky, S. S., Wilcox, B. L., Wright, M. L. C., & Randall, B. A. (2004). The impact of religiosity on adolescent sexual behavior: A review of the evidence. *Journal of Adolescent Research, 19*(6), 677–697.

Rubin, Z. (1970). Measurement of romantic love. *Journal of Personality and Social Psychology, 16*(2), 265–273.

(1973). *Liking and loving: An invitation to social psychology.* New York: Holt, Rinehart and Winston.

& Mitchell, C. (1976). Couples research as couples counseling: Some unintended effects of studying close relationships. *American Psychologist, 31,* 17–25.

& Peplau, L. A. (1975). Who believes in a just world. *Journal of Social Issues, 31*(3), 65–89.

Rusbult, C. E. (1980). Commitment and satisfaction in romantic associations: A test of the Investment Model. *Journal of Experimental Social Psychology, 16*(2), 172–186.

Agnew, C. R., & Arriaga, X. B. (2012). The Investment Model. In P. A. M. Van Lange, A. W. Kruglanski, & E. T. Higgins (Eds.), *Handbook of theories of social psychology* (Vol. 2, pp. 218–231). Thousand Oaks, CA, Sage.

Olsen, N., Davis, J. L., & Hannon, P. (2001). Commitment and relationship maintenance mechanisms. In J. H. Harvey & A. Wenzel (Eds.), *Close romantic relationships: Maintenance and enhancement* (pp. 87–113). Mahwah, NJ: Erlbaum

Zembrodt, I. M., & Gunn, L. K. (1982). Exit, voice, loyalty, and neglect: Responses to dissatisfaction in romantic involvements. *Journal of Personality and Social Psychology, 43*(6), 1230–1242.

Ryan, R. M., & Deci, E. L. (2017). *Self-Determination Theory: Basic psychological needs in motivation, development, and wellness.* New York: Guilford Press.

Rybak, A., & McAndrew, F. T. (2006). How do we decide whom our friends are? Defining levels of friendship in Poland and the United States. *Journal of Social Psychology, 146,* 147–163

Sánchez, V., Ortega, F. J., Ortega, R., & Viejo, C. (2008). Las relaciones sentimentales en la adolescencia: Satisfacción, conflictos y violencia. *Escritos de Psicología, 2*(1), 97–109.

Saphire-Bernstein, S., & Taylor, S. E. (2013). Close relationships and happiness. In S. A. David, I. B. Boniwell, & A. C. Ayers (Eds.), *Oxford handbook of happiness* (pp. 821–833). New York: Oxford University Press.

Sarantakos, S. (2000). Marital power and quality of marriage. *Australian Social Work, 53*(1), 43–50.

Sawaumi, T., Yamaguchi, S., Park, J., & Robinson, A. R. (2015). Japanese control strategies regulated by urgency and interpersonal harmony: Evidence based on extended conceptual framework. *Journal of Cross-Cultural Psychology, 46*, 252–268.

Schachter, S., & Singer, J. (1962). Cognitive, social, and physiological determinants of emotional state. *Psychological Review, 69*, 379–399. doi:10.1037/h0046234

Scheele, D., Striepens, N., Gunturkun, O., Deutschlander, S., Maier, W., Kendrick, K. M., . . . & Hurlemann, R. (2012). Oxytocin modulates social distance between males and females. *Journal of* Neuroscience, *32*, 16074–16079. doi:10.1523/jneurosci.2755-12

Schmidt, C. D., Luquet, W., & Gehlert, N. C. (2016). Evaluating the impact of the "Getting the love you want" couples workshop on relational satisfaction and communication patterns. *Journal of Couple & Relationship Therapy, 15*, 1–18.

Schug, J., Yuki, M., & Maddux, W. (2010). Relational mobility explains between- and within-culture differences in self-disclosure to close friends. *Psychological Science, 21*, 1471–1478.

Yuki, M., Horikawa, H., & Takemura, K. (2009). Similarity attraction and actually selecting similar others: How cross-societal differences in relational mobility affect interpersonal similarity in Japan and the USA. *Asian Journal of Social Psychology, 12*, 95–103.

Schwalb, D. W., & Hossain, Z. (Eds.). (2017). *Grandparents in cultural context.* Florence, KY: Routledge.

Schwartz, S. H. (1990). Individualism-collectivism: Critique and proposed refinements. *Journal of Cross-Cultural Psychology, 21*(1), 139–157.

(1992). Universals in the content and structure of values: Theoretical advances and empirical tests in 20 countries. In J. M. Olson & M. P. Zanna (Eds.), *Advances in experimental social psychology* (Vol. 25, pp. 1–65). Orlando: Academic Press.

(2012). An overview of the Schwartz Theory of Basic Values. *Online Readings in Psychology and Culture, 2*(1). http://dx.doi.org:10.9707:2307–0919.1116

Cieciuch, J., Vecchione, M., Davidov, E., Fischer, R., Beierlein, C., Ramos, A., . . . & Konty, M. (2012). Refining the theory of basic individual values. *Journal of Personality and Social Psychology, 103*(4), 663–688.

& Rubel, T. (2005). Sex differences in value priorities: Cross-cultural and multi-method studies. *Journal of Personality and Social Psychology, 89*(6), 1010–1028. http://dx.doi.org/10.1037/0022-3514.89.6.1010

Scorgie, K., & Sobsey, D. (2000). Transformational outcomes associated with parenting children who have disabilities. *Mental Retardation, 38*, 195–206. doi:10.1352/0047-6765(2000)038<0195:TOAWPC>2.0.CO;2

Scott, C. L., & Blair, S. L. (2017). *Intimate relationships and social change: The dynamic nature of dating, mating, and culture.* Bingley, UK: Emerald Publishing Ltd.

Seligman, M. E. P. (1972). Learned helplessness. *Annual Review of Medicine, 23*(1), 407–412.

(2012). *Flourish: A new understanding of happiness and well-being.* New York: Simon and Schuster.

Shalev, I., & Ebstein, R. P. (2013, December). Frontiers in oxytocin science: From basic to practice. *Frontiers in Neuroscience.* Retrieved from https://doi.org/10.3389/fnins.2013.00250

Shamay-Tsoory, S. G., Fischer, M., Dvash, J., Harari, H., Perach-Bloom, N., & Levkovitz, Y. (2009). Intranasal administration of oxytocin increases envy and schadenfreude (gloating). *Biological Psychiatry, 66*, 864–870. doi:10.1016/j.biop-sych. 2009.06.009

Shek, D. T. (1995). Marital quality and psychological well-being of married adults in a Chinese context. *The Journal of Genetic Psychology, 156*(1), 45–56.

Shenaar-Golan, V. (2016). The subjective well-being of parents of children with developmental disabilities: The role of hope as predictor and fosterer of well-being. *Journal of Social Work in Disability & Rehabilitation, 15*(2), 77–95.

——— (2017). Hope and subjective well-being among parents of children with special needs. *Child & Family Social Work, 22*(1), 306–316.

Showalter, K. (2016). Women's employment and domestic violence: A review of the literature. *Aggression and Violent Behavior, 31*, 37–47.

Siddaway, A. P., Wood, A. M., & Taylor, P. J. (2017). The Center for Epidemiologic Studies-Depression (CES-D) scale measures a continuum from well-being to depression: Testing two key predictions of positive clinical psychology. *Journal of Affective Disorders, 213*, 180–186.

Simpson, J. A., & Campbell, L. (Eds.). (2013). *The Oxford handbook of close relationships*. New York: Oxford University Press.

Singh, V., Lopez, R., & Chowbey, A. (2015). When love conquers all: Scenes from cross-cultural weddings. Retrieved from www.hindustantimes.com/brunch/scenes-from-indian-weddings-less-ordinary/story-yvY3QKfTGoTMahAtYohl7I.html

Singh, D., & Goli, S. (2011). Exploring the concept of mixed marriages in Indian and selected states: First time evidences from large-scale survey. Retrieved from http://paa2011.princeton.edu/papers/111966

Singla, R. (2015). *Intermarriage and mixed parenting, promoting mental health and wellbeing: Crossover love*. Basingstoke, UK: Palgrave Macmillan.

Sitnikov, V. L., & Ilchenko, V. V. (Ситников В. Л., Ильченко В. В.) (2016). Premarital attitudes of adolescent girls in multicultural environment [Добрачные половые установки девушек в поликультурной среде].*Scientific Notes of Transbaikal State University, 11*(5), 107–114.

Skowrońska-Pućka, A. (2016). *(Przed)wczesne macierzyństwo- perspektywa biograficzna. Diagnoza, pomoc i wsparcie*. Poznań: Wydawnictwo Naukowe UAM.

Slany, K. (2002). *Alternatywne formy życia małżeńsko-rodzinnego w ponowoczesnym świecie*. Kraków: Nomos.

Smith, L. E., Greenberg, J. S., & Seltzer, M. M. (2012). Social support and well-being at mid-life among mothers of adolescents and adults with autism spectrum disorders. *Journal of Autism and Developmental Disorders, 42*(9), 1818–1826.

Smith, P. B., & Bond, M. H. (1993). *Social psychology across cultures*. Hartfordshire, UK: Harvester/Wheatsheaf.

Smithsonian Museum of Natural History. (no date). What does it mean to be human? Retrieved from http://humanorigins.si.edu/evidence/genetics

Sorokowski, P., Randall, A. K., Groyecka, A., Frackowiak, T., Cantarero, K., Hilpert, P., . . . & Sorokowska, A. (2017). Marital satisfaction, sex, age, marriage duration, religion, number of children, economic status, education, and collectivistic values: Data from 33 countries. *Frontiers in Psychology*, 8, 1199. doi:10.3389/fpsyg.2017.01199

Sprecher, S., Christopher, F. S., Regan, P., Orbuch, T., & Cate, R. M. (2018). Sexuality in personal relationships. In A. L. Vangelisti & D. Perlman (Eds.), *Handbook of personal relationships*, 2nd ed. (pp. 311–326). New York: Cambridge University Press.

& Felmlee, D. (1997). The balance of power in romantic heterosexual couples over time from "his" and "her" perspectives. *Sex Roles*, 37(5–6), 361–379.

& Hendrick, S. S. (2004). Self-disclosure in intimate relationships: Associations with individual and relationship characteristics over time. *Journal of Social and Clinical Psychology*, 23(6), 857–877.

Regan, P., & Orbuch, T. (2016). Who does the work? Partner perceptions of the initiation and maintenance of romantic relationships. Interpersonal, 10(1), 13–27.

Schmeeckle, M., & Felmlee, D. (2006). The principle of least interest. *Journal of Family Issues*, 27(9), 1–26.

Sprenkle, D. H., Davis, S. D., & Lebow, J. L. (2009). *Common factors in couple and family therapy: The overlooked foundation for effective practice*. New York: Guilford Press.

Staff, H. R., Didymus, F. F., & Backhouse, S. H. (2017). The antecedents and outcomes of dyadic coping in close personal relationships: A systematic review and narrative synthesis. *Anxiety, Stress & Coping: An International Journal*, 30 (5), 498–520.

Stańczak, J., Stelmach, K., & Urbanowicz, M. (2016). *Małżeństwa oraz dzietność w Polsce*. Warszawa: Główny Urząd Statystyczny Departament Badań Demograficznych i Rynku Pracy [online] http://stat.gov.pl/

Stanley, S. M., Rhoades, G. K., Scott, S. B., Kelmer, G., Markman, H. J., & Fincham, F. D. (2017). Asymmetrically committed relationships. *Journal of Social and Personal Relationships*, 34(8), 1241–1259. doi:10.1177/0265407516672013

Whitton, S. W., Sadberry, S. L., Clements, M. L., & Markman, H. J. (2006). Sacrifice as a predictor of marital outcomes. Family Process, 45(3), 289–303.

Stein, P. J. (Ed.). (1981). *Single life: Unmarried Adults in Social Context*. New York: St. Martin's Press.

Sternberg, R. (1986). A triangular theory of love. *Psychological Review*, 93(2), 119–135.

Straus, M. A. (1979). Measuring intrafamily conflict and violence: The Conflict Tactics Scales. *Journal of Marriage and the Family*, 41, 75–88.

(2012). Blaming the messenger for the bad news about partner violence by women: The methodological, theoretical, and value basis of the purported invalidity of the Conflict Tactics Scales. *Behavioral Sciences and the Law*, 30, 538–556.

Striepens, N., Scheele, D., Kendrick, K. M., Becker, B., Schafer, L., Schwalba, K., . . . & Hurlemann, R. (2012). Oxytocin facilitates protective responses to aversive social stimuli in males. *Proceedings of the National Academy of Sciences of the United States of America*, 109, 18144–18149. doi:10.1073/pnas.1208852109

Stryker, S., & Burke, P. J. (2002). The past, the present, and the future of identity theory. S*ocial Psychology Quarterly*, 63, 284–297.

Stutzer, A., & Frey, B. S. (2006). Does marriage make people happy, or do happy people get married? *The Journal of Socio-Economics*, 35(2), 326–347. doi:10.1016/j.socec.2005.11.043

Surra, C. A., & Hughes, D. K. (1997). Commitment processes in accounts of the development of premarital relationships. *Journal of Marriage and the Family*, 59(1), 5–21.

Tay, L., & Dierner, E. (2011). Needs and subjective well-being around the world. *Journal of Personal Social Psychology, 101*(2), 354–365.

Thibaut, J. W., & Kelley, H. H. (1959). *The social psychology of groups.* New York: John Wiley and Sons.

Thomson, R., Yuki, M., & Ito, N. (2015). A socio-ecological approach to national difference in online privacy concern: The role of relational mobility and trust. *Computers in Human Behavior, 51*, 285–292.

Thomson, R., Yuki, M., Talhelm, T., Schug, T., Kito, M., Ayanian, A. H., ... & Visserman, M. L. (2018). Relational mobility predicts social behaviors in 39 countries and is tied to historical farming and threat. *Proceedings of the National Academy of Sciences of the United States of America.* Retrieved from https://doi.org/10.1073/pnas.1713191115.

To, S. (2015a). Contesting discriminatory constraints. In *China's leftover women: Late marriage among professional women and its consequences* (pp. 81–106). London: Taylor and Francis.

(2015b). "My mother wants me to jiaru-haomen (marry into a rich and powerful family)!" Exploring the pathways to "altruistic individualism" in Chinese professional women's filial strategies of marital choice. *SAGE Open, 5*(1), 1–11. doi:10.1177/2158244014567057

Tolman, R. M., & Rosen, D. (2001). Domestic violence in the lives of women receiving welfare: Mental health, substance dependence, and economic well-being. *Violence Against Women, 7*(2), 141–158.

Torres, C. V., Schwartz, S. H., & Nascimento, T. G. (2017). The refined Theory of Values: Associations with behavior and evidences of discriminative and predictive validity. *Psicologia USP, 27*(2), 1–16.

Tower, R. B., & Kasl, S. V. (1996). Depressive symptoms across older spouses: Longitudinal influences. *Psychology and Aging, 11*, 683–697.

Triandis, H. C. (1992). Cross-cultural research in social psychology. In G. Sarup & D. Grandberg (Eds.), *Social judgment and intergroup relations: Essays in honor of Muzafer Sherif* (pp. 229–244). Berlin: Springer-Verlag.

(1993). Collectivism and individualism as cultural syndromes. *Cross-Cultural Research, 27*(3–4), 155–180. Retrieved from https://doi.org/10.1177/106939719302700301

(1995). *Individualism & collectivism.* Boulder, CO: Westview Press.

(1989) The self and social behavior in differing cultural contexts. *Psychological Review, 96*(3), 506–520.

Valor-Segura, I., Expósito, F., Moya, M., & Kluwer, E. (2014). Don't leave me: The effect of dependency and emotions in relationship conflict. *Journal of Applied Social Psychology, 44*(9), 579–587.

van de Vijver, F., & Leung, K. (1997). *Methods and data analysis for cross-cultural research.* Thousand Oaks, CA: Sage.

Van Selm, M., & Jankowski, N. W. (2006). Conducting online surveys. *Quality and Quantity, 40*(3), 435–456.

VanderDrift, L. E., & Agnew, C. R. (in press). Interdependence perspectives on relationship maintenance. In B. G. Ogolsky & J. K. Monk (Eds.), *Relationship maintenance: Theory, process, and context.* Cambridge: Cambridge University Press.

Vangelisti, A. L., & Perlman, D. (Eds.). (2018). *The Cambridge handbook of personal relationships,* 2nd ed. Cambridge: Cambridge University Press.

Vélez, L. S. (2017). *Relación de pareja: satisfacción e insatisfacción conyugal* (Tesis de maestría). Pontificia Universidad Javeriana, Santiago de Cali.

Viejo, C., Ortega-Ruiz, R., & Sánchez, V. (2015). Adolescent love and well-being: The role of dating relationships for psychological adjustment. *Journal of Youth Studies, 18,* 1219–1236.

Voicu, B., & Telegdy, B. (2016). Dynamics of social values: 1990–2012. *Acta Universitatis Sapientiae. Social Analysis, 6*(1), 7–30.

Voorpostel, M., & Blieszner, R. (2008). Intergenerational solidarity and support between adult siblings. *Journal of Marriage and the Family, 70,* 157–167.

Waller, W. (1938). *The family: A dynamic interpretation.* Austin, TX: Holt, Rinehart & Winston.

Wang, H., & Amato, P. R. (2000). Predictors of divorce adjustment: Stressors, resources, and definitions. *Journal of Marriage and the Family, 62,* 655–668.

Wangmann, J. M. (2011). Different types of intimate partner violence: An exploration of the literature. Retrieved from www.adfvc.unsw.edu.au/ PDF%2ofiles/ IssuesPaper_22.pdf

Waszyńska, K. (2016). Analiza podstawy programowej. In I. Chmura-Rutkowska, M. Duda, M. Mazurek, & A. Sołtysiak-Łuczak (Eds.), *Gender w podręcznikach. Projekt badawczy. Raport, t. 3: Raporty przedmiotowe i rekomendacje* (pp. 167–170). Warszawa: Fundacja Feminoteka.

Weigel, D. J., Bennett, K. K., & Ballard-Reisch, D. S. (2006). Influence strategies in marriage: Self and partner links between equity, strategy use, and marital satisfaction and commitment. *Journal of Family Communication, 6*(1), 77–95. doi:10.1207/s15327698jfc0601_5

Weiss, R. S. (1974). *Loneliness: The experience of emotional and social isolation.* Cambridge, MA: MIT Press.

Wellings, K., Collumbien, M., Slaymaker, E., Singh, S., Hodges, Z., Patel, D., & Bajos, N. (2006). Sexual behaviour in context: A global perspective. *Lancet, 368*(9548), 1706–1728. doi:10.1016/S0140-6736(06)69479-8

Weisfeld, C. C., Weisfeld, G. E., & Dillon, L. M. (2018). *The psychology of marriage: An evolutionary and cross-cultural view.* New York: Lexington Books.

Whitton, S. W., James-Kangal, N., Rhoades, G. K., & Markam, H. J. (2018). Understanding couple conflict. In A. L. Vangelisti & D. Perlman (Eds.), *Cambridge handbook of personal relationships,* 2nd ed. New York: Cambridge University Press.

Stanley, S., & Markman, H. (2002). Sacrifice in romantic relationships: An exploration of relevant research and theory. In A. L. Vangelisti, H. T. Reis, & M. A. Fitzpatrick (Eds.). *Stability and change in relationships* (pp. 156–181). Cambridge and New York: Cambridge University Press.

Stanley, S. M., & Markman, H. J. (2007). If I help my partner, will it hurt me? Journal of Social and Clinical Psychology, 26(1), 64–92.

Wichmann, T., Buchheim, A., Menning, H., Schenk, I., George, C., & Pokorny, D. (2016). A reaction time experiment on adult attachment: The development of a measure for neurophysiology. *Frontiers in Human Neuroscience, 10.* doi:10.3389/fnhum.2016.00548

Winch, R. F., & Goodman, L. W. (Eds.). (1968). *Selected studies in marriage and the family,* 3rd ed. New York: Holt, Rinehart, and Winston.

Woodin, E. M. (2011). A two-dimensional approach to relationship conflict: Meta-analytic findings. *Journal of Family Psychology, 25*(3), 325–335. doi:10.1037/a0023791

World Health Organization. (2010). *Preventing intimate partner and sexual violence against women: Taking action and generating evidence.* Geneva: World Health Organisation and London School of Hygiene and Tropical Medicine.

(2014). *Health care for women subjected to intimate partner violence or sexual violence: A clinical handbook.* Geneva: WHO. World Health Organization.

(2002). *World report on violence and health: Summary.* Geneva: World Health Organization.

Wu, T.-F., Cross, S. E., Wu, C.-W., Cho, W., & Tey, S.-H. (2016). Choosing your mother or your spouse: Close relationship dilemmas in Taiwan and the United States. *Journal of Cross-Cultural Psychology, 47*, 558–580.

Xiaohe, X., & Whyte, M. K. (1990). Love matches and arranged marriages: A Chinese replication. *Journal of Marriage and the Family, 52*(3), 709–722.

Xu, A., Xie, X., Liu, W., Xia, Y., & Liu, D. (2007). Chinese family strengths and resiliency. *Marriage & Family Review, 41*, 143–164.

Yamada, J., Kito, M., & Yuki, M. (2015). Relational mobility and intimacy in friendships and romantic relationships: A cross-societal study between Canada and Japan [in Japanese]. *Japanese Journal of Experimental Social Psychology, 55*, 18–27.

(2017). Passion, relational mobility, and proof of commitment: A comparative socio-ecological analysis of an adaptive emotion in a sexual market. *Evolutionary Psychology, 15*(4), 1–8. doi:10.1177/1474704917746056

Yan, H. K. T. (2017). Is filial piety a virtue? A reading of the Xiao Jing (Classic of Filial Piety) from the perspective of ideology critique. *Educational Philosophy and Theory, 18*(1), 1–11.

Yáñez, H., Ferrel, F., Ortiz, A., & Yáñez, G. (2017). Efectos de la mentira en las relaciones de pareja entre jóvenes universitarios heterosexuales. *Psicología desde el Caribe, 31*(1), 1–24.

Yeh, K.-H., & Bedford, O. (2003). A test of the dual filial piety model. *Asian Journal of Social Psychology, 6*, 215–228.

Yelsma, P., & Athappilly, K. (1988). Marital satisfaction and communication practices: Comparisons among Indian and American couples. *Journal of Comparative Family Studies, 19*(1), 37–54.

Yuki, M., & Schug, J. (2012). Relational mobility: A socioecological approach to personal relationships. In O. Gillath, G. Adams, & A. Kunkel (Eds.), *Relationship science: Integrating evolutionary, neuroscience, and sociocultural approaches* (pp. 137–151). Washington, DC: American Psychological Association.

Zamudio, L., & Rubiano, N. (1991). *Las separaciones conyugales en Colombia.* Bogotá: Universidad Externado de Colombia.

Zhen, N., Zhang, S., Li, M. H., Mao, G. Y., & Wang, J. (2000). *Sexuality among contemporary Chinese college students.* Tienjing: Tienjing University Press.

Zuo, X., Lou, C., Gao, E., Cheng, Y., Niu, H., & Zabin, L. S. (2012). Gender differences in adolescent premarital sexual permissiveness in three Asian cities: Effects of gender-role attitudes. *Journal of Adolescent Health, 50*(3), S18–S25.

INDEX

Concepts and measures explored in the study are indexed when they are first defined, and again if their meaning is elaborated further. Authors are indexed only if they are the source of concepts and measures explored in the study. Capitalized terms refer to measures used in the study.

additional variance, 24
Alpha, 17
alternative partner, 106
alternative relationships, 8
alternatives to compliance, 102
analysis of variance, 15
ANOVA. See Analysis of Variance
anxiety, 156, 157
Anxious Attachment, 44
approval of outside sex, 91
approval of the current Partner, 133
arranged marriages, 132
attachment, 75
attitude, 73
Attractiveness Factor, 58
Attractiveness Important, 54
Attractiveness Similarity, 55
Avoidant Attachment, 44

bases of power, 101
Beck, Aaron, 157
benefits, 107
benevolence, 50
Berscheid, Ellen, 74, 198
Blake, Robert, 114
Blau, Peter, 7, 102
Boston Couples Study, 1, 5, 53, 60, 76, 103, 159, 161, 194
breaking up and coming back, 119
breakups, 139
Brown, Roger, 199

Campbell, Angus, 157
caring, 75
central factors, 23, 173
central traits, 24
CFI. See Comparative Fit Index
chance consequences, 199
circles of support, 204
collectivist cultures, 9
commitment mechanisms, 201
commitment readiness, 63
commitment rituals, 200
companionate love, 74
Comparative Fit Index, 19
comparison levels, 8, 103
Comprehensive Commitment Model, 19, 178
Comprehensive Factors, 173
Comprehensive Partner Model, 175
Comprehensive Relationship Model, 203, 205
conceptual tools, 4, 217
confidence for having a current partner, 175
conflict, 112
Conflict Resolution, 179, 186, 191, 195
conservation, 38, 42
Converse, Philip, 157
coping with stress, 134
correlations, 16
couple commitment, 21
couples counseling, 196
Cruz del Castillo, Cinthia, 112
cultural regions, 12
current rewards and costs, 8, 102

delegation of power, 105
dependent variable, 23
depression, 156, 157
Diaz-Loving, Rolando, 112
Diener, Edward, 155
difficulty finding a partner, 44
dimensions of social relationships, 199
direct predictions, 23
domestic violence, 117

Eastwick, Paul, 198
economic exchange, 8
effect size, 17
Equal Interest in Sex, 89
eros, 75
Ethnicity Similarity, 55
evolutionary psychology, 52
Exchange Processes, 179, 186, 191, 195
Expectations Conflicts, 113
explained variance, 16
expressions of affection, 76
expressions of intimacy, 82

factor analyses, 17
filter Theory, 52
Finkel, Eli, 198
four responses to dissatisfaction, 116
French, John, 101
friendly relations, 199
friendship, 199
F-tests, 15

gamma (γ), 23
gender role attitudes, 107
gender-role attitude scales, 107
general life satisfaction, 159
generalizability, 13
genetic research, 181
Gottman. John, 115
Greve, Bent, 156
Gunn, Lawanna, 116

Happiness, 155, 156
Hazen, Cindy, 44
Hendrick, Clyde, 75
Hendrick, Susan, 75
hierarchy of needs, 36
Highest Sources of Conflict, 112
homogamy, 52
honesty, 80
Hunt, Morton, 131

ideal frequency of sex, 88
impacts of life domains, 133
importance of the decisions, 105

incremental exchange, 8
independent variables, 23
indirect predictions, 23
individualist cultures, 9
Intelligence Factor, 58
interpersonal attraction, 198
intimacy, 75
Intimacy Dimensions, 179, 186, 190, 195
intimate, 4
intimate partner violence, 117
intimate relationships, 4
invested, 107
investment costs, 8, 102

jealousy, 118

Kanter, Rosabeth, 201
knowing the current partner, 132
knowing the partner, 80
Kurth, Suzanne, 199

legal commitment, 22
life as fulfilling and meaningful, 160
life goals, 39
life satisfaction, 155, 159
limitations of the study, 193
Living Together Conflicts, 113
Lucas, Richard, 155

mate selection, 52
means, 14
measurement invariance, 13
motivation for having a current partner, 175
Mouton, Jane, 114
multiple regression, 17

Negative Responses, 115
negotiation styles, 114

Oishi, Shigehiro, 155
one race, 181
openness to change, 38
opportunity costs, 8, 103
opportunity for having a current partner, 175
overarching theory of relationships, 198
Own Disclosure scale, 79
oxytocin, 37

Partner Disclosure scale, 79
Partner Suitability, 179, 186, 190, 195
passion, 75
passionate love, 74
Peplau, Anne, 1, 5, 84, 103
personal commitment, 21

Personality Important, 54
Personality Similarity, 55
physical attractiveness, 58
physical violence, 117
point-biserial correlation, 17
Positive Responses, 115
predict in common, 24
pre-marital sex, 138
principle of least interest, 102
probability distribution, 15
Proximity, 199
Public Displays of Affection, 78

Racial-ethnic Identities, 136
ratings of self and partner, 57
Raven, Bertram, 101
readiness for having a current partner, 175
reciprocating a negative, 115
reciprocity of liking, 199
relational mobility, 82, 106, 200
Relationship Commitment, 21
relationship reasons, 38
Relationship Satisfaction, 20
relationship types, 11
relative dependency, 102
relative disclosure, 104
relative involvement, 103
relative power, 102, 103
reliability, 13
reliability analyses, 17
religious commitment, 22
religious identities, 137
repeated measures ANOVA, 15
replication, 15
Rivera Aragón, Sofia, 112
Rogers, Willard, 157
romantic love, 131
Romanticism Scale, 44
R-squared, 17
Rubin, Zick, 1, 5, 73, 84
Rusbult, Caryl, 21, 116

s.d.. See Standard Deviation
Sacrifices, 107
same-sex partners, 138
scale, 17
Schwartz, Shalom, 38
Secure Attachment, 44
Segall, Marc, 181
self-disclosure, 79
self-enhancement, 38

self-esteem, 156, 160
self-reflection, 195
self-transcendence, 38, 42, 50
Seligman, Martin, 155
SEM Measurement Models, 18
SEM Structural Models, 18
sex outside the current relationship, 89
Sexual Activities, 86
sexual approval, 85
sexual liberals, 84
sexual moderates, 84
sexual satisfaction, 87
sexual traditionalists, 84
sexual violence, 117
Sexuality, 90
Shaver, Phillip, 44
Similarity, 199
Simpson, Jeffry, 198
social commitment, 21
social exchange, 7
social networks, 204
Social Status Important, 54
Social Status Similarity, 55
socially structured, 61
standard deviation, 14
standardized regression coefficients, 23
statistical tools, 4, 217
statistically significant, 15
Sternberg, Robert, 21, 74
Strauss, Murray, 117
Structural Equation Modeling, 18
styles of influence, 105

timing of external events, 139
Traditional Gender Role Attitudes scale, 107
trivial correlations, 16
T-tests, 14

Uncertainties Conflicts, 113
Universalism, 50
unwanted sex, 87

Validity, 13
Values, 41
verbal violence, 117

Walster, Elaine, 74, 198
well-being, 155, 196
wider applicability, 180

Zembrodt, Isabella, 116